REVOLUTION
AS TRAGEDY

REVOLUTION AS TRAGEDY

The Dilemma of the Moderate from Scott to Arnold

JOHN P. FARRELL

Cornell University Press

ITHACA AND LONDON

Cornell University Press gratefully acknowledges a grant from the Andrew W. Mellon Foundation that aided in bringing this book to publication.

First published 1980 by Cornell University Press.
Published in the United Kingdom by Cornell University Press Ltd., 2-4 Brook Street, London W1Y 1AA.

International Standard Book Number 0-8014-1278-1
Library of Congress Catalog Card Number 79-26000
Printed in the United States of America
Librarians: Library of Congress cataloging information appears on the last page of the book.

To Judy, Sheri, and Marcy
for the comedy of
our days

Contents

Preface

This book analyzes the origin and development in nineteenth-century Britain of a literary tradition formed by writers who tried to comprehend the position of the moderate in revolution by appealing to the tragic spirit. A remarkable consistency characterizes this appeal. In every case, the tragic scene set by these writers tends to depict man as "Wandering between two worlds, one dead, / The other powerless to be born." And in every case, tragedy functions to dignify the moderate's position and to support the act of conscience that leaves him isolated in a world polarized by extreme ideologies.

My treatment of tragedy is nominalistic. I have attempted to explicate each writer's subjectively derived sense of tragedy and to show how each used his own version of tragedy to defend, privilege, and transvalue the moderate's position. Large categories of political and imaginative experience, however, underlie and nurture, and thus intimately connect, literary works that explore the moderate's struggle with revolution. I have traced these connections to Romantic valorizations of tragedy, on the one hand, and on the other to the perception shared by many writers of a complex, inherently tragic content dominating the moral order of revolution.

9

The tragedy of the moderate in revolution appears with full force in works by Scott, Byron, Carlyle, and Arnold. In studying these writers, I have endeavored to respect the very great differences in style, temperament, and political consciousness that separate them from one another. But I do see them as crucially linked figures in the tradition I describe, a tradition that erases some of the boundaries orthodox literary history would still place between Romantics and Victorians. Many writers, both in other literatures and in other ages, stand in the same tradition, and of some of these I have taken note. It has seemed to me best, however, to concentrate on the development of this tradition in the literature of nineteenth-century Britain. Because Britain did not undergo a political revolution, we sometimes have difficulty seeing revolution as more than an indefinite, though troubling, background to literary texts. Yet it was more than that. Again and again it appears as the moral environment that governs both the themes of the artist's work and the work's deepest strategies.

"What is the gross sum that I owe?" I may do no better than Falstaff in arriving at a just reckoning, though it gives me very great pleasure to acknowledge here the generosity of others.

A gift of time, in the form of a fellowship from the National Endowment for the Humanities and a semester sabbatical granted by the Regents of the University of Kansas, enabled me to get started on this project. The time was made even more productive by a travel grant from the American Philosophical Society.

While teaching at the University of Kansas, I had the benefit of learning from a stimulating group of Victorian scholars: Peter J. Casagrande, Roy Gridley, Harold Orel, William D. Paden, Max K. Sutton, and George J. Worth, to whom, in his capacity as chairman of the English Department, I am also obligated for unvarying kindness and support for this project in many practical ways.

My debts to many other scholars are, I hope, indicated by the footnotes, though they certainly extend beyond what formal citation can record. I am conscious of having been saved from error by Charles Richard Sanders and helped on doubtful points by Walter Houghton and Jerome McGann, all of whom took time and trouble to answer queries. There is simply no getting near the gross sum of my debts when it comes to assessing the value of David J. DeLaura's advice, criticism, encouragement, and example over many years. As both scholar and friend, he has aided me at every stage of this work. I also wish to thank Betty Sue Flowers, Blair Labatt, Wayne Lesser, and Charles Sherry, past and present colleagues of mine at the University of Texas, who willingly read and very helpfully criticized portions of the manuscript. The contributions of R. J. Kaufmann, Walter L. Reed, Warwick Wadlington, all of the University of Texas, and my wife, Judith, have been on a scale equaled only by the demands I made of them. Again and again their judgment helped me to tie what I had only managed to tangle, and they gave me, my wife most of all, a steadily renewed sense of possibility.

With allies so numerous and gifted, I should have left no errors of fact or judgment remaining in the field. But the gross sum of these errors, whatever it may be, must be charged exclusively to my account.

Part of the material in Chapter 5 appeared as "Matthew Arnold's Tragic Vision" in *PMLA*, 85 (1970), 107–17. It is used again by permission of the Modern Language Association.

Acknowledgment is also due for permission to quote excerpts from the following books: Albert Camus, *The Rebel*, translated by Anthony Bower, © 1956, Alfred A. Knopf, Inc., reprinted by permission of Alfred A. Knopf, Inc.; Boris Pasternak, *Doctor Zhivago*, translated by Max Hayward and Manya Harari, © 1958, Pantheon Books, Inc., by permission of Pantheon Books, a Division of Random House; William Butler Yeats, *The Autobiog-*

J. P. F.

Austin, Texas

Abbreviations

OM	Walter Scott, *Old Mortality*. Everyman's Library. London: Dent, 1906.
P	*The Works of Lord Byron: Poetry*. Ed. E. H. Coleridge. London: John Murray, 1898–1904. 7 vols.
PMLA	*Proceedings of the Modern Language Association*.
TL	Chauncey B. Tinker and Howard F. Lowry, *The Poetry of Matthew Arnold: A Commentary*. London: Oxford University Press, 1940.
TNB	*Two Note Books of Thomas Carlyle*. Ed. Charles E. Norton. New York: Grolier Club, 1898.
TR	Albert Camus, *The Rebel: An Essay on Man in Revolt*. Trans. Anthony Bower. 1954; rpt. New York: Vintage Books, 1956.
UTQ	*University of Toronto Quarterly*.
WTC	*The Works of Thomas Carlyle*. Centenary Edition. Ed. H. D. Traill. London: Chapman & Hall, 1896–99. 30 vols.

REVOLUTION
AS TRAGEDY

CHAPTER ONE

Revolution as Tragedy: Being at the Center

Kenneth Burke once made a rough catalog of the *points d'appui* with which men have identified the logic of human purpose: God, nature, community, utility, history, and self.[1] To these we may add revolution. Revolution was devised as a pragmatic instrument to extend the scope and legitimacy of public decision, but it was soon swept with a grandeur of spirit that acquired for it the status of a transcendent act. It restructured the logic of human purpose by vastly expanding the conception of freedom that originally inspired the revolutionary mind. Something prodigious occurred when the space for public decision was opened to the public at large, when the propositions of the philosophical few were redefined by the oppressed many, when the uncertain measures of men became the dogmas of history, and when the imagery of human purpose was shifted from the world of memory and recentered in the world of hope. The revolutionary process then became unimaginably complex, and though it was designed as a clarification, it developed as an ambiguity. Its history is replete with paradox and tension. The spirit of this history was pointedly evoked by Octavio Paz when he called revolution

1. *Attitudes toward History*, 2d ed. (1959; rpt. Boston: Beacon Press, 1961), p. 271.

17

the major invention of the Western world, and added: "Like the early Christians expecting the Apocalypse, modern society has been watching since [the late eighteenth century] for the coming of the Revolution. And revolution comes; not the expected one but another, always another."[2] The revolution that comes is the wrong revolution. And the wrong revolution always expresses itself in the same way: as the expense of spirit in a waste of shame.

Of course, this is the history of revolution from the special viewpoint of those who are neither entrenched elites nor *engagés* in the ordinary sense. It is, rather, the viewpoint of that heterogeneous group known as moderates and it is offered from the depths of their political disorientation. Though members of this group are the focus of the present study, an enormous prologue from political science would be required to define the group in any satisfactory way. Clearly some adherents of "middlingness" (George Eliot's term) such as Macaulay and Guizot developed the stance of moderation as a formal creed. The English Whigs and the French Doctrinaires made "middlingness" the program of organized political parties.[3] But I am less concerned with moderates who are adherents of a formal creed than with that looser aggregation of individuals in the nineteenth century who, while sometimes able to imagine the grand possibilities of revolution, were almost always unable to accept either the frightening practices of revolution or many of its general aims. We may not know how to define their position very precisely, but we know who they are. They are the people wheeling with fantastic steps through what E. J. Hobsbawm has called "the dramatic dialectical dance," that tearing process brought on by the pull and tug of right-wing

2. "The Revolt of the Body," trans. Monique Fong, *Hudson Review*, 23 (1971), 659.
3. The program is described in Vincent E. Starzinger, *Middlingness: "Juste Milieu" Political Theory in France and England, 1815–48* (Charlottesville: University Press of Virginia, 1965).

and left-wing extremists.[4] The moderates caught in this dance are, indeed, men whose mood is apt to be deeply antipolitical. Their desire for the social transformation glowingly offered in revolution is accompanied by a reluctance to use political machinery at all. They find themselves, for this reason and many others, steadily outflanked and stymied by political zealots; their philosophical position splits in a series of refractions, divisions, and reformulations. They are vulnerable in this way essentially because of the one trait they can be said to have shared since the French Revolution: an uneasy alliance of liberal consciousness with the conservative conscience. In the nineteenth century (and in our own as well), their humanistic appreciation for the expansion of consciousness drew them toward the revolutionary idea; but the conservative conscience, with its foundation in classical ethics, made them always cautious of excess and travesty.

Revolution does not work cautiously. If revolutions have shared any one trait in common, it has been a commitment to totality. The victims of the dramatic dialectical dance are trapped because they try to follow revolution in some of its developments but not in its totality. Their measured sympathy is always at odds with revolution's fury against fine distinctions. As a result, the feeling they know most intimately is the feeling of cultural estrangement. Many writers who faced this situation tried to identify its terrible burdens by invoking the tragic vision.

THE SCHEME OF TRAGEDY

This study proposes to examine how Scott, Byron, Carlyle, and Arnold used tragedy as a speculative instrument in order to explore the imperative of revolution in their world. This is not to say that their attitudes toward revolution were identical.

4. *The Age of Revolution, 1789–1848* (New York: New American Library, 1962), pp. 84–85.

There is much that separates Scott from Carlyle and Byron from Arnold. But in trying to grasp the meaning of revolution, these writers, like many of their contemporaries, gave particular attention to the destiny of the moderate within a scheme that exposes revolution as a tragic action. Though each writer interprets the scheme differently, its basic materials are essentially the same for all of them.

It ought to be said at the outset that the problem before us is a matter of literary history rather than literary theory, a distinction that must be made since the analysis of revolution and tragedy from the perspective of theory inevitably develops in quite another direction from the one taken here. The sticking point for theoretical and formal studies of revolution and tragedy is the question of what constitutes "genuine" or "authentic" tragedy. The reason is clear. Any association of the tragic spirit with the idea of revolution becomes immediately contentious because of an implied valuation that some critics see as a distortion of tragedy and others as a distortion of revolution. George Steiner is one of many critics who has argued that the true spirit of tragedy is offended by the optimistic and egalitarian motives of revolution. More recently and more heatedly, Jacques Ellul has attacked revolution for having blinded us to the tragic vision by giving us an inchoate appetite for innovation. On the other hand, such Marxist critics as Georg Lukács and Raymond Williams have tried to establish the human meaning of revolution by relating it to a form of tragedy. To be sure, the form has little in common with what Milton referred to as tragedies of stateliest and most royal argument. These critics argue instead for a newly evolved and yet demonstrably authentic version of tragic experience contained in class conflicts.[5]

5. George Steiner, *The Death of Tragedy* (New York: Knopf, 1961). Ellul's comments occur throughout his *Autopsy of Revolution* (New York: Knopf, 1971), especially pp. 45, 79, and 173–74. In citing Lukács, I am thinking particularly of *The Historical Novel*, 2d ed., trans. Hannah and Stanley

The problem of what constitutes genuine tragedy is not at issue here. I wish to proceed, with respect to the writers studied in the following chapters, more or less nominalistically. What is actually in question is not the nature of tragedy but the appropriation of the tragic vision by moderates in their effort to describe the struggle between conscience and consciousness brought about by revolution. Their appeals to tragedy are not necessarily profound or free from evasiveness, but they are clearly definitive of the intellectual and emotional dislocations such writers experienced in the environment of revolution. In the case of nineteenth-century British writers the appropriation of tragedy has not been adequately connected to its causes. Revolution is characteristically treated as a factor in the general background of their work, occasionally coming to life as a threat. This treatment blurs the immanence of revolution in the nineteenth-century world; even British writers experienced revolution as something more fully played out than a threat. What they saw in revolution was precisely its comprehensiveness, its power to affect everything, its refusal to be stayed by artillery or legislation or geographical boundaries. It might be said, in fact, that these writers sought the comprehensiveness of tragedy in order to withstand the comprehensiveness of revolution.

I shall return at the end of this chapter to the specific situation of the four British writers with whom we are mainly concerned. We have first to consider more generally the historical and the aesthetic reasons for the moderate's appeal to tragedy. What is obvious, initially, is that the aesthetic motives underlying this appeal are more suggestive of pathos than of tragedy. Robert Heilman, for example, has distinguished between tragedy and melo-

---

Mitchell (1962; rpt. Boston: Beacon Press, 1963). In spite of my different view and approach, Raymond Williams, *Modern Tragedy* (London: Chatto & Windus, 1966), has been indispensable. I owe the term "tragic deadlock" to this book. I also profited from Walter Stein's critique of Williams in *Criticism as Dialogue* (Cambridge: The University Press, 1969), pp. 183–246.

drama by seeing melodrama as a structure in which "man is pitted against some force outside himself—a specific enemy, a hostile group, a social pressure, a natural event, an accident, or a coincidence." Most of the works that figure in the present study would qualify as melodramas in Heilman's terms. Similarly, E. M. W. Tillyard once identified such dramatic tragedies as *The Duchess of Malfi* as works that present an "action of suffering" where the sufferers "are not greatly to blame" and where the distinct point of interest is "the sufferer's quality of mind [which] causes him to protest and to reflect." This, too, is a salient feature of the works before us, and Tillyard might well have defined the effect as characteristic of pathos.[6]

But, of course, the writers who produced these melodramas and actions of suffering thought of them as grounded in tragedy. Their presumption might be seen simply as a reflex of the age's taste for pathos and particularly of what Steiner calls "the strain of melancholy historicism" evident in so much Romantic and post-Romantic literature. This view, however, excessively generalizes the pattern of feeling that lies behind the moderate's sense of tragedy. If the literature we are considering places a declamatory stress on disillusionment, it also implies that the disillusionment experienced in revolution is somehow unique. Revolution promoted itself as a form of redemption and its failure could be perceived, in Byron's chilling terms, as "Man's worst—his second fall." Alexander Herzen, in his sprawling memoir, *My Past and Thoughts,* adroitly analyzed how the failure of revolution engendered what he believed was a special and powerful pattern of feeling that is not reducible to pathos. Herzen recounted how in 1848 revolution "fell like Agrippina, under the blows of its own children," and how his own involvement left him with "a sedi-

6. Robert B. Heilman, *Tragedy and Melodrama: Versions of Experience* (Seattle: University of Washington Press, 1968), p. 79; and E. M. W. Tillyard, *Shakespeare's Problem Plays* (London: Chatto & Windus, 1964), p. 12.

ment of bitterness, anguish, and weariness at the bottom of [his] heart."[7]

> Disillusionment is a vulgar, hackneyed word, a veil under which lie hidden the sloth of the heart, egoism posing as love, the noisy emptiness of vanity. . . . [These] have long wearied us in life and in novels. . . . That is perfectly true; but is there not something real, peculiarly characteristic of our times, at the bottom of these frightful spiritual sufferings which degenerate into absurd parodies and vulgar masquerade?" [p. 385]

Herzen answers this question affirmatively. It is worth noticing that he points to the example of Byron. He saw clearly that Byron was not a poser and that he represented in his work forms of thought and experience that were the authentic, if alarming, discoveries of his age.

Herzen proceeds from his remarks on Byron to state, in terms similar to those used by Paz, the case for seeing the age's disillusionment as distinctive. The great trial of his times, he says, is that man, having unshackled himself from the religion of Christianity and rushed joyously toward the religion of liberalism, has had to acknowledge that liberalism itself is just another void.

> Triumphant and then defeated liberalism has revealed the rift in all its nakedness; the painful consciousness of this is expressed in the irony of modern man, in the scepticism with which he sweeps away the fragments of his shattered idols. Irony gives expression to the vexation aroused by the fact that logical truth is not the same as the truth of history, that as well as dialectical development it has its own development through chance and passion. . . . *Disillusionment in our sense of the word was not known before the Revolution.* [pp. 386–87; italics added]

7. *My Past and Thoughts*, rev. trans. Humphrey Higgens, abridged by Dwight Macdonald (1973; rpt. New York: Vintage Books, 1974), pp. 384–85.

Herzen is here implicitly accounting for the mosaic of disillusionment that is displayed in the literature of his age, and he goes
on, almost immediately, to describe the disillusionment of which
he speaks as having "a tragic and passionate character" (p. 388).
He means not a generalized and amorphous recurrence of morbid
feeling, but a quite explicit emotional decorum that his contemporaries could take as appropriate to tragedy in their time. Impotence, isolation, and deadlock are its reiterated signs; the erosion
of hope is its irrevocable result. Almost inevitably Herzen once
more cites Byron. "We, like Byron, do not know what to do
with ourselves, where to lay our heads. . . . He saw that there is
no way out" (pp. 389, 391).

The sense of living through a specially profound disillusionment is the true seed of the tragic idea for the writers we are discussing. But the idea was also reinforced and developed by a convergence of certain intellectual and literary traditions that changed
the face of tragedy in nineteenth-century thought. Most prominent as a factor in this change was the ripening of the historical
consciousness, that sixth sense invented, as Nietzsche thought,
by the nineteenth century under the spell of the French Revolution. What Nietzsche had in mind was the complete historization
of experience, which, though it was accomplished in his time,
had its original growth in the previous century, "when history
rather than nature became the home of man, and society the immediate reference for the individual within the stream of
history."[8] This process of temporal concentration, as Erich Auerbach calls it, abrogated the first principles of a whole social order,
the *ancien régime,* and gave social change and even convulsion a
sort of institutional life.[9] The idea of tragedy shifted in relation to
the process of temporal concentration by placing unprecedented

8. John G. Gunnell, *Political Philosophy and Time* (Middletown: Wesleyan
University Press, 1968), p. 252.
9. *Mimesis,* trans. Willard Trask (1953; rpt. Garden City, N.Y.: Anchor
Books, 1957), p. 404.

emphasis on the discovery not of a tragic flaw in man but of a tragic fact in the world. The tragic ideas of Hegel, Schopenhauer, and Nietzsche form an extended commentary on this fundamental alteration in perspective.

The change was registered in literary works before the philosophers appeared and even before the French Revolution took place. The new mode of tragedy and its implications can be seen most clearly in the turn taken by the drama, that customary vehicle of the tragic vision, during the mid-eighteenth century. The *tragédie classique,* in yielding more and more to bourgeois drama, was in effect yielding to a moral perspective that associated tragic process with the action of history. Arnold Hauser points out that this development depended on a revised understanding of tragic experience.

> Classical tragedy sees man isolated and describes him as an independent, autonomous intellectual entity, in merely external contact with the material world and never influenced by it in his innermost self. The bourgeois drama, on the other hand, thinks of him as a part and function of his environment and depicts him as a being who, instead of controlling concrete reality, as in classical tragedy, is himself controlled and absorbed by it. The milieu ceases to be simply the background and external framework and now takes an active part in the shaping of human destiny.[10]

The emphasis on milieu attained in the nineteenth century so habitual a place in critical thinking that tragic fate could seem purely a matter of the bulk and extensiveness of social action affecting an individual. Benjamin Constant took this view (in 1829) when he argued that "the more numerous the [social] obstacles to be vanquished, the more [a work's] efforts and effects result in tragedy."[11]

10. *The Social History of Art,* trans. by the author and Stanley Godman (New York: Vintage Books, 1951), III, 89–90.
11. "Reflections on Tragedy," trans. Barry Daniels, *Educational Theater Journal,* 23 (1971), 330.

Although this reorientation was spurred by the low mimetic naturalism that came into vogue in the eighteenth century, the preoccupation with milieu was embodied in a grander, more idealized form by the German Romanticists, especially Schiller, and given supreme sanction by the Romantic reinterpretation of Shakespeare.[12] Shakespeare became a veritable Napoleonic figure in this period, cannonading the effete French drama into oblivion and settling a new constitution upon dramatists who were trying to describe history as a tragic action. What began with Lessing as a reconsideration of dramatic form that elevated Shakespeare to the level of the Greek tragedians finally issued in a celebration of Shakespeare for the reason that his world seemed philosophically richer because of the scope it gave to social and historical reality. Where the tragedy of even the Greeks seemed completely indifferent to the texture of history, Romantic writers could see in Shakespeare's characters men whose humanity was very much defined by their standing between an active past and an anticipated future.[13] This model of tragic experience deeply influenced the general aggrandizement of milieu that distinguishes so much Romantic literature.

It happened, then, that writers who wanted to tell the story of the moderate *in extremis* had a subject that was perfectly suited to the age's sense of a tragic occasion. A form of historical disillusionment, widely accepted as a distinctively new and profound cause of emotional crisis, neatly joined (and even stimulated) the contemporary inclination to esteem tragedy for its generic capacity to mirror human fate in history. This access to the prestige of tragedy was, as we shall see, crucial for our writers. It allowed them to tell the story of the moderate at an exalted level of moral

12. The Romantic view of Shakespeare is sketched in Steiner, *Death of Tragedy*, pp. 143–50.

13. For this formulation see Tom F. Driver, *The Sense of History in Greek and Shakespearean Drama* (1960; rpt. New York: Columbia University Press, 1967), p. 97. And see Northrup Frye, *Fools of Time: Studies in Shakespearean Tragedy* (Toronto: University of Toronto Press, 1967).

intention; indeed, they regarded the story as nothing less than a touchstone for the meaning of revolution. They took their cue from the same intellectual environment that could prompt Schelling to assert, quite categorically, that "for the historian tragedy is the true source of great ideas and noble thinking."[14] And, more complexly, they no doubt had some sense that their appropriation of the tragic vision was authorized by a perception that Kenneth Burke has made explicit:

> If tragedy is a sense of man's intimate participation in processes beyond himself, we find that science has replaced the older metaphysical structure with an historical structure which gives the individual man ample grounds to feel such participation. What science has taken from us as a personal relationship to the will of Providence, it has regiven as a personal relationship to the slow, unwieldy movements of human society.[15]

Burke's comment suggests the essential manner in which "temporal concentration" conduced to a general reformulation of the tragic vision. Whether authentic tragedy is possible within this reformulation is, as has been indicated, a now much-debated question. But for many decades at least, the reformulation retained, and even expanded, the prestige of tragedy. This enhancement provided our writers with a determinate way of signifying the exemplary status of the moderate who is at hazard not with a personal enemy but with his historical circumstances. And, insofar as these circumstances are distinguished not only by the unwieldy movements of society but by the trammelings of revolution, the moderate is inexorably attached to the *Zeitgeist* by his dreams and repelled by his foreboding.

The writers we are considering attempted to illuminate the tragic action they saw by using a scheme whose two major elements are a specific kind of protagonist and a special plot, or,

---

14. F. W. J. Schelling, *On University Studies*, trans. E. S. Morgan, ed. Norbert Guterman (Athens: Ohio University Press, 1966), p. 109.
15. *Counter-Statement* (New York: Harcourt, Brace, 1931), p. 253.

more precisely, a microcosmic scene that, sometimes loosely and sometimes strictly, governs the whole structure of a work. The best way to begin describing both protagonist and scene may well be to look at an opposing scheme. Coleridge's important poem "France: An Ode" was written in reaction to revolution, but it makes no appeal to tragedy. The poem concludes with an apostrophe to Liberty.

> Alike from Priestcraft's harpy minions,
> And factious Blasphemy's obscener slaves,
>   Thou speedest on thy subtle pinions,
> The guide of homeless winds, and playmate of the waves!
> And there I felt thee!—on that sea-cliff's verge,
>   Whose pines, scarce travelled by the breeze above,
> Had made one murmur with the distant surge!
> Yes; while I stood and gazed, my temples bare,
> And shot my being through earth, sea, and air,
>   Possessing all things with intensest love,
>   O Liberty! my spirit felt thee there.[16]

The portent of a dialectical dance is evident here in the standard way that we shall see many times: the reactionary world (Priestcraft) and the revolutionary world (Blasphemy) are imagined as twin evils. Yet, no dialectical dance occurs. The poet moves freely beyond the snares of Priestcraft and Blasphemy and even reaches an eminence above them where a harmony of outward forms and the life within—to use the language of "Dejection"—is triumphantly celebrated. In reaching this eminence Coleridge has also laid claim to two enormous achievements. He has created a politics of nature (really an antipolitics) alongside which the machinery of both Priestcraft and Blasphemy looks feeble. And he has ascertained his existence in a plenitude of being that he can give to, and receive from, the world that is his home.

The point of this illustration can be put briefly: the tragic vi-

16. Cited from *The Portable Coleridge,* ed. I. A. Richards (New York: Viking Press, 1950), ll. 95–105.

sion in the tradition described by the present study is a search for
the same two victories in an action that nevertheless concedes the
loss of free movement beyond the engorged camps of rightist and
leftist ideologies. In other words, the loss of free movement, the
experience of blockade, is acknowledged, but the acknowledgment, by taking the form of tragedy, confers upon the moderate
something of the magnitude that Coleridge could feel by having
such apparently unlimited access to a precious eminence.

What is sought in the tragic structure is, first of all, a political
faith (which, again, is more often than not an antipolitics). Like
Coleridge's, it is a faith whose power is authenticated less by its
doctrines than by the structure in which it is found. Tragedy exposes the meanness of the encircling ideologies by highlighting
the nobility of principled resistance. The accusation of political
naiveté, repeatedly heard by moderates, is at last silenced in a
structure that credits the human struggle against—and with—the
temptations of monism. But more important even than the political faith that is offered in the structure of tragedy is the sense of
being it arouses. Coleridge's poem describes an unalienated man
whose political vision is impregnated by his ontological security.
The literature before us, on the other hand, forms one of the classic nineteenth-century meditations on the problem of alienation.
The dialectical dancers are trapped between isomorphic sociopo-
litical forces that, like a pair of reflecting mirrors, swallow up all
the space between them. What the dancers find is that they are
existentially missing in action. Tragedy is their claim to being, a
spectacle of significant form thrown up between the mirrors
which endows the dancers with gravity. Although we are being
explicitly asked to regard the form for the sake of the political
faith it powerfully unfolds, we are also being tacitly asked by it to
recognize the existence of socially occluded men.

The figure who corresponds to the tragic hero in the literature
we are discussing is, then, a cultural derelict. He has recognized
the futility of established institutions and has accepted, to some

degree, a revolutionary view of the world. But just as he cannot participate in the action of established institutions, neither can he participate in the action of revolution. The moral gulf between revolution as a thought and revolution as an action constantly estranges him from the culture that revolution is building. And his own acute perception of injustice constantly renews his repudiation of the old order. This situation can appear with many modifications and can lead to quite distinctive results, but it is always the informing pattern used to define the moderate as a cultural derelict and it has shaped an extraordinary variety of works by writers ranging from Goethe to Malraux.

For a preliminary sampling of this literature we can look at two works whose dates of publication conveniently bracket the period between the earliest years of Scott's life and the latest years of Arnold's. These texts, Goethe's *Götz von Berlichingen* (1773) and Strindberg's *Master Olof* (1872), represent fairly well the degree of variation that could occur within the basic paradigm. And though they can be treated only briefly here, they may be said to represent the background in European literature against which the works of our British authors may properly be set. *Götz*, moreover, has a coincidental relevance for us, not only because Scott translated it in 1798 (it was the first work to bear his name in print) but also because Carlyle made so much of this fact, a point to be taken up in Chapter 3.

The historical character upon whom Goethe's play is based was almost an exact contemporary of Martin Luther and Dr. Faustus. He belonged to the lower nobility of free knights (*Reichsritter*) and he was, according to all accounts, a rogue. Goethe, however, makes him a sturdy and thoughtful man who is unquestionably loyal to the emperor Maximilian. He has every wish to cooperate with the emperor's attempt to end the political chaos caused by interminable feuds between independent lords and knights. But he is not by any means a statist, and he is especially unwilling to surrender any of his own independence as long as the emperor's court is dominated by a clique of ambitious and corrupt princes. His allegiance is to the regnant political order; he only awaits its purification. But Götz is betrayed by an old friend who is actually an agent of the princes and who influences the emperor against him. He is brought to trial on specious charges and is saved only by a sort of cavalry charge led by one of his kinsmen. After that, he accepts house arrrest until the emperor's pleasure is known. For a long time Götz waits patiently, but the emperor dies before deciding. In 1525, after years of isolation, Götz breaks his parole during the Peasants' War. While Martin Luther was writing his diatribes against the revolt that his own rebellion helped to stimulate, Götz is persuaded to take temporary command in the rebels' army. He accepts command only on condition that the revolt be dedicated to the achievement of freedom. The peasant leaders agree, but the old pattern of betrayal repeats itself—the leaders, of course, merely want Götz's good name and reputation to screen their pillaging and plundering. The tragedy ends when Götz, betrayed by both sides, dies in misery and disgrace.

Goethe, whose models of revolution at the time he wrote *Götz* were limited to such events as the Netherlands' revolt against Spain, shows us in a rather uncomplicated way a devout man with a pure passion for freedom. Though at several points Götz appears capable of sinning as well as being sinned against, these moments are never developed. We are left with an appealing man, a minor Lafayette in the rough. And though there is sufficient irony in the play, especially in the episode of Götz's rescue by one of those private armies he has scorned, to assure us that "freedom" is a more mysterious value than Götz recognizes, still the play maintains the clean lines of an object lesson. It ends with a terse epitaph for Götz: "Woe to the future. that cannot know thee." Götz, indeed, may be regarded as a Teutonic version of the Tory radical who was about to emerge in England and who would proclaim that the condition of freedom was to be sought in the past, not in the future.

The typical situation of the derelict is concretely but minimally evoked through such a figure as Götz. He is at heart a conservative man, the most recalcitrant of rebels. The play itself is best seen as an overture to the moderate's tragedy. In *Master Olof,* on the other hand, the typical situation of the moderate is exceeded. Strindberg, whose examples of revolutionary scenes included, most immediately, the Paris Commune of 1871, also focused his drama on a contemporary of Martin Luther. Master Olof is inspired by Luther's rebellion against the church and he attempts to bring the spirit of reform to his own congregation. He is cultivated by the Swedish king, Gustav Vasa, but he discovers the king has only been using him in an attempt to solidify the power of the monarchy by gaining wide popular influence. At the same time, Olof's tutor in revolution, Gert Bookprinter (the name is obviously significant), who professes anarchism, compromises his own revolutionary principles when his daughter's welfare becomes a question. And Olof is never able to adapt his idealism to the murky moral climate created by the revolutionaries. "Why," he keeps asking, "do you behave like wild animals? Why, you desecrate everything holy!"[17]

But Olof, it is clear, inhabits a world whose otherness is more at issue than its politics. Strindberg had once intended to give the play the sumptuous title *What Is Truth?* He uses the situation of the moderate in revolution to explore the somber ambivalence touching every aspect of the protagonist's existence. Olof's sexual identity, his relations with his wife and mother, his erratic deferences, his weakening intimacy with his congregation, and his need for illusion are all as problematic as his position in a political and religious struggle. At the end of the play, he recants under desperate circumstances that charge his action with the opposing energies of love and treachery. He is, as he says, completely lost—

17. *The Vasa Trilogy,* trans. and ed. Walter Johnson (Seattle: University of Washington Press, 1959), p. 53.

to himself most of all. He slumps against his pillory in tortured incapacity to use either life or death, combat or martyrdom, to his advantage. Here the risks of revolution are superseded by the risks of identity.

The development from *Götz von Berlichingen* to *Master Olof* indicates how prepotent the figure of the derelict became for the nineteenth-century literary imagination in its effort to comprehend the bondage of the self to the dialectic of history. Though the course this development takes tends more and more to remove the moderate from the storm center of revolutionary action, revolution, threatened, ineffectual, or contaminated, is always the condition that crystallizes for him the burdens of his existence and that serves as the author's major rationale for locating him within the *mythos* of tragedy. Nineteenth-century writers, we may judge, became so accomplished in working this *mythos* on behalf of the derelict that the process could occur elliptically and yet unmistakably. This happens in Matthew Arnold's lyric "Dover Beach," whose hypnotic power is certainly related in part to its skeletal but wholly plausible evocation of the world in which Götz and Olof suffer. The landscape of Arnold's poem seems, at first, expressive only of private agonies: the doubtful possibilities of romantic love, the cruel anxieties of religious doubt. But the setting is deliberately calculated as the tenebrous place where private grief breaks into abruptly felt connection with the clash of "ignorant armies" who have catastrophically polarized the world of historical opportunity and thus sealed off all roads to renewal.

Just as the figure of the moderate as derelict appeared persistently in nineteenth-century literary works, so also did he assume a place as the hypostatized image of man in much of the meditative writing of the age. Schiller, in his treatise *On the Aesthetic Education of Mankind,* which has the French Revolution for its immediate frame of reference, describes his age as divided between a stubborn defense of anachronisms and a brutal forcing of change:

Man portrays himself in his actions. And what a figure he cuts in
the drama of the present time! On the one hand, a return to the
savage state; on the other to complete lethargy: in other words,
to the two extremes of human depravity, and both united in a
single epoch! . . . Thus do we see the spirit of the age wavering
between perversity and brutality, between unnaturalness and
mere nature, between superstition and moral unbelief; and it is
only through an equilibrium of evils that it is still sometimes kept
within bounds.[18]

The man Schiller sees as desperately needed is the man who can
unite nature and culture, but the equilibrium of evils blocks his
emergence.

Similarly, Constant, who spent most of his adult life trying to
find a reasonable relationship to revolution, ended by seeing man
as unable to do anything with the freedom he had achieved.
"What shall man do," he asked in 1824, "without memory,
without hope, between the past which abandons him and the future which is closed before him"? Constant shifts the perspective
away from Schiller's world of nature and imagines the derelict in
the context of time. The point, however, is the same. The model
man is cut off from the organic processes of growth, development, and fulfillment.[19] The culminating writer is Tocqueville,
who recorded in his *Recollections* the anguish of bearing steady
witness to the fading of hope and the growing isolation of the
moderate. As the barricades went up again in 1848, he was seized
by a desiccation of spirit:

> I began to pass in review the history of our last sixty years, and I
> smiled bitterly when I thought of the illusions formed at the con-
> clusion of each period in this long revolution. . . . I do not know

18. Friedrich Schiller, *On the Aesthetic Education of Mankind,* trans. and ed.
Elizabeth Wilkinson and L. A. Willoughby (Oxford: Clarendon Press,
1967), p. 25.
19. Cited by Georges Poulet, *Studies in Human Time,* trans. Elliott Cole-
man (Baltimore: Johns Hopkins University Press, 1956), p. 212.

when [our] voyage will be ended; I am weary of seeing the shore in each successive mirage, and I often ask myself whether the *terra firma* we are seeking does really exist, and whether we are not doomed to rove upon the seas forever.[20]

As usual, Tocqueville is especially suggestive. Not only does he understand the feelings of the derelict, he also gives us in miniature what we have already seen as the recurrent plot, the tragedy of deadlock, in which the figure of the derelict inevitably appears. It should be said that there are relatively few immaculate examples of this plot. Moreover, the plot has significantly different forms of closure: patient hope; irremediable despair; gnostic breakthrough; analgesia; futile collaboration with one of the false ideologies; existential rebellion; annihilation. Nevertheless, a decided similarity remains: revolution creates a schismatic political universe in which reconciliation constantly seems the mirage of which Tocqueville speaks. The position of the reconciler, then, is ultimately disqualified as being itself a mirage. Condemned to a ghostly existence by his attempts at moral clarification, the derelict becomes a spectator who can protest, but apparently not affect, the cumulative efficiency of *Realpolitik*.

And yet, to come back to the contrast with Coleridge, the moderate is not helpless. The device of tragedy answers the challenge of *Realpolitik*. This answer begins, as I have suggested, in the valorizations of tragedy created in the Romantic tradition. Our writers did not improvise upon this tradition so far as to discover the consummate mode of transcendence that Yeats later claimed for tragedy. But they at least attributed to tragedy a luminous and ennobling orientation in the deep meanings of human action, an orientation that no merely partisan or polemical spirit could attain. Holding tragedy in such immense regard, they solic-

20. *The Recollections of Alexis de Tocqueville,* trans. A. T. de Mattos, ed. J. P. Mayer (New York: Meridian Books, 1959), pp. 68–69. On Tocqueville as "tragedian," see Hayden White, *Metahistory* (Baltimore: Johns Hopkins University Press, 1973).

ited for the moderate himself the moral splendor they associated with the form.

The deflection of tragedy's prestige to the central character is largely a result of the way in which the tragic process (the derelict's victimization) distances, clarifies, and counters the revolutionary process. The Romantic valorizations of tragedy were pressed in several ways for this purpose. The writers we are dealing with ascribed to tragedy the authority of an ancient wisdom achieved through what Arnold called seeing life steadily and seeing it whole. By sustaining this vision, tragedy reached its special and ageless illumination of what is missing from the human endowment. Our writers could, then, turn to tragedy in order to demystify revolution by exposing it as only the latest instance of man's oldest griefs.

In another direction, as we have earlier observed, tragedy could be esteemed as a resource of the historical imagination. If it was the destiny of modern man to live in a world ridden by the historical sense, tragedy's newly emphasized foundation in the processes of history could give him perspective on his disillusionment. In this sense tragedy acted not as a means of tapping an ancient wisdom but rather as a means of embracing the uniquely relevant structures of modern thought in order to confront the exceptional oppressions of modern life.

These functions of tragedy are clearly united in their common assertion of an aesthetic framework that can make revolution intelligible. While revolution seemed to the men in the middle a bizarre alloy of the ineffable and the unspeakable, tragedy seemed, conversely, a loosening of the tongue. To say that our writers appropriated the prestige of tragedy on behalf of the moderate is really to say that they privileged the moderate with a potent language. In this language he could give utterance to the very conditions that deprived him of action. Carlyle, in his dazzling letter to Emerson of August 12, 1834, railed against the insufficiency of all contemporary "Poetics and Rhetorics and Sermonics," and declared that the speech of man must "anew environ itself with fit modes."[21] Tragedy, especially as rehabilitated by both the poetics and the sermonics of Romanticism, offered itself as a "fit mode" in the moderate's search for a decisive idiom. In other words, the age of disillusionment sought in tragedy precisely what T. S. Eliot, much later, acclaimed in Joyce's use of myth: the necessary means "of controlling, of ordering, of giving a shape and a significance to the immense panorama of futility and anarchy which is contemporary history."[22] Deprived though he was of a Coleridgean eminence, the derelict commanded, in the tragic vision, the enlarged description of reality that revolution itself falsely claimed as its prerogative in the modern world.

This is the rallying and aesthetically aggressive purpose assigned to tragedy by our writers. What actually happens in their use of tragedy entails, of course, another purpose. The powers of historical definition attributed to the tragic vision are, finally, less frequently realized than the potential for self-reflection that tragedy implicitly bestowed upon the derelict. In a quite basic sense, the appeal to tragedy functions as a way of dignifying the moderate's position and contesting the valueless, abysmal place that has been reserved for him in the new dispensation. The literature we are discussing thus has as a major aim the commemoration of the reconciler's consciousness. And inasmuch as this aim can assume distinct priority, it should be clear that the tragedy of deadlock takes its ground tone from elegy. It is elegy that has always performed the service of capturing the prestige of some honorific tradition in order to locate, by a process of magnification, the being of an exemplary man whose local existence has been obliterated. We may say, then, that visibility is the double purpose of the

21. *The Correspondence of Emerson and Carlyle,* ed. Joseph Slater (New York: Columbia University Press, 1964), pp. 103–4.
22. "Ulysses, Order, and Myth," *The Dial,* 75 (1923), 480–83, rpt. in *The Modern Tradition: Backgrounds of Modern Literature,* ed. Richard Ellman and Charles Feidelson, Jr. (New York: Oxford University Press, 1965), p. 681.

tragic literature written about the moderate. Tragedy makes visible the world the moderate sees; it is the "fit mode" he needs to define the world. But it also makes the moderate himself visible. Though the tragic action presented in a work may revolve about a problem of conscience or an ideal of social justice, the reflexive rhetoric of all such literature is pointedly elegiac. The rhetoric is persistently reminiscent of Ophelia's flower ceremony, the action that raises her from insubstantial to poignant existence. The great fire of Sardanapalus, the sepulchral utterances of Balder, the solitary trace of Ravenswood above the quicksand, the disjointed records of Cromwell's great suffering—these are the legacies proffered by the derelict to a world that has ordained his extinction. And, as with Ophelia, the legacy circles back to the subject to become the motive for his elegiac translation into a new order of being.

THE TRAGIC CONTENT OF REVOLUTION

Nothing disappears in revolution. Revolution is simply the ironic form in which history comments on its own continuity. Such, at any rate, is the bleak conception arrived at by many moderates. Their representations of this point, which occur pervasively in the revolutionary age, can be guarded as in Shelley or axiomatic as in Conrad, who saw his world alternately menaced "by the lawlessness of autocracy—for autocracy knows no law—and the lawlessness of revolution."[23] The importance of this point lies in what it exemplifies. It is exactly the sort of perception that guided moderates to their conviction that revolution is inherently tragic.

The conviction is indispensable. An interpretation of revolution on the model of tragedy was certainly prompted by that ana-

23. On Shelley see Gerald McNeice, *Shelley and the Revolutionary Idea* (Cambridge: Harvard University Press, 1969). Conrad is quoted from *Under Western Eyes* (Garden City, N.Y.: Anchor Books, 1963), p. 64.

logical "enriching" of the tragic vision which we observed in the previous section. But this matching, though mediated by the climate of critical opinion and cultural inclination, depended in many ways on the ability of moderates to see revolution as a tragic action, an action as vividly within the spectrum of tragedy as the cease of majesty or the fall of Troy. The recognition of a grievous parity between the aims of autocracy and the aims of revolution is but one instance, though perhaps the one most frequently cited, of the discoveries about revolution that typed it as a tragic phenomenon.

It is hardly necessary to enumerate all the features of revolution that contributed to this identification. Many of them were already commonplaces by the time Wordsworth wrote the 1805 *Prelude*. More to the point than the number of these features is the structure of their relationships. The sources for a tragic view of revolution are evident in each of the major categories for the analysis of revolution that moderates typically used. Though moderates might, by their very nature, adopt various perspectives in seeking the essence of revolution, the sense of tragedy could attend all of them. This is what I mainly wish to illustrate in the following discussion of revolution's tragic content. The discussion is, moreover, intended to suggest several other points relevant to our subject. By noticing how the motives of tragedy connect with one another, one can imagine why moderates found it so difficult to cauterize the wound to conscience which revolution always inflicted. Though they might attempt to tolerate some morally problematical aspect of revolution in the hope that revolution would secure its just aims, the interconnectedness of its tragic content made selective sanctioning nearly impossible. This, in any case, is an inference that may be drawn on the basis of what follows. Finally, and more pointedly, the structure of revolution's tragic content, as analyzed here, makes a preface to the themes we find in Scott, Byron, Carlyle, and Arnold. The structure itself is especially important for Carlyle.

We can begin with the heuristic advantage that revolution most clearly offers us—its name. Revolution came as a word into the political vocabulary of Europe meaning something quite opposite to what it does now. It originated as an astronomical term and gained increasing importance in the natural sciences with the publication in 1543 of Copernicus' *De revolutionibus orbium coelestium*. Its scientific usage emphasized order and repetition; essentially, it drew attention to an inevitable cycle in the natural world. When the term was borrowed by political writers, it was used to explain the relation of worldly changes to an orderly scheme. Its political usage was not, however, confined to this meaning. In sixteenth-century Italy, *rivoluzione* gradually replaced such older terms as *mutazione* in discussions of the sudden reversals of fate to which political leaders are subject. Machiavelli, of course, is chiefly responsible for this development. He treats revolution as an ethically neutral political phenomenon that challenges the existing order with violence and which can be contained only by the proper use of force. By emphasizing the role of force in political action, he secularized the authority of rulers. Machiavelli did not in any sense inspire the modern idea of revolution, but his work is symptomatic of a changing perspective that implied that a whole political order could be transformed through the successful use of violence by ordinary men, men who never imagined they were appointed by birth to rule. Such a transformation required only that ordinary men subscribe to the program of violence. Whether they would do so, however, depended, as Hannah Arendt points out, on a further modification in the idea of revolution. The old astronomical metaphor, with its implacable cycles, had first to give way to the idea that revolution inaugurates "a process which spells the definite end of an old order and brings about the birth of a new world"—a *novus ordo saeculorum*.[24]

24. I am quoting Hannah Arendt, *On Revolution* (1965; rpt. Harmondsworth: Penguin Books, 1973), p. 42. Arendt is using Karl Griewank's crucial

We have a record of what is presumably the first use of the word with this world of implication behind it. Carlyle dramatized the famous moment. The date was July 14, 1789.

> In the Court, all is mystery, not without whisperings of terror. . . . His Majesty, kept in happy ignorance, perhaps dreams of double-barrels and the Woods of Meudan. Late at night, the Duke de Liancourt . . . gains access to the Royal Apartments; unfolds, with earnest clearness . . . the Job's news. *"Mais,"* said poor Louis, *"c'est une révolte!"*—"Sire," answered Liancourt, "it is not a revolt,—it is a revolution." [*WTC*, II, 200]

But if Louis heard this version of the Job's news, moderates eventually heard quite another, which was that the old astronomical metaphor with its implacable cycles, rather than decaying, had a new pertinence. Nothing, indeed, had disappeared in revolution. Modern revolution's attempt to reduce the past to a fallacy and raise the future to a principle soon seemed a specious wizardry that merely recycled the oppressions of the past under a new name. The implacable cycles thus moved remorselessly on. If the tyrannical stars had fallen out of the heavens, they had only bequeathed their iron will to a company of men who insisted always not on liberty but on absolute sovereignty.

Given the actual experience of revolution, similar forms of disillusionment sprang up like fears in a violent night. As Robert Nisbet remarks, every turn of events in the nineteenth-century revolutions seemed to suggest that "impending tragedy [inhered] in the very conditions that . . . spelled mankind's progressive emancipation from the past."[25] And thus there emerged what we

---

essay, "Emergence of the Concept of Revolution," trans. and ed. Heinz Lubasz, in his *Revolutions in Modern European History* (New York: Macmillan, 1966), pp. 55–61. For other detailed discussion, see Peter Calvert, *Revolution* (London: Macmillan, 1970), pp. 69–73, and Raymond Williams, *Keywords: A Vocabulary of Culture and Society* (New York: Oxford University Press, 1976), pp. 226–30.

25. *Social Change and History: Aspects of the Western Theory of Development* (New York: Oxford University Press, 1969), p. 130.

may call the structure of revolution's tragic content: its positive, latent, and negative drives. For the moderate each of these drives is a source of the idea that revolution is an intrinsically tragic phenomenon. Stated concisely, the problem of revolution's positive content corresponds to the problem of democracy, its latent content to the problem of false gods, and its negative content to the problem of nihilism.

The positive content of revolution, in the eyes of moderates and liberals, was the combined work of freedom, equality, and rationalism.[26] Above all else revolution was conceived as the development of the rule of reason in all the departments of human society, a triumph of mind over the arbitrary, the autocratic, and the chimerical. Men had come to be confident that they understood the processes of progress and that the goods of this life could be obtained, in Meyer Abrams's apt figure, without the need for a sudden relief expedition from the skies.[27] Saint-Just, in one of his unparadoxical moods, gave expression to the fundamental use of reason envisioned by the men of the revolution when he said he imagined "that if men were given laws in accordance with nature and their own hearts, they would no longer be unhappy and corrupt."[28] Reason, embodied in the forms of law, would extirpate, simultaneously, both misery and vice. Liberal optimism did not, of course, make the rule of reason contingent upon revolution; the classic liberal philosophies argued that reason could achieve what revolution could not achieve. Still, revolution presented itself as the inspiration of reason and the fulfillment of man's strug-

26. Robert Nisbet, *The Sociological Tradition* (New York: Basic Books, 1966), p. 39. The naive assumptions about revolution implicit in this view are dramatically evident in a characteristic source: [Henry Reeve and B. E. Desainteville], "France and Her Revolutions," *Westminster Review,* 15 (1831), 406–32.

27. *Natural Supernaturalism: Tradition and Revolution in Romantic Literature* (New York: Norton, 1971), p. 59.

28. Cited in Norman Hampson, *A Social History of the French Revolution* (1963; rpt. University of Toronto Press, 1966), p. 222.

gle against the darkness. John Dunn points out that it could not have been otherwise.

> What revolutionaries offer themselves and their own societies is above all else an image of power, control, certainty and purpose in a world in which impatience, incomprehension and the terror of sheer meaninglessness are permanent threats. It is a very rationalist offer—and only insofar as it *is* a very rationalist offer is it any more than the most trivial *actes gratuits,* the veriest idiocy.[29]

The trouble was that the revolution did not sustain the distinction between rationalist offer and veriest idiocy. It showed one becoming the other. The damage done to the image of reason by this experience was not wholly irreparable. Arguments for "evolution" rather than revolution could be expanded. And other efforts to free reason from its disastrous alliance with revolution could be made. Arnold's "Function of Criticism at the Present Time" is an important example of such efforts. Nevertheless, reason failed to contain the chaos of revolution and so lost its luster. In addition, there was a more ironic and disturbing result: looked at in another way, revolution somehow seemed an autonomous power greater than reason, a power that was acquiring in the nineteenth century the prestige that reason had enjoyed in the eighteenth. For those men who looked back to Voltaire and Montesquieu, and who dreamed of a secularized and humanized classicism as the final result of the demand for change, the ascendency of revolution over reason shattered the first principle of their faith.[30]

Revolution not only eclipsed the sovereignty of reason, it replaced it with the sovereignty of the people. As Leopold von Ranke said, no political idea has had so profound an influence as the idea of the modern democratic state; "it is the eternal ferment

29. *Modern Revolutions: An Introduction to the Analysis of a Political Phenomenon* (Cambridge: The University Press, 1972), p. 256.

30. This is argued by Christopher Dawson, *The Gods of Revolution* (London: Sidgwick & Jackson, 1972), p. 23.

of the modern world."[31] The attractions of democracy were manifest. Greek democracy gleamed in the historic background and
the American experiment in democracy was full of recent promise. Both Greece and America, however, were spared what we
have come to call the social question. There was no Saint-Just to
say, ominously, that *les malheureux sont la puissance de la terre*. The
French Revolution, and the coeval Industrial Revolution, made
an indissoluble link between the political question and the social
question, between the hunger for freedom and rudimentary, biological hunger. As Hannah Arendt writes: "When the poor,
driven by the needs of their bodies, burst upon the scene, [revolu-
tion] lost its old connotations and acquired the biological imagery
which underlies and pervades the organic and social theories of
history, which all have in common that they see a multitude—the
factual plurality of a nation or a people or society—in the image
of one supernatural human body driven by one superhuman, irresistible 'general will.' "[32]

It was in this image that the European democratic state was
founded. Arendt again: "Those who needed and desired liberation from their masters or from necessity, the great master of
their masters, rushed to the assistance of those who desired to
found a space for public freedom—with the inevitable result that
priority had to be given to liberation and that the men of the
Revolution paid less and less attention to what they had originally considered to be their most important business, the framing
of a constitution."[33]

The construction of a constitution, which would permit public
spirit to override the caprices of individual—and despotic—whim,
was conceived in the traditional terms of republicanism (as set
out, for example, in the *Federalist* papers). But the eternal ferment

31. Cited in Marcus Raskin, *Being and Doing* (New York: Random
House, 1971), p. 54.
32. *On Revolution*, pp. 59–60.
33. Ibid., p. 132.

of the modern world, the demand that the people be sovereign, assured the triumph of popular democracy. What was not quite assured, but what nevertheless came to be the main pursuit of the new social forces, was happiness. Arendt concludes her discussion of the social question by citing Crèvecœur.

> Crèvecœur was right when he predicted that "the man will get the better of the citizen, [that] his political maxims will vanish," that those who in all earnestness say, "The happiness of my family is the only object of my wishes," will be applauded by nearly everyone when, in the name of democracy, they vent their rage against the "great personages who are so far elevated above the common rank of man" that their aspirations transcend their private happiness, or when, in the name of the "common man" and some confused notion of liberalism, they denounce public virtue . . . as mere ambition, and those to whom they owe their freedom as . . . possessed by a "colossal vanity." [*On Revolution,* p. 140]

Public freedom was superseded by private happiness; the citizen was superseded by the individual; and the generous few, as Shelley called them, were superseded by the factual plurality in such a way that the stratified procedures of majority decision were replaced by the summary procedures of majority rule.[34] These exchanges form, in essence, the litany of complaints against democracy in the literature of the nineteenth century—or at least the literature written by men and women who expressed an interest in founding a space for public freedom. What they imagined was what Tocqueville imagined, that "freedom alone is capable of lifting men's minds above mere mammon worship. . . . It alone replaces at certain critical moments their natural love of material welfare by a loftier, more virile ideal . . . and sheds a light en-

---

34. Nineteenth-century analyses of democratic government often emphasized this distinction, as in Tocqueville, *The Ancien Régime and the French Revolution,* trans. Stuart Gilbert (1955; rpt. London: Fontana, 1966), p. 27; and see Arendt, *On Revolution,* pp. 164–65.

abling all to see and appraise men's vices and their virtues as they truly are."[35] But, as Arendt tries to show, this high purpose depended primarily on the act of foundation: the making of a constitution. The revolution failed in this enterprise; it accepted, instead of a constitution, the rule of opinion. Shelley made the key point. He said that if faith is a virtue, "it is so in politics rather than in religion," for there it has the power of producing the kind of belief that "is at once a prophecy and a cause."[36] He meant that in public affairs the world could assume a virtue if it had it not, and by assuming it, acquire it. But instead of assuming a virtue, it merely launched an opinion.

Shelley's comment on the efficacy of political faith is also suggestive because it makes a distant disclosure of the second area of tragic tension that we must consider, revolution's latent content. Mazzini's analysis of this content is more direct.

> Ideas rule the world and its events. A Revolution is the passage of an idea from *theory* to *practice*. Whatever men have said, material interests never have caused, and never will cause, a Revolution. Extreme poverty, financial ruin, oppressive or unequal taxation, may provoke risings that are more or less threatening or violent, but nothing more. Revolutions have their origin in the mind, in the very root of *life*; not in the body, in the material organism. A Religion or a philosophy lies at the base of every Revolution. This is a truth that can be proved from the whole historical tradition of Humanity.[37]

Men who may have had neither the instinct nor the taste for the practice of revolution were nonetheless susceptible to its latent religious and metaphysical dimensions. John Stuart Mill could say, when revolution came to France again in 1830, "It aroused my utmost enthusiasm, and gave me, as it were, a new

35. *Ancien Régime*, p. 30.
36. *The Letters of Percy Bysshe Shelly*, ed. Frederick L. Jones (Oxford: Clarendon Press, 1964), II, 191.
37. Joseph Mazzini, *The Duties of Man and Other Essays* (London: Dent, 1907), p. 266.

existence."[38] So closely is religion related to revolution in structure that Paul Schrecker, in his seminal essay "Revolution as a Problem in the Philosophy of History," argued that there could be no true revolution "so long as religion was recognized as the sphere which dominated all civilization and from which all others received their supreme laws."[39] But once the religious structure manifested significant entropy, the competing political structure of revolution could, as Tocqueville saw, "overrun the whole world" with its own "apostles, militants, and martyrs."[40]

The personal immortality defined by the Christian dispensation was imitated by the revolution's capacity to aggrandize the significance of human action. If Wordsworth could find intimations of immortality in the splendor of the grass, the men of the revolution were not incapable of detecting in the spectacle of historical action reflections of their eternal selves. Revolution filled the imaginations of men with visions of a heavenly state, a future entirely disconnected from the egregious errors of the past and safe from the institutional matrix of its corruption. Again like Wordsworth, the men of the revolution wondered why "groves Elysian and Fortunate Fields" should always belong only to the history of departed things, and why they should not be found in what men are, or are about to become. This tradition persisted among writers for whom philosophical consistency was less immediately important than the spiritual inspiration that revolution brought them. *Doctor Zhivago* is a late but highly representative example of the tradition: "Mourning for Lara, [Zhivago] also mourned that distant summer . . . when the revolution had been a god come down to earth from heaven, the god of the summer . . . when everyone's life existed in its own right, and not as an

38. *Autobiography*, ed. C. V. Shields (Indianapolis: Bobbs-Merrill, 1957), p. 111.

39. "Revolution as a Problem in the Philosophy of History," trans. R. B. Hamilton, in *Nomos VIII: Revolution*, ed. Carl J. Friedrich (New York: Atherton Press, 1966), pp. 34–35.

40. *Ancien Régime*, p. 44.

illustration for a thesis in support of the rightness of a superior policy."[41]

The latent religious spirit of the revolution was accompanied by an evangelical zeal that it evoked to establish the purity of its motives and the integrity of its acts. Shallow as this zeal may often have been, it is important to remember that, as Hobsbawm remarks, revolutionaries not only set for themselves and for others a higher standard of morality than that of anyone except saints, but also, at moments, really acted on those standards. The effect of their extraordinary dedication and incorruptibility was to promote the feeling that revolution had instilled in men a higher sense of responsibility than religion itself had achieved.[42] And far from projecting a "value-free" world, revolution genuinely did, and still does, represent to many men a historical action in which the laxness and turpitude of humanity in its ordinary state is transformed by a spirit of moral awakening.

Beyond the quasi-religious elements that initially mark revolution's latent content, there is an even more powerful expectation. It was identified by Thomas Paine in his "Letter to the Abbé Raynal": "Our style and manner of thinking have undergone a revolution, more extraordinary than the political revolution of the country. We see with other eyes; we hear with other ears; and think with other thoughts, than those we formerly used."[43] The great cognitive revolution that we know as the Romantic frame of mind did not develop because of the political revolution,

41. Boris Pasternak, *Doctor Zhivago*, trans. Max Hayward and Manya Harari (New York: Pantheon, 1958), p. 454.

42. Eric J. Hobsbawm, *Primitive Rebels: Studies in Archaic Forms of Social Movement in the Nineteenth and Twentieth Centuries* (Manchester: Manchester University Press, 1959), pp. 61–62.

43. *The Writings of Thomas Paine*, ed. Moncure D. Conway (New York & London: Putnam, 1894), II, 105. Recent studies of revolution have heavily emphasized the latent content, as Isaac Kramnick indicates in "Reflections on Revolution: Definition and Explanation in Recent Scholarship," *History and Theory*, 11 (1972), 26–63.

but the revolution immensely influenced it. We have only to think of Wordsworth on the one hand and Hegel on the other to understand the way in which the modern experience of revolution created a parable for the explication of mind and a focal point for the discovery of man's buried instincts. The four writers with whom this study is mainly concerned display the effects of the cognitive revolution in all that they wrote. Scott's novels, no matter how deeply indebted they are to his encyclopedic knowledge of civil wars and aristocratic revolts in British history, would not have been conceived in the same way that they were had it not been for the French Revolution, which had made the sense of history a fundamental constituent of mind. Carlyle said more than once that the French Revolution educated men in the processes of symbolic thinking. Byron's exploration of the nature of the self is guided by what he perceived as man's rediscovered instinct for rebellion. And Arnold saw man's renewed need for "spontaneity of consciousness" as the real, if misunderstood, significance of modern revolution. These writers, and many of their contemporaries, accepted revolution as a modification of sensibility.

I have already cited one of the most important works in this tradition, Schiller's *On the Aesthetic Education of Mankind*. Meyer Abrams's comments on Schiller in *Natural Supernaturalism* (a book that is in many ways a history of the latent content of revolution) acutely describe the nature of revolution's appeal even for those who were politically disengaged.

> Throughout the treatise the French Revolution and the drastic problems which it posed for European politics and culture are both the explicit and implicit frame of Schiller's reference. His systematic procedure is to internalize the political concepts and ideals, as well as the millennial hope of the Revolution, by translating them into mental, moral, and cognitive terms. . . . The "aesthetic state" offers [man] an alternative realm in which he can even now achieve the great revolutionary aims of liberty, equality, and fraternity. [p. 350]

The internalizing of the political ideals and millennial hope of the revolution produced a major tension for writers who tried to use their art as an "alternative realm." To a significant extent the creative act itself came to be regarded as an effort in the transformation of man's fate analogous to the purposes of revolution. Seen in conjunction with the religious parallels, this tremendous spiritual attachment to the idea of revolution becomes the almost inevitable prelude to a sense of catastrophe. For writers who responded to the latent content of revolution, in any of its several forms, neither the failure of political revolution nor its periodic repetitions could occur without producing a sense of immeasurable loss. Those who were imaginatively enthralled by the quasi-religious spirit of revolution would find in its failures the disappearance of the only god that mattered: Prometheus. And those who hoped to make the aesthetic state an alternative realm could find in the wearying reenactments of revolution only a political and social detour from the apocalypse of the imagination.

At this point we can relate the "tragic" effects of the positive content and the latent content of revolution. The politics of revolution were designed by the philosophes, who made reason the keystone of their enterprise. Reason remained the official guardian of the revolutionary spirit. But the practice of revolution withered faith in reason, and consequently faith in democracy. On the other hand, the myth of revolution, its suprarational and unofficial identity, was designed by the founders of Romantic literature to achieve the ascendancy of man's creative and spiritual powers. The revolution of myth suffered the same fate as the revolution of reason. If the latter could not produce a constitution, the former could not persuade Prometheus to return. The hand that would lift the veil of the unborn hour was stayed by the "darkness [that] dawned in the East."[44]

44. The references are to Shelley's *Hellas*. My discussion of the latent content has been influenced by Harold Bloom's suggestive comment on a group of nominally "tragic" works in the period: "To find tragedy in any of these,

With the failure of the sun to rise either upon a cautiously democratic and rational community or upon the privileges of the self's cleansed perception, revolution could inculcate another set of lessons, those of its negative content. These lessons, no less than its positive political goals and latent millennial dreams, were to be made part of the "thinking with new thoughts" that revolution initiated and that historical experience converted into the imagination of disaster.

On posters and public monuments the slogans of the French Revolution broadcast the new conditions of human destiny. Everyone knows the most celebrated slogan: *Liberté, Egalité, Fraternité ou la Mort.* Revolution had this lesson to teach. The lesson, however, is not contained in the grim threat of the last phrase, though that also had its place, but in the either/or of the whole pronouncement. Revolution proved to be a confederation of absolutes, the chief modalities of which were, as they still are, violence and ideology. Violence became the major legislative instrument of revolution; decrees were passed by the guillotine. Ideology became its mental habit, its frigid climate of opinion. Together they operated as revolution's methods for changing society. Engels himself said that there is nothing more authoritarian than revolution.

Violence is essential. The basic element in the phenomenon of revolution is now most often seen as the attempt to effect political change through violent means, a process for reorganizing the style of politics by altering the state's monopoly on armed violence.[45] The need for emphasis on the element of violence is obvious: rather than being an unfortunate by-product, it is central to

---

you must persuasively redefine tragedy, as Shelley implicitly did. Tragedy becomes the fall of the imagination, or rather the falling away from imaginative conduct on the part of a heroically imaginative individual" ("The Unpastured Sea: An Introduction to Shelley," in *Romanticism and Consciousness: Essays in Criticism,* ed. Harold Bloom [New York: Norton, 1970], p. 391).

45. "Introduction" to Krishan Kumar, ed., *Revolution: The Theory and Practice of a European Idea* (London: Weidenfeld & Nicolson, 1971), p. 15.

the praxis of revolution. Revolution assaults a set of legitimizing norms, the prevailing paradigm. One of the distinguishing features of this paradigm is that it explicitly excludes whatever it is that the revolution wants. There is nothing in the paradigm to sanction its revolutionary replacement. Violence alone can alter this situation by enforcing the authority that revolution confers upon itself. Revolution assumes the genius for knowing, if not right reason, right violence. In order to create a new paradigm, it has as much need for violence as the state has for prisons. Moreover, violence can be extended as a practice and transvalued as a concept in much the same manner that the authority of the state can undergo bureaucratic expansion and pragmatic philosophical buttressing. The escalation of violence from unorganized fury to a reign of terror is part of revolution's search for legitimacy. And so is the transvaluing process. For to the extent that the act of foundation is frustrated, delayed, and, in effect, abandoned, the act of terror is usually cultivated, sanctioned, and accorded sacramental status.

Revolution also requires absolute confidence in its own rectitude; it can achieve this confidence only by remaining ideologically coherent and intact. If violence attempts to exercise absolute control over the world of the body, ideology seeks the same kind of control over the world of the mind. The gross form of this control, propaganda, is, given the sort of issues we are pursuing, less to the point than the severely intellectualized polemics that in many ways generated revolutionary action. Few writers were disillusioned by the cruder forms of propaganda that normally accompanied revolution. But intellectual pretentiousness, the dogged adherence to a formula, and the arrogant claim to scientific accuracy appalled moderates. Ideology mechanized the revolutionary spirit; it deprived it of human significance; and it returned society to the environment of dogma. The reaction against ideology, since it forms so recurrent a theme in Scott, Byron, Carlyle, and Arnold, can be represented here very briefly. What is at issue is the decay of consciousness and spontaneity, the leaden weight that revolution's negative content thrust upon its latent content. Herzen very clearly observed the deadening of sensibility to be discerned among the *habitués* of the revolution. He saw them gathered at the Café Lamblin looking like so many lapidary inscriptions seated at table. "Dealing all their lives with a small number of political ideas, they only know their rhetorical side, so to speak, their sacerdotal vestments."[46] Herzen's mockery is, however, deceptive. The ideologues of the revolution could be treated contemptuously, but they incarnated the perversities of the analytical intellect. They did, in good earnest, murder to dissect. Their political ideology was the advance guard of the secular and inductive mind that had made method the latest despotism. They are those for whom Tocqueville reserved his greatest scorn and whom he saw as the architects of modern man's grief. "These strange beings [were not] mere ephemera, born of a brief crisis and destined to pass away when it ended. They were, rather, the first of a new race of men who subsequently prospered and proliferated in all parts of the civilised world, everywhere retaining the same characteristics. They were already here when we were born, and they are still with us."[47] The astringency of Tocqueville's response is symptomatic. The literary imagination frequently reacted to ideology in the same way. It had seen mind, as Yeats said, dwindling into "a bitter, an abstract thing." We may turn once again to *Doctor Zhivago* for a compelling late echo of this theme in the tragedy of revolution. Zhivago, having lost everything, has returned to a devastated Moscow. With him is Vasia Brykin, a youth who has become Zhivago's companion as well as a reminiscence of his own lost boyhood. After a time, however,

> . . . the friendship between Yurii Andreievich and Vasia cooled. Vasia had developed remarkably. He no longer thought or spoke like the ragged, barefoot, dishevelled boy from Veretenniki. The obviousness, the self-evidence, of the truths proclaimed by the

46. *My Past and Thoughts*, p. 349.
47. *Ancien Régime*, p. 178.

revolution attracted him increasingly, and the doctor's language, with its obscurities and its imagery, now struck him as the voice of error, doomed, conscious of its weakness and therefore evasive. [*Doctor Zhivago*, p. 478]

It is significant that Pasternak writes, immediately before this, that in their wanderings the doctor and Vasia "moved from one dilapidated place to another, each uninhabitable and uncomfortable in a different way."[48] In the contest for a habitable position, the assertion of a large design seemed more cogent and appealing than the acceptance of incessant, ambiguous, and multitudinous intellectual activity, which may, indeed, at times cover its evasions by a taste for doubt. But many writers preferred the risks of the latter to the freezing certainties of the former.

The absolutes of revolution imitated the function of zero. Everything was to be measured with reference to them. Revolution could be located, with some propriety, under the sign of zero, for at the deepest level of its activity it toyed with nihilism. Its furious work of destruction implied a cosmic contamination from which it could not shield even itself. Again and again, men found cause to observe that revolution eats its children. In its confederation of absolutes, absolute negation inevitably found a place. Sergei Nechayev, the model for Verkhovensky in *The Possessed,* left in his *Catechism of the Revolutionist* an outline for a nihilist manifesto: "A revolutionary enters the world of the State and its so-called intellectual world, and he lives in that world with the sole purpose of its complete and speedy destruction. . . . It is all the worse for him if he has family, friendship, or love relationships; he is not a revolutionary if they can stay his hand."[49]

Dostoevsky has Verkhovensky confess himself a nihilist in just the sense that is relevant to our purpose. Verkhovensky says, "I

48. Pasternak, *Doctor Zhivago,* pp. 474–75.

49. Cited from "The Catechism of the Revolutionist," in *Revolutionaries on Revolution,* ed. Philip B. Springer and Marcello Truzzi (Pacific Palisades: Goodyear, 1973), pp. 185–86.

am a nihilist, but I love beauty. Don't nihilists love beauty"?[50] The point here is that the potential nihilism of revolutionaries is concealed, usually even from themselves, by veneers of sentiment. Their nihilism is equivalent to the dark in the tunnel of love. Dostoevsky was convinced of this. For other writers, much less hostile to the spirit of revolution, the discovery of the dark was not an exposure of hypocrisy but an exposure of the tragic, an apprehension of the fateful way in which dedication, compassion, and hope connect by strange routes to the denial of life. Obviously these writers do not begin with such a patently unstable figure as Nechayev. Their interest is not in active nihilism but in the lurking potential for nihilism that revolution harbors among its ideological absolutes. This is what we see in Georg Büchner's extraordinary drama, *Danton's Death*.[51] Danton, near his end as a political figure and spiritually wrecked by the bloodbath of the September Massacres, seeks in sensuality some respite both from his enemies and from the torpid gloom that has come to possess him. As the play develops, it becomes clear that his appetite for sensuality is no more than a desperate effort to remain in contact with life itself. In making this effort, he is resisting the nihilistic impulse that sprang up within him when he recognized how clearly his bloody actions had reflected and abetted Robespierre's ideological and moral insanity. He knows that he has been victimized by revolution's absolutes.

Who can condemn the hand on which the curse of "must" has fallen? Who spoke the "must"? Who was it? Was it that part of ourselves which lies, whores, steals, and murders? We're pup-

50. Fyodor Dostoevsky, *The Devils*, trans. David Magarshack (Harmondsworth: Penguin, 1971), p. 420. For Dostoevsky's use of Nechayev, see Magarshack's "Introduction" to this edition; for the emergence of the term "nihilism" in nineteenth-century revolutionary rhetoric, see Avrahm Yarmolinsky, *Road to Revolution: A Century of Russian Radicalism* (New York: Collier Books, 1962), pp. 148–68.
51. In *Classical German Drama*, trans. Theodore H. Lustig (New York: Bantam Books, 1963). Büchner's striking affinities with Carlyle are explored

pets, and unknown powers manipulate our wires. Ourselves
we're nothing, nothing! We are the swords wielded by ghosts
who fight each other, their hands remain unseen as in a fairy tale.
Now I am calm.   [II, v]

His calmness is, of course, emptiness. He struggles against this
emptiness, but the horror that he confronts and that accompanies
him to the guillotine is overwhelming. He gives form to it in an
image that grotesquely identifies his sense of the revolution's ultimate assumptions about man and the nature of the world.

There is this damned maxim that something cannot become
nothing! I am something, that is the trouble! . . . Nothingness
has committed suicide, Creation is its wound, we are the drops of
its blood and the world is the grave in which it rots.   [III, vii]

It is worth observing that Büchner's assessment of revolution
is echoed by a writer so distant from him as André Malraux.
Man's Fate is a chronicle of the flaring nihilism in revolution, and
it uses the wound as its central metaphor. But Malraux sees the
nihilism of the revolutionaries as a calculated risk in a magnificent
gamble against oppression. Their failure is predicted in the opening event of the novel. The devout terrorist Ch'en wounds himself in the process of killing a sleeping man, and this scene makes a
pattern for the whole book. The pattern repeats itself even in Old
Gisors, Ch'en's Buddhist mentor, who has passed beyond the
concerns of the political realm, but who seeks his own version of
transcendence—and moves toward it with opium. It is impossible
to distinguish Gisors's meditative tranquillity from his opiated
vacancy. Malraux applies the same ambiguity to the novel's revolutionary action. Psychic and moral self-destruction exist side by
side with the compassionate heart and the enlightened mind. In
the climactic episode of the novel, all the principal revolution-

_____

in R. Majut, "Georg Büchner and Some English Thinkers," *MLR,* 48 (1953),
310–22.

aries, each suffering from a wound, await their execution by rifle squad or, for some, by incineration. What we see are doomed men "in the darkness full of menaces and wounds, among all those brothers in the mendicant order of the Revolution." And Malraux writes: "Each of these men had wildly seized as it stalked past him the only greatness that could be his."[52] Their deaths testify to their heroism; but their wounds testify to the moral damage they have done to themselves in the darkness. Their spirit of self-sacrifice is nearly overshadowed by the self-annihilating ceremonies to which their mendicant order has pledged them.

The writer who has made the most influential analysis of revolution as a nihilistic act is, no doubt, Albert Camus. I want to summarize his analysis in some detail because *The Rebel* figures in several of the later chapters of this study, and quite extensively in the chapter on Byron.

Both Camus's admirers, such as Richard Wollheim, and his best Marxist critics, such as Raymond Williams, see him, rightly, in the line of nineteenth-century liberal humanists. For Wollheim, Camus has brilliantly dissociated liberal humanism from the Romantic "voice" in politics, that dangerous propensity for passionate submission with which the Romantic imagination approaches its several deities. For Williams, Camus, in his struggle against submission, expresses "the last rhythm of liberal tragedy." It is an authentic rhythm, but greatly diminished in significance because of its typical inability to extend to collective suffering the empathy it reserves for the struggle of the individual. Williams argues this point after being candid enough to cite Camus's own statement that "today tragedy is collective."[53]

Camus begins with the existentialist revelation of *absurdité*. The

---

52. André Malraux, *Man's Fate*, trans. Haakon M. Chevalier (1934; rpt. New York: Random House, 1961), p. 300.

53. Williams, *Modern Tragedy*, p. 174; and see his whole discussion of Camus and Sartre, pp. 174–89. Richard Wollheim discusses Camus in "The Political Philosophy of Existentialism," *Cambridge Journal*, 7 (1953), 3–19.

universe is indecipherable. We may react to this discovery by accepting a state of passive nihilism. Or we may create on our own a system of values that the world necessarily does not give us. Finally, as Wollheim puts it, "there is the realization that any such act to be consistent must be done not merely on one's own behalf but on behalf of all."[54] *L'homme révolté* is the man who moves through all three of these phases. The revolutionary, on the other hand, betrays the act of rebellion by contravening one stage or another of the rebel's logic.

"Our purpose," Camus says, "is to find out whether innocence, the moment it becomes involved in action, can avoid committing murder" (*TR*, p. 4). If the world is absurd, murder is, at most, morally neutral. His argument is that the rebel who murders simply imitates the world of the Everlasting No, thereby destroying the only thing of value that he may trust: his human no, which he declares from within that "passionate side of his nature [which] serves no other purpose than to be part of the act of living" (*TR*, p. 19). The rebel finds honor—and value—in a paradox. In spite of the interminable negation in which he lives, he affirms the existence of a borderline. "In a certain way, he confronts an order of things which oppresses him with the insistence on [his] right not to be oppressed beyond the limit that he can tolerate" (*TR*, p. 13). At that very point of action in which he declares his right to exist, he declares the right of all men to exist. Man's solidarity is thus based on rebellion, and rebellion, in its turn, can justify itself only by this solidarity. Any rebellion that destroys brotherhood is therefore "in reality an acquiescence in murder" (*TR*, p. 22). On the other hand, by sustaining the paradox that informs it, rebellion transcends nihilism.

The Rebel begins with a consideration of what Camus calls metaphysical rebellion and it traces the process by which metaphysical rebellion becomes political revolution. The crucial link in this

---

54. Wollheim, "Political Philosophy of Existentialism," p. 13.

process is the nineteenth century's transformation of metaphysical rebellion into historical rebellion. The latter is an outgrowth of radical Hegelianism and it prepares for the Marxist-Stalinist revolution of the twentieth century. The book's development, then, may be seen as depending on a three-part summary of Camus's attitude toward nihilism: a rejection of passive nihilism; a celebration of the rebel's discovery of an alternative to nihilism; and a description of the tragedy of active, revolutionary nihilism.

Camus's description of revolutionary nihilism is based on the politicizing of rebellion that is evident in the French Revolution. For then began the desperate effort "to create, at the price of crime and murder if necessary, the dominion of man" (*TR*, p. 25). The energy that impelled this effort was the search for new absolutes, a search that was initiated by a catastrophic weakening of the rebel's allegiance to the paradox that gives him his dignity.

The true spirit of rebellion, though it kills God, also builds a church, which is to say that the rebel, while he finds that nothing is true, refuses to act as if everything were permitted. The major legacy of the nineteenth-century revolutions is their obscuring of this commitment through a rationalizing of murder in the name of abstract principles.

> The revolution based on principles kills God in the person of [the King]. The revolution of the twentieth century kills what remains of God in the principles themselves and consecrates historical nihilism. Whatever paths nihilism may proceed to take, from the moment it decides to be the creative force of its period and ignores every moral precept, it begins to build the temple of Caesar. To choose history, and history alone, is to choose nihilism, in defiance of the teachings of rebellion itself. [*TR*, p. 246]

Hegel made the most influential choice of history. By granting history the status that had been denied to God, Hegel opened the way for the possessed to take power. History becomes a protracted punishment since the only real reward available to man will come at the end of time. In the meanwhile, the deification of history makes it possible to say once and for all, that the revolution itself is more important than the people it wanted to save. With this acknowledgment the betrayal of rebellion emerges in its last and most brutal phase in which man is once again required to become a slave. "The tragedy of this revolution is the tragedy of nihilism" (*TR*, p. 240). Camus describes the tragic action of revolution by adverting to the ancient myth that gives *The Rebel* its moral focus.

> Here ends Prometheus' surprising itinerary. Proclaiming his hatred of the gods and his love of mankind, he turns away from Zeus with scorn and approaches mortal men in order to lead them in an assault against the heavens. But men are weak and cowardly; they must be organized. They love pleasure and immediate happiness; they must be taught to refuse, in order to grow up, immediate rewards. Thus Prometheus, in his turn, becomes a master who first teaches and then commands. Men doubt that they can safely attack the city of light. . . . The hero tells them that he, and he alone, knows the city. Those who doubt his word will be thrown into the desert, chained to a rock, offered to the vultures. The others will march henceforth in darkness, behind the pensive and solitary master. Prometheus alone has become a god and reigns over the solitude of men. But from Zeus he has gained only solitude and cruelty; he is no longer Prometheus, he is Caesar. The real, the eternal Prometheus has now assumed the aspect of one of his victims. The same cry, springing from the depths of the past, rings forever through the Scythian desert. [*TR*, pp. 244–45]

So compressed an account of *The Rebel* must serve for the moment as a summary of Camus's thought. I shall expand the account when we discuss Byron, whose understanding of revolution's negative content led him to investigate the difference between rebellion and revolution.

The triadic structure offered here as a way of displaying revolution's tragic content relates certain issues given predominance by one writer or work to those that preoccupy another. In the case of Carlyle, this structure is even a subtextual format controlling his description of the French Revolution as a tragic action. I am far from claiming, however, that the structure makes an impermeable background for the reading of literary texts. Its major purpose is to indicate the entanglement of motives working to convince moderates of revolution's intrinsically tragic nature. One or another of these motives is often stressed. But, mainly, the derelict could not fail to know them all. For his sense of tragedy came to him, fundamentally, not in his cool analysis of the saw's teeth but in his shocked experience of the edge. There is a scattered imagery in the prose and poetry of the age which, though it is not consistent, summarizes the three kinds of tragic occurrence in revolution's three kinds of content, and intimates, as well, their ultimate unity as modes of affliction.

> *Deluge*—the overwhelming of the simple designs for freedom and justice originally drawn up by the heirs of the Enlightenment.

> *Pollution*—the corruption of the secular redemption within man's reach by revolution's refusal to quit the political realm and become purely an activity of spirit.

> *Drought*—the disappearance of negotiated renewal in a world that has subscribed to violence and ideology.

The imagery highlights the major points of recurrent tension that led nineteenth-century writers to see revolution as a tragic action. A great many additional sources for this idea could be adduced, but one source reiterates all that is essential. There is a passage in Thucydides so remarkable as a reflection of the tragedy of revolution that it was commandeered by nineteenth-century editors and translators as a veritable prophecy. In Book III of his history Thucydides moralized upon the chaos caused by the Peloponnesian War. His term for the conflict he was describing is *stasis,* which until the nineteenth century had been translated as "sedition." But in the widely used Crawley translation, *stasis* becomes revolution.

> So bloody was the march of revolution [that] the whole Hellenic world was convulsed. . . . The sufferings which revolution entailed upon the cities were many and terrible. . . . Moderation was held to be a cloak for unmanliness; ability to see all sides of a question inaptness to act on any. . . . To succeed in a plot was to have a shrewd head, to divine a plot still shrewder; but to try to provide against having to do with either was to break up your party and to be afraid of adversaries. . . . Even blood became a weaker tie than party. . . . On the one side [there was] the cry of political equality of the people, on the other of an ordered aristocracy. . . . Meanwhile the moderate part of the citizens perished between the two, either for not joining in the quarrel, or because envy would not suffer them to escape. Thus every form of iniquity took root in the Hellenic countries. . . . Society became divided into camps in which no man trusted his fellow.[55]

55. *The History of the Peloponnesian War,* trans. Richard Crawley (London: Longmans, Green, 1876), pp. 224–27. The relatively late date of this translation is deceptive. Crawley worked on it for many years ("Preface," p. vii). But more to the point is the way "revolution" crept into the text much earlier in the century. William Smith's translation, first published in 1753, retained "sedition" in its 4th edition (London: W. Baynes, 1805). *The History of Thucydides,* trans. S. T. Bloomfield (London: Longman, Rees, 1829) also uses "sedition," but Bloomfield could not refrain from editorializing in his notes to the passage in question: "This [situation] again occurred during the Peloponnesian war of our own times, the *French Revolution,* when there was the same struggle between aristocracy and democracy . . . and when men of ability, who had flattered the vanity and prejudices of the multitude . . . were soon pulled down by others who were ready to go to *greater* lengths to obtain the same objects" (II, 152n). By 1840 Thomas Arnold had raised "revolution" to a place in the marginal gloss that he supplied for his edition of the Greek text, *The History of the Peloponnesian War,* 8th ed. (Oxford and London: Parker, 1882), I, 441. (Editions subsequent to the 2d in 1840 merely add indexes by R. P. G. Tiddeman.) In addition, Dr. Arnold was moved to explicit commentary on the key passage: "Compare the overthrow of the Presbyterians by the Independents, and that of the Brissotine, or Girondist party, by the Jacobins. In ordinary times in civilized countries intellect has the superiority over physical strength and energy; but revolutions . . . place men in the condition of barbarians" (I, 460). After Arnold, "revolution" became the estab-

This chapter from Thucydides was read, *mutatis mutandis,* as a study in contemporary history. The writer whom Macaulay called the world's greatest historian had composed, with dramatic accuracy, a portrait of an age that seemed to moderates to be reenacting itself. In Dr. Thomas Arnold's words, "the work of Thucydides . . . belongs to modern and not to ancient history. [It] affords a political lesson more applicable to our own times, if taken all together, than any other portion of history which can be named anterior to the eighteenth century."[56]

FOUR BRITISH WRITERS

Scott, Byron, Carlyle, and Arnold judged revolution to be a tragic action. It is true that these four writers are not tragedians of the highest order. It is also true that, as British citizens, they had no contact with the solemn venture of revolution. But if revolution was for them an atmospheric rather than a personal crisis, the atmosphere was sufficiently electric. It fundamentally influenced the sense of tragedy they brought to their work. In American literature the association of revolution and tragedy hardly occurs. Revolution in America was subject to a special dispensation from terror. Many explanations for the dispensation have been given, perhaps none so cogent as Richard Hofstadter's observation that "the United States was the only country in the world that began with perfection and aspired to progress."[57] Continental writers, on the other hand, have dramatized the possibilities of revolution in a literature that is reinforced by the pungency of

---

lished term for English translations (e.g., Benjamin Jowett's in 1881 and Rex Warner's in 1954).

56. *History of the Peloponnesian War,* III, xiv. Arnold has in mind the whole historical period from Pericles to Alexander.

57. *The Age of Reform: From Bryan to F.D.R.* (New York: Vintage Books, 1960), p. 36. The question is discussed in detail in Edward Pessen, "Why the United States Has Never Had a Revolution—Only 'Revolutions,' " *South Atlantic Quarterly,* 72 (Winter 1973), 29–42. And see White, *Metahistory,* p. 210.

firsthand reports. Britain is distinguished by its divergence from both the American and European developments. It could neither plumb the depths of modern revolutionary experience nor remove itself, at a stroke, from the revolutionary environment. It was crisscrossed by the warm breeze of gradualism and the east wind of imminent revolt. As I suggested earlier, this is hardly the preclinical condition implied by conventional emphasis on the "threat" of revolution. It is a condition with its own pathology, a condition in which restless hopes and frayed nerves can approximate the damage of actual trauma. Scott, Byron, Carlyle, and Arnold were steadfastly bound by this condition, and they wrote in a spirit of tragedy that is pervasively affected by it.

The *kind* of tragedy they wrote is affected in the same way. The highest order of tragedy makes a different claim on us than the works we are to deal with. Some remarks by Lionel Trilling on the nature of high tragedy come usefully into place here:

> Tragedy . . . invites us to find in it some pedagogic purpose, but the invitation cannot really be thought to be made in good faith. We cannot convince ourselves that the two Oedipus tragedies teach us anything. . . . We decide that tragedy has indeed nothing to do with the practical conduct of life except as it transcends and negates it, that it celebrates a mystery debarred to reason, prudence, and morality.[58]

On the whole, Scott, Byron, Carlyle, and Arnold acquiesce in the pedagogic purpose promised by tragedy—which they do, in fact, accept in good faith. They do not attain the transcendence of which Trilling speaks. And though their inhibition may have something to do with the limits of their genius, it has more to do with the functions of tragedy described in the first section of this chapter. The scheme of tragedy was for them, perhaps even more than for others, an oracular design. To say this is to place upon

58. *Sincerity and Authenticity* (Cambridge: Harvard University Press, 1972), pp. 83–84.

them the onus of didacticism. But our knowledge of nineteenth-century literature has by now made it clear that the didactic and imaginative functions of literature are capable of cohabitation. There is another important point to be made. Though they lived on the nether slopes of a volcano, the point of their appeals to the tragic spirit was not always—or even usually—to turn men back to the slumbers of the valley. They themselves had, more or less, given up those slumbers. For the most part (Carlyle always being somewhat irregular), they invoked the spirit of tragedy in their perplexed recourse to what Camus has called "the extenuating intransigence of moderation" (*TR*, p. 303). They could recommend neither the valley nor the volcano.

The severity of their moderation found expression in their appeals to the tragic spirit. The spirit of tragedy, not the formal tradition, is at issue here. Only Byron and Arnold made major attempts to write tragedies in the formal literary sense. In the case of Byron, I have relied upon his use of the formal tradition as a guide to his sense of tragedy. But what matters most is what all four writers conceived tragedy to be and the way their thought was shaped by the pressure of revolution. Modern literature has more and more extended our understanding of the tragic in literature beyond the formal tradition and has made us conscious, in Unamuno's phrase, of the tragic sense of life in men and in peoples. This sense may be the deeply rooted habit of mind characteristic of a whole culture. But it may also be a special view of reality developed in response to historical crisis and shock.[59] As such, it becomes a search for elasticity. It seeks not only a continuing capacity to deal with disorder, but also, at its best moments, the retrieval of man from the marginal existence that chaos would allow him. The four writers we shall analyze had an ingrained attachment to the formal tradition, especially in its classical models,

59. Murray Krieger, *The Tragic Vision: Variations on a Theme in Literary Interpretation* (Chicago: University of Chicago Press, 1966), pp. 3, 30.

but in their own works they emphasized a tragic response to milieu, and they used for their purpose whatever genres and forms they could command.

In developing this sense of tragedy they did not, of course, altogether cease to be influenced by the dramatic tradition, and especially by the decisive event in formal tragedy, the catastrophe. We shall, however, see a number of instances in which these writers render tragic experience in works that manage to avert catastrophe. Sentimentality is not the definitive element in these instances; revolution is. Scott, Byron, Carlyle, and Arnold sometimes communicated their sense of tragedy in works that forestall tragic conclusions, or in ones that at least leave open the possibility of rescue. They sometimes write, that is, not transacted tragedies, but agendas for tragedy. There is little point in regarding works in this class as evasions. All four writers were concerned with what could be done to insulate Britain from the agony of revolution. It was their purpose to suggest the possibilities of rescue from cultural annihilation. Sometimes the integrity of their art disintegrated in the search for escape. But these instances are themselves significant examples of how imposing the alternatives, the tragic alternatives, seemed. As records of their sense of reality, the agendas are more representative, more telling, than the evasions.

There is no linear development in the idea of tragedy from one writer to the next. A large arc does extend from Scott's appeal to the sense of tragedy, which is almost always punctuated by confident expressions of hope, to Arnold's, whose confidence is often forced. But the four writers studied here establish four distinct kinds of relationship between tragedy and revolution. Overlaps and parallels occur, and they help us to establish connections; nevertheless, the consciousness of tragedy in these writers comes to them from their proximity to revolution, not from their proximity to one another. The point is to be emphasized in order that an opposite point can be made. And that concerns the very important sense in which Scott, Byron, Carlyle, and Arnold *did* influence one another. They are the four writers in nineteenth-century Britain who are most responsible for the development, the inculcation, and the transmission of the historical consciousness in their age. I suggest that a prolegomenon to this study might establish these four writers as a natural tetrad, and show that they relied upon one another's works in important ways in order to refine and distinguish their individual attitudes toward history. What can be said is that their diverse meditations on tragedy and revolution were initiated by their similar meditations on history. For this reason I have made a point of noting, if only briefly at times, some of the major lines of influence or stimulus that ramify in their works. If, as David DeLaura has argued, Arnold's "historical nightmare" prefigures the formation of the post-Victorian sensibility, then we can see in Scott, Byron, and Carlyle, together with Arnold, a chain of connection that links *Waverley* with *The Wasteland*.[60]

Whether one ought to say something of the same sort about the central theme studied here is doubtful. The tragic views of revolution manifested in Scott, Byron, Carlyle, and Arnold, though they resonate with the attitudes of such writers as Pasternak, Silone, Malraux, and Camus, are attended by critical nuances that are impressively unfamiliar to us. The very institutions that the nineteenth-century revolutions attacked are now, many of them, the curiosities of history. The major role that religion played as both instigator and antagonist of the revolutionary consciousness has dwindled dramatically in the political upheavals of the twentieth century. Most of all, contemporary revolution has entirely abandoned the concept of itself as a transitional act. The word "transition" was not coined in the nineteenth century, but it should have been. The word was a comfort to many people who

60. "Matthew Arnold and the Nightmare of History," *Victorian Poetry*, Stratford-upon-Avon Studies no. 15 (London: Edward Arnold, 1972), pp. 37–57.

used it as a synonym for survival. These same people might have agreed with Karl Jaspers that "transition is the zone of tragedy" but they could have drawn some hope from being able to define their condition in those terms.[61] The concept of transition sometimes bestowed a certain reasonableness on the crisis of revolution, suffusing it, almost, with overtones of a sweet malady. The idea of transition, in other words, blurred much of what a later age has come to know about the dynamics of change. The British writers who developed a sense of the tragedy of revolution were often responding to the shock of initiation. They did not expect transition to be balked; they did not know that the dynamics of change included deadlock. Their concessions to the dynamics of change become more and more dispiriting and create tones of surprise and depletion that mark the trials of their initiation. It was left to Tennyson, writing in the waning years of the century, to collect in a striking image the realities about change that the great age of revolution had finally—inexorably—unveiled:

Ah if I
Should play Tiresias to the times,
I fear I might but prophesy
Of faded faiths, and civic crimes,
And fierce Transition's blood-red morn.[62]

61. *Tragedy Is Not Enough,* trans. H. A. T. Reiche et al. (Boston: Beacon Press, 1952), p. 49.
62. The lines occur in a canceled stanza from "To E. FitzGerald," which Tennyson published in 1885. He no doubt canceled them as too gloomy for a birthday tribute (*The Poems of Tennyson,* ed. Christopher Ricks [London: Longmans, 1969], p. 1320).

CHAPTER TWO

Scott: The Implicit Note of Tragedy

In 1831 Sir Walter Scott was a man upon whom the glooms of age, sickness, and indebtedness had fixed themselves tenaciously. He had come to the end. Curiously, for a man so fascinated by the movements of history, an epoch was also at this time coming to its end. His son-in-law, John Gibson Lockhart, wrote to him from London on February 28: "Tomorrow is the grand day for Lord John Russell & by Friday night we shall, I suppose, be able to see what the first act of the *English* Tragedy comes to. . . . I witness a deep & bitter fierceness such as never met my observation before."

Scott replied, quoting, as he often did, from *King John*: "I have your desponding letter and can only answer 'you breathe these dead news in as dead an ear.' I have had no hope that the Reform or rather the Revolution bill would [not] pass. . . . I have resolved not to break my knuckles striking uselessly at a flint & steel to kindle wet tinder. Time which all refer to must be trusted."[1] History kept its compact with Scott. The Reform Bill did not become law until 1832; Scott did not die until 1832. Car-

1. *The Letters of Sir Walter Scott,* ed. H. J. C. Grierson (London: Constable, 1932–37), XI, 487–89.

lyle wrote the event down in his diary: "Sir Walter Scott died nine days ago. Goethe at the spring equinox, Scott at the autumn."[2] A new age had clearly come about. Carlyle would arrive at a better understanding of the reform movement than the dejected Walter Scott could manage. The world had gotten beyond him. Scott really did think that the passing of the Reform Bill was an act of revolution. Shortly after he replied to Lockhart's desponding letter, he wrote in his journal: "It has fallen easily the old Constitution, no bullying Mirabeau to assail, no eloquent Maury to defend. . . . The curse of Cromwell on those whose conceit has brought us to this pass."[3]

Such reflections on the history of his own times are to be found not only in Scott's letters and in his often moving and melancholy journal; they are also to be found in his novels. What finally matters about Scott's fiction is not its supreme evocation of the past but its exploration of the present. The device of historical narrative was, in Scott's hands, as in the hands of later historical novelists, a means of probing the present indirectly by filtering out the circumstantial and evanescent, and so turning the reader's mind to the deep core of historical meaning in his cultural experience. The mediating term, at least in the most powerful of the Scottish novels, is revolution.

The connection of past and present through the image of revolution generates, to a large extent, the quality in Scott's novels that David Daiches calls their "implicit tragic note."[4] Daiches' term is a convenient shorthand for the distinct, if restrained, sense

2. Quoted in James Anthony Froude, *Thomas Carlyle: A History of the First Forty Years of His Life* (1882; rpt. New York: Scribner's, 1906), II, 251.

3. *The Journal of Sir Walter Scott*, ed. W. E. K. Anderson (Oxford: Clarendon Press, 1972), p. 478.

4. "Scott's Achievement as a Novelist," *NCF*, 6 (1951), 153–73; rpt. in *Scott's Mind and Art*, ed. A. Norman Jeffares (Edinburgh: Oliver & Boyd, 1969), p. 34. W. P. Ker notices the same quality in his discussion of Scott; see *On Modern Literature: Lectures and Addresses* (Oxford: Clarendon Press, 1955), p. 109. Alexander Welsh finds the withholding of tragic finality in the novels

of doom that seems always to be pressing for recognition in the novels, and that occasionally, as in the famous pages devoted to the last hours of Fergus MacIvor and Evan Maccombich, emerges quite deliberately in a "tragic" set piece. It must be said that the implicit tragic note has several sources. Many critics have explained it with reference to Scott's nostalgia for a simple, heroic culture. In John Henry Raleigh's view, for example, the Waverley novels expose a development from "History as tragic myth, to History as the unambiguous present." For Georg Lukács, tragic effect in the novels is rendered by "the inability of the clans to defend their common interests against nobility or bourgeoisie." It is "historical necessity" that creates "the tragic atmosphere."[5]

And yet, while the novels do emphasize the reluctant farewell Scott bade to the heroic world, my argument here is that the implicit tragic note derives more basically from apprehensiveness than from regret. The image of revolution haunts the novels as a rattling of the past against the gates of the future—Scotland's future. Francis R. Hart has shown that Scott's novels frequently analyze the upheavals of history as a conflict of "opposing fanaticisms," a cataclysmic struggle of sanguinary combatants, one side fiercely defending a dilapidated tradition, the other cunningly advancing the cause of an ambitious but heartless modernism.[6] Seen from this perspective, Scott's fiction identifies for his contemporaries the prospect for tragic calamity inherent in the historical con-

a natural consequence of the romance form, upon which Scott drew so heavily. His analysis of Scott's "tentative fiction," *The Hero of the Waverley Novels* (New Haven: Yale University Press, 1963), pp. 189–98, is especially relevant.

5. John Henry Raleigh, "*Waverley* as History; or 'Tis One Hundred and Fifty-six Years Since," *Novel*, 4 (1970), 29; Georg Lukács, *The Historical Novel*, 2d ed., trans. Hannah and Stanley Mitchell (1962; rpt. Boston: Beacon Press, 1963), pp. 57–58.

6. *Scott's Novels: The Plotting of Historic Survival* (Charlottesville: University Press of Virginia, 1966). Hart's section called "Opposing Fanaticisms and the Search for Humanity" includes discussion of *Old Mortality, Woodstock, Peveril of the Peak, A Legend of Montrose,* and *The Heart of Mid-Lothian.*

ditions precipitated by the French Revolution. The conflicts of opposing fanaticisms are commentaries on the political polarization
that terrorized the European world during a considerable part of
Scott's own lifetime. As a reviewer of *Waverley* said (in 1814),
"the history of those bloody days, which is embodied in this tale,"
is an "awful warning" against the "fearful and deadly scenes of
civil commotion" that Britain had so recently witnessed in France.[7]
For Scott the politics of polarization were bound to have the
resonance of tragedy, because his sense of tragedy was always a response to the degradation of the social affections. It was, appropriately, in one of his unsuccessful attempts to write a tragic
drama that he managed to define most concisely the tragic idea
implicit in his novels dealing with opposing fanaticisms: "Wo to
those who would advance the general weal by trampling on the
social affections! They aspire to be more than men—they shall become worse than tigers."[8] The relationship between tragedy and
revolution projected in this speech derives from Scott's deepest
convictions about politics and society. Like Edmund Burke, he
saw in modern revolution an unexampled disordering of the human contexts that allow the social affections to flourish.

Tragedy in Scott works as an alarm sounded in response to revolution's camouflaged assault on "the general weal." Because
tragedy has this nearly semaphoric quality for Scott, his novels
might be described as narratives that passionately receive their
own signals. Ordinarily, the tragic note is embedded in the narrative as an inducement to the rediscovery of moral order. It is,
then, the precatastrophic phase of the tragic process that interests
Scott, since he is convinced that the amelioration of social crisis

7. The comments are made in an unsigned review of *Waverley* in the *British Critic* for August 1814; rpt. in *Scott: The Critical Heritage,* ed. John O. Hayden (London: Routledge & Kegan Paul, 1970), p. 68.
8. *The House of Aspen,* in *The Poetical Works of Sir Walter Scott* (Edinburgh: Adam & Charles Black, 1868), XII, 431.

may be possible once the dangerous conditions weakening the social order have been experienced for what they are. This is the case in two of the novels I shall discuss, *Old Mortality* (1816) and *The Heart of Mid-Lothian* (1818). A third novel, *The Bride of Lammermoor* (1819), is an important exception. Because it has a bleak, explicitly tragic ending, it has often been seen as an anomaly among Scott's works. It seems to me more suggestive to notice that this book may be read as a revealing structural transformation of the situation that dominates the other two novels. In *The Bride of Lammermoor* Scott allows the tragic rhythm to complete itself, as though to acknowledge the fragility of the resolutions achieved in his earlier books and the weight of the tragic element in them.

THE FALL FROM COMMUNITY

Nassau Senior, in an astute essay on Scott, called his novels "the most striking literary phenomena of the age," and, while noting the features praised by other critics, argued that the secret of their success was to be found in their skillful joining of "the most irreconcilable forms, and the most opposite materials. . . . tragedy and romance, comedy and the novel."[9] Senior's claim might be regarded as an early perception of the hybrid character of the novel as a literary form which has interested such later theoreticians as Lukács.[10] Scott himself, though no theoretician, was clearly in league with a literary tradition that encouraged rather

9. *Essays on Fiction* (London: Longman, Green, 1864), pp. 2–3. These remarks did not appear in the 1821 *Quarterly Review* version of Senior's essay. They occur in a sort of preamble to the essay which, as James T. Hillhouse speculates, was apparently cut by the *Quarterly* editor; see Hillhouse, *The Waverley Novels and Their Critics* (Minneapolis: University of Minnesota Press, 1936), p. 51.
10. See Georg Lukács, *The Theory of the Novel*, trans. Anna Bostock (Cam-

than stifled a breaking of the boundaries traditionally set between different genres. He once vividly recalled his excitement upon hearing Henry Mackenzie lecture in 1788 on the new literature of Germany. "Those who were accustomed from their youth to admire Milton and Shakespeare, became acquainted, I may say for the first time, with [poets] who, disclaiming the pedantry of the unities, sought . . . to present life in its scenes of wildest contrast." What he found in the Germans were writers who mingled, without hesitation, livelier with more serious incidents, and who exchanged "scenes of tragic distress, as they occur in common life, with those of a comic tendency."[11] These observations suggest that the tragic note implicit in the Waverley novels has much to do with Scott's underrated interest in the possibilities of fictional form as well as with the effect on him of his age's changing perception of the scene and motives of tragedy.

The major question that concerns us, however, is the content of tragedy as Scott himself tended to identify and describe it. As I have indicated, the preeminent tragic subject for Scott is the degradation of the social affections in Scotland. Scott came to his particular sense of tragic experience because he lived in, and loved, a country with a long heritage of rancorous civil disputes. It was a heritage of designing political factions polarizing Scotland in a way that constantly threatened what Scott once called life's greatest good (next to a clear conscience): "The quiet exercise and en-

bridge, Mass.: M.I.T. Press, 1971), and, for a more recent approach, Walter L. Reed, "The Problem with a Poetics of the Novel," *Novel,* 9 (1976), 101–13. Avrom Fleishman makes the point from a particularly germane perspective: "The historical novelist uses the universals of literature—such categories of esthetic experience as romance and satire, tragedy and comedy—to interpret the course of historical man's career" (*The English Historical Novel: Walter Scott to Virginia Woolf* [Baltimore: Johns Hopkins University Press, 1971], p. 8).

11. "Essay on Imitations of the Ancient Ballad" (1830), in Scott's *Minstrelsy of the Scottish Border,* ed. Thomas Henderson (New York: Thomas Y. Crowell, [1931]), p. 548.

joyment of social feelings."[12] He wrote about this heritage in
Tales of a Grandfather (1828-31):

> [A] bloody and tragic tale it has been. The generation of which I
> am an individual . . . have been the first Scotsmen who appear
> likely to quit the stage of life, without witnessing either foreign
> or domestic war within their country. Our fathers beheld the
> civil convulsion of 1745-6,—the race who preceded them saw the
> commotions of 1715, 1718, and the war of the Revolution in
> 1688-9. A third and earlier generation witnessed the two insur-
> rections of Pentland Hills and Bothwell Bridge, and a fourth lived
> in the bloody times of the great Civil War, a fifth had in memory
> the civil contests of James the Sixth's minority; and a sixth race
> carries us back to the long period when the blessings of peace
> were totally unknown, and the state of constant hostility be-
> tween England and Scotland, was only interrupted by insecure
> and ill-kept truces of a few years' endurance. And even in [my]
> own time, though this country was fortunate enough to escape
> becoming the theatre of bloody conflict, yet we had only to look
> abroad to witness such extensive scenes of war and slaughter,
> such subversion of established states, and extinction of ancient
> dynasties, as if the European world was again about to return to
> the bondage of an universal empire. [*MW*, XXV, 109-10]

This vision of history has much more to do with the note of
tragedy in Scott than his occasional renderings of personal disaster
in such novels as *Kenilworth* and *St. Ronan's Well.* Just as Scott
looked back to Scotland's romantic past and imagined its decline
into the bourgeois present, so also did he look back to its crises of
social and political enmity and imagined them in the light of
modern revolution. Though Scott certainly was attracted to a
progressive view of history, and though he understood the advantages of a rationalized life, he never believed that history guaran-
teed anything, and he saw a world of evidence to suggest that
extremists and fanatics would once again create a machinery of

12. *Letters of Sir Walter Scott*, V, 421.

hatred. *Tales of a Grandfather* is a book for the coming generations, and in it Scott also said that the

> spirit of party faction, far from making demigods of the one side,
> and fiends or fools of the other, is itself the blot and stain on our
> annals—*has produced under one shape or another its most tragic events*—
> has blighted the characters of its best and wisest statesmen, and
> perhaps reserves for Britain at a future day, a repetition of the
> evils with which it has already afflicted our fathers. [*MW*,
> XXV, 114; italics added]

What Scott is saying here is far from incidental. The passage reveals a historical imagination radically disturbed by the premoni-
tion of tragedy. The very passion of Scott's attachment to his
native country made him acutely sensitive to its menacing political impulses.

In the novels tragic action is checked by the social affections
and the community they inspire. Donald Davie is right to see almost everything Scott wrote as implying that the guiding principle of all public and much private morality is "the fact of community considered as a state of being or a state of feeling" and that it
is a "feeling of and for community" that we apprehend when we
speak, as we are compelled to do, of Scott's humanity.[13]

Any effort to understand the tragic implications that Scott perceived in the conflict of opposing fanaticisms must begin, then,
with an understanding of his trust in the idea of community.
Scott belongs to that oddly assorted group of post-Hobbesians,
which would include such men as Montesquieu, Burke, Coleridge, Comte, and Tocqueville, who agreed, despite their many
and deep differences, that political institutions derived their au-

---

13. *The Heyday of Sir Walter Scott* (London: Routledge & Kegan Paul,
1961), pp. 19–20. For a more detailed view, see Joan S. Elbers, "Isolation and
Community in *The Antiquary*," *NCF*, 27 (1973), 405–23. Glenn Tinder,
"Community: The Tragic Ideal," *Yale Review*, 65 (1976), 550–64, though
not on Scott, cogently challenges Scott's sort of assumptions.

thority from the organic structure of society. The governing order of civilized life was, in their view, inherent in the numberless private loyalties and communal arrangements that developed in small social units. Sheldon Wolin has described the assumptions behind this view:

> These elements furnished the necessary cohesives which held society together; should they be weakened, as occurred towards the end of the *ancien régime,* the political order would topple of its own weight. The focal point of inquiry, therefore, was to be directed at the system of social gradations; at the complex of nonrational "prejudices" which disposed men toward obedience and subordination; at the ties spun by local community, parish, and manor into a web of association stronger than any conscious thought could conceive.[14]

Scott was dedicated to this version of the relationship between politics and society. Like his own Chrystal Croftangry, he was "a Borderer between two ages."[15] He lived, as Edgar Johnson has said, between the fell encounters of mighty opposites: Highlander and Lowlander, pastoral Scotland and commercial England, Established Church and Covenanter, freedom of conscience and orthodoxy, Edinburgh's rationalism and Germany's imagination, tyranny and constitutional government, barbarism and culture, tradition and progress.[16] These mighty opposites, Scott knew, could turn themselves into opposing fanaticisms if the values for which they stood became the hinges of political extremism. Politics for Scott was a chaotic meddling in the neural web

---

14. *Politics and Vision* (Boston: Little, Brown, 1960), pp. 290–91.

15. For Chrystal Croftangry, see the First Series of *Chronicles of the Canongate* (1827). The comparison of Scott with Croftangry cited here was made by John Gibson Lockhart, *Memoirs of the Life of Sir Walter Scott* (Edinburgh: Robert Cadell, 1837–38), VII, ix–x.

16. I have somewhat extended the terms Johnson uses in his "Scott and the Corners of Time," in *Scott Bicentenary Essays,* ed. Alan Bell (Edinburgh: Scottish Academic Press, 1973), p. 27.

upon which the social order was founded. And in his own time it
was all too evident that politics was steadily enlarging its base of
operations.[17]

These attitudes were most influentially articulated for Scott by
Burke, but they also grow out of the effect on him of key figures
in the Scottish Enlightenment, a tradition whose profound importance for Scott has been increasingly documented since Duncan
Forbes published his pioneering essay in 1953.[18] Scott's valuation
of the social affections is itself best understood as a development
of Francis Hutcheson's and David Hume's conception of a non-
cognitive moral sense in human nature which issues in human benevolence. Hume, in a well-known passage, argued that "some
spark of friendship for human kind; some particle of the dove
[must be] kneaded into our frame, along with the elements of the
wolf and serpent." He based his case on the perception that "the
social virtues are never regarded without their beneficial tendencies, nor viewed as barren and unfruitful. The happiness of mankind, the order of society, the harmony of families, the mutual
support of friends, are always considered as the result of their
gentle dominion over the breasts of men."[19]

Scott reflects this line of thinking in much of his work and of-

17. The development is analyzed in J. H. Plumb, "Political Man," in *Man
versus Society in Eighteenth-Century Britain,* ed. James L. Clifford (London:
Cambridge University Press, 1968), pp. 1–22.

18. "The Rationalism of Sir Walter Scott," *Cambridge Journal,* 7 (1953),
20–35. Peter D. Garside has further explored the background in a series of essays, especially "Scott, the Romantic Past, and the Nineteenth Century," *Review of English Studies,* n.s. 23 (1972), 147–61, and "Scott and the Philosophical Historians," *Journal of the History of Ideas,* 36 (1975), 497–512.

19. *Enquiries Concerning Human Understanding and Concerning the Principles
of Morals* [1777], ed. L. A. Selby-Bigge and P. H. Nidditch (Oxford: Clarendon Press, 1975), pp. 181–82, 271. See also Francis Hutcheson, *Illustrations on
the Moral Sense,* ed. Bernard Peach (Cambridge: Harvard University Press,
1971). Peach's introductory discussion (especially pp. 74–88) analyzes the
"moral sense" theory in a way that suggests crucial parallels between Hutcheson and Scott.

ten makes it quite explicit. "Nature," he said, "when she created man a social being, gave him the capacity for drawing happiness from his relations with the rest of the race which he is doomed to seek in vain in his own bosom"(*MW*, XVII, 359). Thus it is not Scott's antiquarian interests that elicited from him his deep loyalty to the ties spun by local community. His loyalty is founded on the prospect of community as the goal of man's unique moral sense, an endowment that could be trusted in contrast to the operations of reason, which Scott, like Burke, distrusted as the potential agent of doctrinaire policy and political revolution. He saw the exchange of simple benevolence for rational ideology as inevitably enticing political mania out of civilization's spiritual deserts and endowing it with a lamia-like power over the discipline of the social affections.

Scott, however, is not Burke or a reflecting apparatus for the Scottish Enlightenment. His social vision has its own imaginative structure and content, and is marked, as we might expect, by a set of internal tensions that decisively influence his fiction.

It is a tradition in Scott studies to observe the remarkable difference between the rasping Toryism so often evident in his commentary on contemporary affairs and the spirit of tolerance that is a salient feature of the novels. The rasping Tory is fully on display in Scott's reply to Lockhart quoted at the beginning of this chapter. The spirit of toleration is everywhere on display in his fiction. This misalignment is still, perhaps, most pungently described by Hazlitt in *The Spirit of the Age*. Noting that Scott is a man who "shudders at the shadow of innovation," and accusing him of venting "his littleness, pique, resentment, bigotry and intolerance on his contemporaries," Hazlitt was moved to a light mockery when he considered the moderation so characteristic of Scott's fiction.

> The political bearing of the *Scotch Novels* has been a considerable recommendation to them. . . . The candour of Sir Walter's his-

toric pen levels our bristling prejudices . . . and sees fair play between Roundheads and Cavaliers, between Protestant and Papist.
He is a writer reconciling all the diversities of human nature to
the reader. . . . There was a talk at one time that our author was
about to take Guy Faux [sic] for the subject of one of his novels,
in order to put a more liberal and humane construction on the
Gunpowder Plot.[20]

The case is just as Hazlitt says: Sir Walter's historic pen levels
our bristling prejudices. But this does not mean that Scott en-
dorses in his novels a middle-of-the-road politics. Actually, the
Scotch novels attempt to level all political positions and to reach
an image of community as *telos*. There are, without question, political implications inherent in this climax, and the implications
are mainly conservative.[21] Nevertheless, it is a crucially altered
conservatism that appears as the goal toward which the novels
strive. It is purged of all dialectical content; it exists only as a reflex of the prudence required to assure the hegemony of the social
will. The image of community as *telos* has, in other words, an inevitable political dimension, but it is a dimension completely submerged in the triumph of the social affections.

What Scott's historic pen thus effects is the transfiguration of
political dialectics, or, as A. O. J. Cockshut puts it, a mode of
"reconciliation at a level far deeper than the political."[22] That
Scott was in so many ways a rasping Tory probably accounts in
part for the strength of the transfiguration achieved in the novels.
He knew too well the signs of a violent political temper. And if

20. William Hazlitt, "Sir Walter Scott," *New Monthly Magazine* (April
1824); rpt. in *The Spirit of the Age* (1825; London: World's Classics, 1904),
p. 86.
    21. Some important remarks on this issue may be found in George Levine,
"Politics and the Form of Disenchantment," *College English,* 36 (1974), 422–
35. But cogent as I find Levine's general argument that "the minutest narrative choices . . . become political" (p. 427), I think the essay overplays the
persistence of Scott's Toryism in the deliverances his heroes achieve.
    22. *The Achievement of Walter Scott* (London: Collins, 1969), p. 60.

he did not know them from himself, he knew them from Scotland's political heritage. For it was surely Scotland that aroused in Scott his feeling for the sanctity of local custom and practice as well as his apprehension of fierce political divisions. Scott, who in this regard resembles Yeats, immersed himself in the idiomatic life and legends of his homeland, the things that "married its people to rock and hill," while he worried ceaselessly about the strident dogmatizing and rhetoric of terror that dominated Scotch politics.[23] His apprehension shows up frequently in his journal and letters. Beyond the rasping Tory propagandist there is the Scott who recoiled at the appalling consequences of political divisions. He clearly believed that "politics are the blowpipe beneath whose influence the best cemented friendships too often dissever."[24] What concerned him most was the difficulty of fixing limits on the sphere of political action so that the cooperation essential to social life would not be destroyed.

> The Tories and Whigs may go be damned together as names that have distracted Old Scotland and torn asunder the most kindly feelings since the first day they were invented. . . . They are spells to rouse our angry passions. . . . God knows I would fight in honourable contest with word or blow for my political opinions but I cannot permit that strife to "mix its waters with my daily meal," those waters of bitterness which poison all mutual love and confidence betwixt the well disposed on each side, and prevent them if need were from making mutual concessions and balancing the constitution against the Ultras of both parties. The good man seems something broken by these afflictions. [*Journal of Sir Walter Scott*, pp. 63–64]

The distinction Scott himself draws here between a rather adventurous response to overt political challenge and the tolerance necessary to cohesive social life enables us to see the structure of

23. My reference is to *The Trembling of the Veil*, in *The Autobiography of William Butler Yeats* (New York: Collier Books, 1965), pp. 131–32.
24. *Journal of Sir Walter Scott*, p. 47.

value in whose name the novels move toward a redefined conservatism. Scott, in making this distinction, had, as I have indicated, the vivid example of Scotland to instruct him. The root of the distinction, however, lies in a larger European preoccupation with the difference between idiomatic and institutional life. A writer so philosophically distant from Scott as Proudhon, for example, formulated the distinction in a way that is directly relevant to the kind of conflict envisioned by the Waverley novels. In the "Second Study" of his *General Idea of the Revolution in the Nineteenth Century* (1851), Proudhon writes: "We must understand that outside the sphere of parliamentarism, *as sterile as it is absorbing,* there is another field, incomparably vaster, in which our destiny is worked out; that beyond these *political phantoms whose forms capture our imagination,* there are phenomena of social economy, which, by their harmony or discord, produce all the good and ill of society."[25]

Proudhon's comment is apposite because it acknowledges the mesmeric power of the political sphere while insisting that this power distorts the transcendent significance of communal action. At issue here, for Proudhon and for a great many other writers beginning with Herder, and before him Vico, is a question of historical consciousness. It was just about the time Scott was born (1771) that the nature of historical reality was being called into question in a way that would ultimately negate the heavily political meaning of historical action and bring to preeminence the notion of "culture" as history's most significant content. The popularity of Scott's novels is itself, of course, a major sign of this transformed historical consciousness.

The novels, by creating a fearful tension between the overbearing, extruded scene of political action and the idiomatic life, awaken the rhythms of Romantic tragedy. The focus on milieu,

---

25. P.-J. Proudhon, *General Idea of the Revolution in the Nineteenth Century,* trans. J. B. Robinson (London: Freedom Press, 1923), pp. 45–46 (italics added).

the emphasis on historical disorder and chaos, the isolation of the moderate by his burden of disillusionment, the inability of nearly all characters to see the immanence of meaning in human experience—these typical themes of Romantic tragedy all emerge in the Waverley novels. But, as I have indicated, tragedy is for Scott a semaphoric, not a symbolic, design. The tragic rhythms are not expanded into complex structures within which meaning and order are ultimately or even tentatively grasped. Instead, the note of tragedy becomes a kind of anathema that the novels cast upon the phantasmal world of political action. Warning us in this severe and troubled way against political mystifications, the novels redirect us in a search for the enduring wholesomeness of the presumptive life, the life that orthodox historical analysis had consistently minimized and obscured.

The search is conducted in a way that helps us to define the nature of narrative in Scott's "tragic" fiction. The crucial element is double plotting. There is a primary plot in which the hazards, opportunities, inducements, and, most important, the polarizations of political action are dominant. And there is a counterplot, superimposed on the primary plot, in which the abandoned or lost treasure of community becomes the focus of discovery. This superimposing or enjambment of plot and counterplot is essential. It replicates Scott's sense of the institutional and the idiomatic life at odds with one another. It is also important to see that the novels are not constructed so that the ideal of community belatedly appears as a comfortable sanctuary or marvelously achieved alternative after the titanic struggles formed in the primary plot have been brought to some sort of negative climax or impasse. The narratives are structured in such a way that the life of community, the life shaped by the social affections, is always substantiating itself in the very midst of the ideological contests that seem to dominate the action.

The double plotting is the narrative correlative of Scott's feeling for the adamantine strength of community as *telos,* on the one

hand, and his restless consciousness of momentous political movements and displacements, on the other. The note of tragedy is a
medium for locating the moral boundaries of plot and counterplot. The tragic element endows with appropriate dignity the
Ozymandian mightiness of the political realm, but it anathema-
tizes this realm, and alerts us to an entirely different social order
that is founded on "the spirit's weaving, the self-true mind, the
trusty reflex."[26]

These contending structures of value interact in relation to a
central character who has the lineaments but not the full endow-
ments of a hero.[27] The typical Scott hero is a representative individual who is best described, in Scott's own language, as the
"good man" caught between the "Ultras" of opposing parties.
This figure is Scott's embodiment of the moderate *in extremis*. In
his *Life of Napoleon* (1827), Scott frequently chastised "the defeated factions of Moderates" for "consulting their own safety"
(*MW*, IX, 31). But the moderates of the French Revolution,
Scott tried to show, were unable to seek anything but political solutions. The representative moderate in Scott's fiction is another
sort of figure entirely, and the role he must play defines both the
nature and the values of the life engendered by the social affections.

Capable of comprehending oppression, repelled by the many
modes of institutional tyranny that touch them, and attracted in
some measure to revolution's positive content, Scott's central
characters find themselves futilely drawn into the struggle between opposing fanaticisms. It is not, however, their task to resolve or harmonize these forces. The real task of the moderate *in*

26. The line is from Richard Wilbur's beautifully apposite poem, "Speech
for the Repeal of the McCarran Act," in *The Poems of Richard Wilbur* (New
York: Harcourt, Brace & World, 1963), p. 100.
27. The question of the "insipidity" of Scott's heroes has been much discussed since Scott himself first raised it in an unsigned review (Hayden, ed.,
Scott: The Critical Heritage, p. 115); it is the starting point for Welsh's *Hero of
the Waverley Novels*.

extremis is to discover their equally false natures and to pass, as through a temporal membrane, into the world of community. What the good man finally possesses is a saving conviction that the communal world reveals a social framework that is the true matrix of human behavior, and not its contingent result or product.[28] He thus frees himself from the dialectical confusions and egotistical fanaticisms that are the common trade of any social framework dominated by ideological initiatives. This, essentially, is the story of Waverley, who, as has often been noted, never resolves any of the specific political issues that initially provoke him. He simply recedes. But in receding, he does not disappear. We can find him relocated in a world where the crisis of wavering is terminated by the process of membership.

This pattern, of course, has many variations. They range from the experience of Jeanie Deans, who is never without sustaining faith in community, but who must make it prevail in a world threatened by deadlock, to the experience of Edgar Ravenswood, who, though exceptionally equipped, cannot escape the indurated polarization of his social environment. In spite of their important differences, however, these characters, together with Henry Morton in *Old Mortality,* stand in significant relation to one another. They are all (unlike Waverley) Scots, and the novels make us see them as closely connected to the tragic drama of Scotland's revolutionary history. Even as Scott admired the evidence of civilization's progress, he continued to recognize that in his own age tragedy remained a key term in the cluster of historical possibilities he could envision.

The consequence of his ambivalence is to turn the novels we are discussing into "paratragedies," according to Oscar Mandel's description of that form: "works of intrigue, works concerning

---

28. The idea is defined in these terms in J. G. A. Pocock, "Time, Institutions, and Action: An Essay on Traditions and Their Understanding," in *Politics and Experience: Essays Presented to Professor Michael Oakeshott,* ed. Preston King and B. C. Parekh (Cambridge: The University Press, 1968), pp. 213–14.

passive victims, works of grave but successful action."[29] This classification is especially appropriate for *Old Mortality* and *The Heart of Mid-Lothian*, which are undoubtedly novels concerning grave but successful action. And *The Bride of Lammermoor* presents us with a passive victim. There is, however, a relationship among these novels that Mandel's classification captures only inadvertently. In the first two novels the grave situation is redeemed precisely because vital action is possible. In *The Bride of Lammermoor* the passivity of the victim *is* the tragedy; all access to community is blocked.

These three novels, and, indeed, nearly all the novels that now stand as Scott's most distinguished achievements, were published between 1815 and 1820. That is to say, they were published during the ominous years of Britain's passage from Waterloo to Peterloo. The revival of radical politics in Britain during this period was matched only, as Elie Halévy has pointed out, by the ferocity of the British government's reliance on counterrevolutionary terror.[30] Scott, in working out the tale of revolution during this period, became, through his complex feeling for the divided tradition of Scottish history, the sort of author he pointedly described when he reviewed John Galt's "novel of character," *The Omen*: "The author is one of those whose 'sense of being is derived from the past.' . . . He does not form his conjectures of the future by comparing it with that which is present, but by the auguries derived from events long passed, and deeply engraved upon the tablets of recollection. These are of a solemn mystic air and tragic character" (*MW*, XVIII, 339–40).

29. *A Definition of Tragedy* (New York: New York University Press, 1961), p. 26.
30. *A History of the English People in the Nineteenth Century,* trans. E. I. Watkin (New York: Barnes & Noble, 1961), II, 25, and *passim,* provides a detailed account of radical activity in Britain after 1815, and notes the government's use of counterrevolution as a weapon.

TRAGEDY IN SCOTLAND

The revolutionary action explored in the three novels we shall discuss stresses, as Raymond Williams would say, the whole action of living men in their experience of disorder and alienation at the level of social crisis. In *Old Mortality,* the Revolution of 1688 is the broad background, but the main focus is on the rising of the Scottish Covenanters against the English Royalists at Drumclog in 1679 and their subsequent defeat at Bothwell Bridge shortly thereafter. Scott's interest, however, is not in the battles but in the nature of social crisis they reflect. *The Bride of Lammermoor* is set in the years immediately preceding the union of England and Scotland in 1707; it deals with the feudal world that was shattered by the Revolution Settlement and the bourgeois world it created. In *The Heart of Mid-Lothian,* whose action begins in 1736, the unresolved alienation of Scotland from England is balanced against a newer, explicitly modern form of revolutionary temperament. All three novels represent Scotland as a community divided by class conflict, internecine religious contentions, and a political struggle acted out in the name of what would come to be called the "British Constitution."

Alexander Welsh makes the point about *Old Mortality* that Scott, in exploring the "popular rising of 1679 . . . came much closer to the heart of all this change than he would have if he had chosen to describe the flight of James II from England."[31] The stability of British life was at stake, and stability counts for much more, in the action of the novel, then the displacement of the reigning dynasty. The novel covers the period from 1679 to 1689, though most of its action takes place in the early summer of the opening year.

The opposing fanaticisms of the novel are embodied in John

---

31. "Introduction" to *Old Mortality* (Boston: Houghton Mifflin, 1966), p. viii.

Balfour of Burley, who led the insurgents at Drumclog, and in Viscount "Bonny" Dundee, who is known to us through most of the novel as John Grahame of Claverhouse. Claverhouse, impeccably aristocratic, readily admits the parallel between himself and Burley: "We are both fanatics; but there is some distinction between the fanaticism of honour and that of dark and sullen superstition" (OM, p. 333). The novel refuses to let Claverhouse's distinction stand. Later, in a sequence central to Scott's whole view of revolution, these two fanatics will find themselves yoked in political alliance.

Behind each of these men is arrayed a special group of characters. Each group seems to coalesce because of its members' political interests and ideology, but in fact all of the characters are convincingly individuated. On the Royalist side there is Lord Evandale, who, while resembling and admiring Claverhouse, is a truly humane man. Another of the soldiers, Sergeant Bothwell, actually has royal blood in him, but he is much more deeply engaged in the life of a moderately debauched Cavalier than he is in resuscitating the privileges of his rank. Lady Margaret Bellenden values Bothwell's lineage far more than he does. She is a charming Royalist simpleton who plays cat's cradle with the forms and rituals of the feudal past. Her son, Major Bellenden, less headstrong than Evandale, delights primarily in protecting his family and has the distinctive warmth that is always called avuncular. Edith Bellenden, his young niece, though genteel, is patently without political consciousness of any kind.

There is equal diversity on the other side. Mause Headrigg rants in the grand Covenanter style, but she is really a terrific harpy who would be much given to ranting whatever her political or religious persuasion. Peter Poundtext, in spite of his name, is more at home "perusing an ancient theological treatise, with a pipe in his mouth, and a small jug of ale beside him," than he is in the councils of an insurgent army (OM, p. 269). He seems fossilized to the twenty-year-old Ephraim Macbriar, whose zeal, eloquence, and intelligence shape a martyr's destiny for him. Then there is the spectral Habakkuk Mucklewrath, a literally insane preacher who illustrates Scott's often-expressed conviction that revolution thrusts actual madmen into positions of power.

Scott's discriminations of character and personality within each camp make a brilliant demonstration of the way political definitions deform personal identity. Evandale's idealism, for example, though rooted in the grandeur of the Royalist tradition, has a fineness that always attests to his qualities as a man and not to the value of his cause. Conversely, Mucklewrath, though a fanatical Covenanter, stands before us a man whose rage is against life itself. As for Claverhouse and Burley, it becomes obvious that their habitual partisanship, though fitted up with loyalty to a cause, is really a style of self-awareness, a governing ego structure. They are entirely devoid of the social will. And just as this is plain to us, so also is it plain that, given the hegemony of the social will, the possibility of mediation between a Peter Poundtext and a Major Bellenden is entirely plausible. The political groups turn out to be disintegral.

The chief consequence of Scott's discriminations is that *Old Mortality* becomes a novel that questions rather than reflects the historical record's monolithic formulations. The novel reads between the lines of history in order to see the tangled threads of human action. For example, one of the most important figures in *Old Mortality* is a character who never appears. He is dead at the time the events of the novel begin. This is "the famous old roundhead, Colonel Silas Morton" (*OM*, p. 134). A moderate, opposed to the government in his time, he nonetheless worked for the restoration of King Charles when he saw that this might achieve social regeneration. He is mentioned by everybody with respect. It is his devotion to tolerance that has been molested by the renewal of enmity and political polarization.

Though Silas Morton does not appear, the novel's central character is his son, Henry. Not as naive as Waverley or as mature as

Woodstock's Everard Markham, Henry Morton is a young man whose task, in many ways, is to free himself from the world of grossly partisan commitments and rediscover the spirit of his father. Morton, who at the novel's outset is much more interested in the affections of Edith Bellenden than in any affairs of state, comes almost by chance to be swept into the political tempest of the time. He is disposed to sympathize with the oppressed dissenters, but he also has the glimmering suspicion of all political parties which seems to have been his father's most significant legacy. At a crucial point of decision, Morton reflects in this way on the nature of his choices:

> Can I be a man, and a Scotchman, and look with indifference on that persecution which has made wise men mad? Was not the cause of freedom, civil and religious, that for which my father fought . . . ? And yet, who shall warrant me that these people [Burley's insurgents], rendered wild by persecution, would not, in the hour of victory, be as cruel and as intolerant as those by whom they are now hunted down? [*OM*, p. 62].

Morton's fateful involvement in the revolution comes about in a manner that, as we shall later see, creates the novel's initial tension between its plot and counterplot. One evening Burley contrives to fall into Morton's company. Morton does not know him, but he immediately senses that Burley is some sort of fugitive. And so he is. He has recently participated in the murder of an archbishop, an act calculated to be a call to arms for disaffected Presbyterians incensed at Charles's increasing persecution of his former benefactors. (The murder is thus coldly technical—something political scientists would now call an "accelerator.")[32] Morton tries to shake Burley off, but Burley reveals himself as the "ancient friend

---

32. See Chalmers Johnson, *Revolutionary Change* (Boston: Little, Brown, 1966), p. 99:

> Accelerators are occurrences that make revolution possible by exposing the inability of the elite to maintain its monopoly of

and comrade" of old Silas Morton and the man who once saved old Morton's life. Henry agrees to hide Burley for one night at Milnwood, where he lives with his parsimonious and indifferent paternal uncle.

Claverhouse later discovers that Morton cooperated to this extent with Burley. Morton is arrested and faced with an order for his execution as a traitor. When he is extricated from this peril, he is psychologically ready for revolution. In Anthony Wallace's terms, he has entered "the mazeway of the culturally disillusioned person."[33] And so, wary though he is of Burley, he nevertheless joins the insurgents. Much in the manner of Waverley, however, he actually spends most of his combat time trying to keep innocent people out of harm's way.

His situation becomes intolerable when the malign Burley decides to place the castle of Tillietudlem under siege. This is the home of Morton's beloved Edith Bellenden, who has found another admirer—and defender—in the gallant Lord Evandale. Morton is deceived by Burley as to the seriousness of the danger to Tillietudlem, and is dispatched to Glasgow to train the irregular troops under his command in preparation for the major battle (which will be fought at Bothwell Bridge, where Claverhouse's soldiers will annihilate the insurgent army).

Morton's experience as a rebel gives him no reason to abandon his suspicion that he has escaped tyranny only to be caught up in anarchy. Burley tells him at one point that "we are enjoined to smite the ungodly, though he be our neighbor" (*OM*, p. 58). And Mucklewrath will also tell him that he must "slay, slay—

force. They are not sets of conditions but single events—events that rupture a system's pseudo-integration based on deterrence. Accelerators always affect an elite's monopoly of armed force, and they lead either mobilized or potential revolutionaries to believe that they have a chance of success in resorting to violence against a hated system.

33. *Culture and Personality* (New York: Random House, 1961), p. 144.

smite—slay utterly—let not your eyes have pity! slay utterly, old and young, the maiden, the child, and the woman whose head is gray— Defile the house and fill the courts with the slain" (*OM,* p. 225).

Although I am abridging the events of the primary plot, it should still be evident that *Old Mortality* keeps representing Henry Morton as a prisoner. He is a prisoner even at Milnwood, where his uncle expects from him humiliating servitude and where "the current of his soul was frozen by a sense of dependence, of poverty, above all, of an imperfect and limited education" (*OM,* p. 138). He does not, in other words, have either personal independence or enriching social attachments. When he takes his first independent action by assisting Burley, he frees himself from the fetters of Milnwood. But, by the same token, he is soon Claverhouse's prisoner. Once he escapes Claverhouse, he becomes no less a prisoner of the rebels, who always keep him under close watch because of his frequent avowals of moderation.

When the rebels are routed at Bothwell Bridge, Morton once again undergoes the typifying ritual of his experience: escape to imprisonment. After hazardous flight, he comes to a solitary farmhouse at Drumshinnel. But here he encounters a small remnant of the defeated rebels, including Macbriar and Mucklewrath. They immediately seize him and make him the scapegoat for their defeat, his valiant efforts at Bothwell Bridge notwithstanding. Alleging that Morton has really been a sympathizer with the Royalists all along, they manacle him and decide to execute him. A pursuit party led by Claverhouse rescues him. Yet once more he becomes a prisoner, being bound over to the Scottish Privy Council. Evandale and Claverhouse, however, recall Morton's attempts at mediation and reconciliation, so that he is exiled rather than hanged.

This reading of Morton's career up to the point of his return to Scotland (which occurs near the end of the novel) suggests one of the major ways in which the novel generates a sense of tragic fail-

ure in Morton's life. Morton is originally placed in jeopardy because he acts in compliance with high moral principle; he assists
Burley out of a sense of obligation to his father. He continues to
act in compliance with high moral principle, insofar as his "limited education" allows him. Yet at every turn he is baffled by a
current of events that chains him within the fratricidal world and
that seems to render absurd his every attempt to act according to
conscience.

In its primary plot, *Old Mortality* concerns itself with Morton's
inability to connect. His inner goodwill has no exchange value in
a domain monopolized by fanaticism. He is a prisoner, most of
all, of his conscience, because conscience, as an attribute of the
moral self, has become caricatured as fidelity to an ideological
program.

This is why the novel has a counterplot through which the hy-
perbolic actions of the warring political camps can be shown as
obscuring—but not negating—the imagination of community,
which is precisely the progenitor of Morton's conscience. The
counterplot is produced by repetition, throughout the novel, of a
single action: the saving of lives. In terms of narrative method,
this action is an epigrammatic formulation that insistently dramatizes the ethic of mutual aid.

With appropriate irony, the impress of this ethic can be found
even in some of the novel's most violent characters. Morton, as
we have seen, originally came under obligation to Burley because
Burley had saved his father's life. The irony attests to the instinct
for social benevolence which, as Hume said, must inhere some-
where in human nature generally. But the counterplot concentrates on more instructive and bounteous cases. Henry Morton
saves Burley by hiding him at Milnwood. When Morton is arrested for this action, Evandale, his rival in love, generously inter-
venes to save him from execution. Morton is then put under
guard as Claverhouse leads the Life-Guards to the battle at Drumclog. There Evandale saves Claverhouse's life. In the confusion of

the battle, Morton is left to his own devices (and thus, effectively, freed). He escapes, but not before risking his own life to save Evandale (p. 185). Later Evandale makes it back to Tillietudlem, and when he finds it besieged by Burley, he offers to negotiate with the rebels for the safety of the Bellendens. Burley contemptuously orders him to be shot. But Morton, defying Burley, once again saves Evandale.

In another of the counterplot's ironies, Claverhouse rescues Morton at Drumshinnel. And then both Evandale and Claverhouse intervene with the Scottish Privy Council in order to mitigate Morton's punishment.

These incidents do not constitute a mere mummery of hairbreadth escapes. When Morton returns from exile, he meets an impoverished Covenanter woman, Bessie Maclure. (" 'If there's an honest woman in the world, it's Bessie Maclure' " [*OM*, p. 398]). Though her two sons had been killed by Claverhouse's soldiers, she herself saved Evandale's life when, wounded and isolated from his troops, he was attempting to reach Tillietudlem. For doing so, she was ostracized by Burley's followers. But she tells Morton, " 'Ye can ken naething waur o' me than that I hae been willing to save the life o' friend and foe' " (*OM*, p. 407). Scott appeals to this simple principle of humanity. It may be regarded as the foundation of his social analysis. The moral vision of the novel is framed by this construction of conscience; the chaos of revolution is judged by it.

To understand this moral vision more fully, we must return to the scene at Drumshinnel. When Macbriar and Mucklewrath seize Morton, they intend to kill him immediately. But Macbriar, holding to a thin thread of conscience, rules that the brethren should not hold an execution on the Sabbath. Morton is thus given a few hours' reprieve. As his mind wavers, "while on the brink between this and the future world," he recites a few words from the Book of Common Prayer. Macbriar, hearing him, is overcome with fury: " 'There lacked but this . . . to root out my carnal reluctance to see his blood spilt. He is a prelatist, who has sought [our] camp under the disguise of an Erastian.'" Mucklewrath, equally outraged, cites a contrived biblical precedent, and, in an act symbolic of revolution itself, he pushes forward the index of the clock "to anticipate the fatal moment" (*OM,* pp. 324–25). It is at this point that Claverhouse's pursuit party arrives and Morton is rescued. But Claverhouse completely empties the act of human rescue of any moral significance. Morton, he declares, was merely lucky. "'It is all a lottery—when the hour of midnight came, you were to die—it has struck, you are alive and safe, and the lot has fallen on those fellows who were to murder you'" (*OM,* pp. 329–30).

His comment is immensely illuminating. For Claverhouse's cynical account of luck is exactly on a par with Mucklewrath's cynical reindexing of the clock. Scott completes the symbolic merging of these characters when Mucklewrath seems to rise from the dead, stares at Claverhouse, and accurately prophesies the manner of Claverhouse's own death (*OM,* p. 330).

The Drumshinnel scene unites Claverhouse and Mucklewrath (who is Burley's surrogate) at the level of their consummate inhumanity. Right-wing fatalism and left-wing anarchy become convertible terms in their degradation of the social affections and in their corresponding reduction of the social order to an infernal machine. Thus Drumshinnel, not Bothwell Bridge, constitutes the climax of the novel's primary plot. The opposed fanaticisms unite there in what Conrad would call the lawlessness of autocracy and the lawlessness of anarchy. These doctrines lose the distancing effects of their ideological gear and announce themselves as alternative styles of emptiness.

And yet Morton is rescued. As the fanaticisms in Scotland's political forces are stripped of their several disguises, the central ethic of the counterplot is reaffirmed. For it was not luck that brought Claverhouse to Drumshinnel in the nick of time. Cuddie Headrigg, Morton's canny "valet," had escaped from the farmhouse, met up with Claverhouse's troops, and directed them to Drum-shinnel.

Cuddie is a vitally important character. We first meet him serving as a ploughman for Lady Margaret Bellenden. But his ranting mother, Mause, who will practice no diplomacy on religious or political questions even when addressing her mistress, gets both herself and her son cast off the Bellenden estate when the feudalistic Lady Margaret finally loses all patience with Mause's harangues. Exasperated with his mother, Cuddie manages to secure for her and himself a meager living at Milnwood. But when Morton is arrested for hiding Burley, so too are the Headriggs, Mause once again refusing to hold her tongue. It is during this period of their joint captivity that Cuddie proposes to Morton, should they ever get free, that he become Morton's servant. Cuddie, who has been caught long enough in the cross fire between his mother and Lady Margaret, is seeking his own escape from opposing fanaticisms. " 'I hae been clean spoilt, just wi' listening to two blethering auld wives; but if I could get a gentleman that wad let me tak on to be his servant, I am confident I wad be a clean contrary creature' " (*OM*, p. 156).

Cuddie's story is a comic restatement of Morton's situation. Each story reflects the other in many ways—Cuddie, for example, being challenged in his love for Jenny Dennison by one of Claverhouse's troopers, just as Evandale and Morton are rivals in their love for Edith Bellenden. Cuddie's bond with Morton, therefore, goes much beyond a banal master–servant relationship. Though they are divided by social class, they are united in the symmetry of their fate. Both are dispossessed of community, but in their finding of one another the image of community is reconstituted. They are prisoners when they connect. And as they connect, they begin to free one another. Morton rescues Cuddie from a dispossession that is menacingly comic. At Drumshinnel, Cuddie rescues Morton from a dispossession that is menacingly tragic. Though their relationship is bounded externally by the signs of a class system, Scott sees it as a living instance of the moral kinship that can be disclosed only by the profound inter-subjectivity of the communal life.

Morton's experience, following the paratragedy of Drumshin-nel, evolves as a spiritual cleansing. His ten-year exile, while it functions as a symbolic death (he is believed to have drowned), really allows him a purgatorial reprieve from the revolutionary ethos of Scotland. Though he is deprived even of Cuddie's com-panionship, it is significant that "he [is] fortunate enough to meet an old officer who had been in service with his father." This "old friend of Silas Morton" counsels Morton with sufficient skill to assure the exile's gradual movement toward renewed social con-nections (*OM,* pp. 390–91).

By the time Morton comes back to Scotland in 1689, the Glori-ous Revolution has taken place. Scott, in yet another attempt to suggest the convergence of all political fanaticisms, emphasizes the ironies of the new political situation. Many of the old Royal-ists are now Jacobites, and both Claverhouse and Evandale have entered into an intrigue with their former enemies, including Burley himself, against the Whigs. Morton comes upon this scene as a phantom. He has no interest in the political factions. Rather, he is seeking a conclusive end to alienation.

His first step is to return to Milnwood. Though the courtyard and front of the house are ruined, he finds that Mrs. Wilson, his dead uncle's kindly housekeeper, is still there. She does not know him, and tells him that "'the name of Morton of Milnwood's gone out like the last sough of an old song.'" Morton assures her she is wrong, and at last she recognizes him. "And how cam ye to pass yoursell for dead?—And what for did ye come creepin' to your ain house as if ye had been an unco body?" (*OM,* p. 389).

Morton had been an "unco body" (a stranger) even in his early years at Milnwood. But he is now ready to find "my humble quiet and tranquility of mind, upon the spot where I lost them"—that is, in his native environment, which had once been only a prison, but which Morton can now conceive as a home (*OM*, p. 400). Moreover, Morton, though deeply dejected by what he perceives as the waste of his life, has seen that "something . . . yet remains for me in the world, were it only to bear my sorrows like a man, and to aid those who need my assistance" (*OM*, p. 384).

The story of Morton's rebirth is completed in the novel's conclusion. The conclusion has been much criticized; there is no doubt that the demons that plague Scott's art have had their hand in it. But the conclusion is not by any means merely adventitious. It represents a thematic resolution of plot and counterplot in the novel.

Morton's immediate concern is for Edith. She is about to be married to Evandale. Morton, of course, cannot interfere. But he does learn that the Bellenden estate is, through Burley's purloining of a vital document, in danger of being lost to its rightful heirs. In the hope of assisting Edith and Evandale anonymously, Morton finds out where Burley (who escaped unscathed from Bothwell Bridge) is hiding, and tries to retrieve the document. Burley, of course, refuses to surrender it.

Morton's wish "to aid those who need [his] assistance," however, is given a larger opportunity. Just as the time for the marriage of Edith and Evandale approaches, Evandale learns that Claverhouse has been killed. Claverhouse, as Viscount Dundee, had been preparing a Jacobite uprising (in tense alliance with Burley and the Covenanters). Leadership devolves on Evandale, and he accepts it. He intends to gain the support of his troops in the Life-Guards and join the Highlanders in revolt. " 'If it is my fate that calls me, I will not shun meeting it' " (*OM*, p. 425).

Unlike the chastened Morton, Evandale now comes to find rectitude in revolution, even though he is fully aware that every political faction has been contaminated by calculated injustices. Noble as he is, Evandale cannot transcend the tragedy of opposing fanaticisms. He has become an addict of the politicized world.

He dies, but he does not die in a glorious cause. While still with Edith, he is made aware that Basil Oliphant, a laird whose estate borders the Bellendens' and for whom Burley has stolen the crucial document, wants Evandale murdered. Oliphant has engaged for this purpose two of Evandale's own soldiers as well as the inexorable Burley. Bessie Maclure hears of this plot, and, acting in her accustomed manner, alerts Morton, who once again desperately tries to save Evandale's life. This time he is too late. "Lord Evandale, determined to face a danger which his high spirit undervalued, commanded his servants to follow him, and rode composedly down the avenue" (*OM*, p. 426). At the end of the avenue he is murdered.

Evandale's behavior with respect to his murderers may be interpreted as either bravery or foolishness. This point is really of no consequence. What matters is that Evandale leaves the sanctuary of Tillietudlem to join with and take command of a revolutionary army. The same sense of "high spirit" that urges him down the avenue has persuaded him to reenter the maelstrom of revolution. The whole novel repudiates his judgment. The legitimacy of the Jacobite rebellion is not being questioned, but Evandale's sense of rectitude is. He does not understand what Scotland needs. His acceptance of Claverhouse's role, on the one hand, and the appearance of Burley among the killers, on the other, are the final, telling points. Morton *cannot* save Evandale's life because Evandale takes his life into his own hands. Such a man is fatally encumbered; he cannot be embraced.

Despite its *longueurs, Old Mortality* is a great and powerful novel. Even Morton's subsequent marriage to Edith cannot be charged against it as sentimental. The marriage is the fulfillment of the counterplot's insistence that political enmity can be subdued by the imagination of community. Tillietudlem and Milnwood, once prisons, are reclaimed as beacons in a social constellation where the idiomatic life can once again emerge. The counterplot, by breaking the dialectical blockade against the social affections, offers us a model of a social structure that is informed by the social affections. Though this structure always has religious implications for Scott, the novel's emphasis is on the order achieved by the social will in a world that perversely represents competing modes of social disorder as historical deliverances.

The Heart of Mid-Lothian is a sort of sequel to *Old Mortality*. It begins in 1736. The Hanoverians are well established; the Jacobite uprising of 1715 is over; the '45 is yet to come. The Covenanter Davie Deans, who fought at Bothwell Bridge, has been allowed several decades of relative tranquillity in which to edge gradually toward a liaison with the prevailing structure of community. If the years of tranquillity have expanded his social affections (or, perhaps more accurately, neutralized his social animosities), they have done little to undermine his dialectical habits of mind. Deans is not a man of formal education, but he has summoned out of the soul of Scottish culture a capacious appetite for speculative truth. Events in the public world pass before his arduous scrutiny like a file of angels parading toward the head of a pin. Scott looks back to the period of *Old Mortality* to give us Deans's view of history:

> It had been a great source of controversy among those holding his opinions in religious matters, how far the government which succeeded the Revolution could be, without sin, acknowledged by true presbyterians, seeing that it did not recognise the great national testimony of the Solemn League and Covenant. . . . At a very stormy and tumultuous meeting, held in 1682, to discuss these . . . points, the testimonies of the faithful few were found utterly inconsistent with each other. . . . This conference took place [in] a wild and very sequestered dell . . . *far remote from human habitation.* . . . David Deans had been present on this memorable occasion, although too young to be a speaker among the polemical combatants. His brain, however, had been thoroughly heated by the noise, clamour, and metaphysical ingenuity of the discussion. . . . When, in the first General Assembly which suc-

ceeded the Revolution, an overture was made for the revival of
the League and Covenant, it was with horror that Douce David
heard the proposal eluded by the men of carnal wit and policy.
[But], more sensible than the bigots of his sect, he did not con-
found the moderation and tolerance of [King William and Queen
Anne] with the active tyranny [of the Stuarts]. Then came the insurrection of 1715, and David Deans's horror for the revival of
the popish and prelatical faction reconciled him greatly to the
government of King George. . . . In short, moved by so many
different considerations, he shifted his ground at different times
concerning the degree of freedom which he felt in adopting any
act of immediate acknowledgment of submission to the present
government. [*HML,* pp. 212–14]

It is difficult to say whether this passage is historical summary
or characterization, so closely are the two blended. In any case, it
provides a version of history that everywhere impinges on the
moral action of *The Heart of Mid-Lothian,* and it gives us, as well,
the essential result of Deans's speculative puzzles. The result, in
personal terms, is a substantial incoherence in his private self. He
has achieved at least marginal social attachments, but his mental
life pulls against their growth and development. In practical
terms, this means that when he is confronted by the impending
execution of his daughter Effie for allegedly murdering her ille-
gitimate child, he reacts with tender though belated compassion,
but he also endures a torment of moral perplexity in trying to decide whether Jeanie, his other daughter, should actually be allowed to testify at her sister's trial. To permit her to do so would
be a tacit recognition of the government's legality.

History in *The Heart of Mid-Lothian* is not guided by revolutionary action. The novel concerns itself with Jeanie Deans's ex-
cruciating moral problem: whether to lie at her sister's trial and
so save her from capital punishment for a crime she did not commit, or to tell the truth and condemn her. Jeanie tells the truth,
and then, by genuinely heroic effort, gains a pardon for Effie
from Queen Caroline herself. The novel thus deals with the prob-

lem of justice and, as one critic very precisely puts it, "the various forms of 'justice' to which appeals are made by this person or that group during the [entire] narrative."[34] Nevertheless, the shadow of revolutionary sentiment is cast across the whole novel. David Deans is one source of the revolutionary vision. The ominous George Staunton is another. The novel is throughout preoccupied with the undercurrent of revolutionary sentiment in a Scotland embittered by capricious law. It begins with a momentous event, the storming of the prison of Edinburgh (the "heart of Mid-Lothian") by a mob of incensed citizens. And it establishes in Jeanie Deans an image of the search for justice that counters the fierce and blind groping of the revolutionary process.

Scott's description of the Porteous riot is one of the most perfectly sustained episodes in his work. A smuggler named Wilson was to be executed and his sentence carried out by Captain John Porteous, commander of the City Guard. Porteous is characterized as a man of vicious habits, but one whose military training made him useful to the city magistrates during the Jacobite uprising of 1715. "His harsh and fierce habits rendered him formidable to rioters or disturbers of the public peace" (*HML*, p. 37). The Wilson execution is interrupted by a muffled figure, George ("Robertson") Staunton, who is Wilson's cohort and, as it turns out, the father of Effie's child. Staunton's derring-do fails, however, to prevent the hanging. On the other hand, Porteous overreacts to the situation. His soldiers fire, and the result is that several innocent citizens are killed and many wounded. Porteous is then convicted of murder, but, to the dismay of the Edinburgh populace, he is granted a pardon by the Queen. The outcry against the pardon is immediate: " 'The profligate satellite, who took advantage of a trifling tumult, inseparable from such occasions, to shed the blood of twenty of his fellow-citizens, is

34. Robin Mayhead, *Walter Scott* (Cambridge: The University Press, 1973), p. 49.

deemed a fitting object for the exercise of the royal prerogative of mercy. Is this to be borne?—would our fathers have borne it? Are we not, like them, Scotsmen and burghers of Edinburgh?'" (*HML,* pp. 47–48).

A great many issues come into play as the burghers of Edinburgh decide to storm the prison and hang Porteous themselves. Clearly, one of these issues is the extreme dissatisfaction with the position of Scotland after the Union. "'Weary on Lunnon, and a' thiet e'er came out o't,'" says an ancient seamstress (*HML,* p. 49). Still, the mob that marches on the Tolbooth is different from the more famous mob of 1789. It is true that the Porteous riot has its inevitable association with the attack on the Bastille, and it counts as one of those episodes that occur sporadically in Scott's novels, where the events of the French Revolution are darkly mirrored. In *Woodstock,* for example, Bletson, the disciple of Harrington, mutters "doctrines of *Animus Mundi* or Creative Power —nor was he . . . inclined absolutely to censor holidays to the great goddess Nature."[35] But the revolutionaries of the Bastille were interested in liberation. The mob in Edinburgh is not so radical; its cause is somewhat more pedestrian and legalistic.

The mob action does confirm, however, the presence of a nidus for revolution. Scott was well aware that the lower class in England and Scotland had been economically depressed. As Arnold Kettle points out, the figure of Madge Wildfire in this novel is something like "the symbol of a class suffering and dispossessed by the enclosure movement and the power of the great landowners."[36] These reflections of popular unrest, together with the reverberations of rebellion that sound in the voice of Davie Deans, make the discovery of justice exigent. Effie's plight is only the

35. *Woodstock,* Everyman's Library (London: Dent, 1906), p. 125.

36. *An Introduction to the English Novel* (1951; rpt. New York: Harper & Row, 1960), I, 116–17. And see Scott's letter to Maria Edgeworth (February 4, 1829): "While the *few* are improved to the highest point, the *many* are in proportion brutalized and degraded" (*Letters,* XI, 128).

most prominent instance of injustice in a society deprived of juridical integrity. Predictably, the official response to the Edinburgh riot is treacherous: "Nothing was spoke of for some time save the measure of vengeance which should be taken, not only on the actors of this tragedy, so soon as they should be discovered, but upon the magistrate who had suffered it to take place, and upon the city which had been the scene where it was exhibited" (*HML*, p. 80).

The significance of Davie Deans, and for that matter of Jeanie, cannot be fully defined except in relation to the portentous figure of George Staunton. As every commentator has observed, Staunton is an open allusion to Byron's heroes. He staggers from scene to scene under the burden of his implausibilities. Even in caricature, however, Staunton is a reality that Byron was making famous and that Scott felt compelled to acknowledge. Scott used traces of the Byronic in John Balfour of Burley. In Staunton, Burley's submerged satanism becomes overt. And to this are added guilt-ridden panache, a potentially noble nature, emotional turbulence, and unguarded sexuality. Above all, there is in him a willful criminality, the outward sign of a personality in which the influence of positive and moral law has been superseded by the influence of the will. It is clear that Scott, so romantically fond of the heroic personality, recognized the pertinence to the modern world of Byron's brooding heroes.

Staunton takes his place in *The Heart of Mid-Lothian* as the terminal type of the revolutionary, the monstrous self-idolator who, as Coleridge said, removes "a world of obstacles by the mere decision that he will have no obstacles."[37] Walter Scott had enough of the skeptic in him to understand the actuality of the self-idolator and the meaning of his newly devised motto: Everything is permitted. *The Heart of Mid-Lothian* is a book in which Scott struggles with his insight into, and horror of, this mutation in history.

---

37. *The Portable Coleridge,* ed. I. A. Richards (New York: Viking, 1950), p. 32. The passage is from Appendix B to *The Statesman's Manual.*

As such, the novel, while envisioning the conflict of opposing fanaticisms, throws its greatest emphasis on the old and new types of rebellion. Reactionary politics in this novel remain pretty much embodied in its brief sketches of the impersonal institutions that have treacherously undercut civil justice in Scotland. This component of the dialectically divided world fills the background of the novel while Scott concentrates his immediate attention on two distinctive specimens of the revolutionary mind in Scotland's historical development. Deans is a known quantity, a perfect example of Scotland's obstinate tradition of ideologically inspired revolt and of her tragic failure to bind up her wounds. But the novel is set in a hopeful moment. A chance for harmony seems to be evidenced in the growing inclination of such a man as Deans for compromise and restraint. Staunton erupts into this tense but remediable state of affairs like a malign force. He is, pointedly, an outsider, a figure who brings to Scotland a new dimension in revolutionary fractiousness.

The Heart of Mid-Lothian places its heroine between the forces of reaction and the forces of revolt, and its tragic element is a consequence of the incipient deadlock she faces. Avrom Fleishman aptly compares Jeanie to Antigone and to "other tragic figures confronted by absolute alternatives."[38] We need to add, however, that Jeanie successfully discovers the condition of justice masked by the polarized world, and even redeems her father from the disease of absolutism. But she can do nothing for Staunton. He is definitively beyond community. At the end of the novel, Staunton is slain, we are led to suppose, by his bastard son. His son then flees to America and joins a tribe of Indians. The purpose of these events is unmistakable. They represent Scott's exorcism of a power that was making a cataclysmic progress through his world. Exorcism is an ultimate negation; the harshness of the remedy is indicative of the virulence that Scott detected in Staunton's version of revolt.

38. *English Historical Novel*, p. 88.

At issue in *The Heart of Mid-Lothian* is the view that law is merely an arbitrary expression of self-interest. More precisely, the issue is the dreadful consequences for human society that attend the unrestricted application of this view. For such a man as Scott, the history of the modern mind virtually pivoted on its display of an ever widening tolerance of the principle of self-interest. In *The Heart of Mid-Lothian* this condition is expressed through a pervasive disposition on the part of the characters to take the law into their own hands. Staunton and Wilson do it as smugglers, their smuggling being condoned as a defiance of the malt tax imposed by the English government in 1725. The thieves on the road do it, Porteous does it, the Edinburgh mob does it. There are more subtle instances. Saddletree does it through the very legalism he espouses. Staunton does it, at a more serious level than that of smuggler, through sophistical justifications of his criminal transactions. And Deans does it in his proud pursuit of doctrinal certainty. All of these assertions of self over the law take place in a world whose legal codes are seen as necessarily imperfect. Effie's calamity is the novel's major illustration of the law's gross imperfection. Yet Scott is uncompromising in his conviction that the man who seduced Effie and the father who nearly disowned her are subversive of the social order in a way that imperfect law administered by imperfect judges is not.

The autocratic self-interestedness of the government is established in the events surrounding the Porteous riot. Scott devotes the remaining action of the novel to Jeanie and to the contrast between Deans, who finally withdraws from the isolating casuistry that is the form self-interest takes in him, and Staunton, whose solipsism becomes so extreme that Scott, with intense irony, depicts him as a self-negation. This contrast gains its full meaning in the context of Jeanie's moral action. Her way of taking the law into her own hands works out as a discovery of the roots of justice. Jeanie's action is so decisive that the tragic realm in which she is ensnared ultimately gives way to its exact opposite, the Arcadian realm of Roseneath.

We may begin our discussion of these relationships with Deans. The critical moment for Deans is made clear to us, but passes by him unrecognized. After Effie's arrest, Deans is trying to convince himself that it would be canonically possible for a true Cameronian's daughter at least to appear at the trial to which Jeanie has been summoned by official subpoena. He is so torn by his doubts that when he hints of his potential approval of this step to Jeanie, he is incapable of coherent communication. Jeanie, to whom it never occurs that the subpoena could be resisted, quite naturally and quite inevitably assumes her father is suggesting to her the very thing that Staunton has already suggested, that she lie on her sister's behalf. " 'Can this be?' said Jeanie, as the door closed on her father—'Can these be his words that I have heard, or has the Enemy taken his voice and features to give weight unto the counsel which causeth to perish?' " (*HML,* p. 218).

Deans is a danger because his dialectic withers the delicate roots of common understanding. Just before he decides on his tremendously misdirected advice to Jeanie, he has been in conversation with Middleburgh, one of the magistrates of the city. Middleburgh, whose name stands for his character, is a considerate and benevolent man. He wishes to help Deans understand the protections the law provides even for such as Effie. More important, he instinctively tries to reconcile Deans with his daughter, to cut beneath Deans's execrations and touch his humanity. In their conversation, Deans takes great offense at what he believes is Middleburgh's dense incapacity to understand his religious position. " 'I am *not* a MacMillanite, or a Russelite, or a Hamiltonian, or a Harleyite, or a Howdenite—I will be led by the nose by none—I take my name as a Christian from no vessel of clay. I have my own principles and practice to answer for, and am an humble pleader for the good auld cause in a legal way.' "

" 'That is to say, Mr. Deans,' said Middleburgh, 'that you are a *Deanite,* and have opinions peculiar to yourself' " (*HML,* p. 211).

Deans is trapped by being a "Deanite." The trap is exactly as he identifies it when he says he walks " 'the middle and straight path, as it were, on the ridge of a hill, where wind and water shears, avoiding right-hand snares and extremes, and left-hand way-slidings' " (*HML*, p. 211). He has described not the *via media* but the isolation of self. It is Scott's view of the public rebel in his private life.

But Deans, through his sufferings as the father of Effie as well as through the example of Jeanie, learns compassion and tolerance. His collapse in agony during the climactic moments of Effie's trial is a suffering greater than any political persecution he has endured. And when Effie for a second time abandons her father in favor of Staunton, Deans has no Calvinistic denunciations to make. He has only an anguished hope for her well-being, and a deep need to "let her pass, and be forgotten" (*HML*, p. 436). More important, Deans finds it possible at last to tolerate deviations from his doctrines. At Roseneath his tortuous reasonings are exercised primarily in order to accommodate himself to what is best for Jeanie. There is an openly comic tone to them. As Scott at one point remarks, "it would be somewhat cruel to inquire too nearly what weight paternal affection gave to these ingenious trains of reasonings" (*HML*, p. 445).

Deans, then, is the rebel for whom the compromises of community eventually work. His life is a reflection of Scotland's gradual movement toward tranquillity. But Staunton stands, as it were, in the future, doing the devil's work under a new name.

> Headstrong, determined in his own sure career,
> He thought reproof unjust, and truth severe,
> The soul's disease was to its crisis come,
> He first abused and then abjured his home;
> And when he chose a vagabond to be,
> He made his shame his glory, 'I'll be free!' [39]

39. George Crabbe, *The Borough* (Letter XII, 261–66), quoted by Scott in *HML*, p. 370. I am indebted to Kathleen Blow, reference librarian, University of Texas at Austin, for identifying these lines.

The last line consummately renders the revolutionary as self-idolator. This is why Scott has Staunton end up as a macerated hypocrite, a dandy English baronet whose personal freedom is as fraudulent as the social mask he must always wear. Nothing betrays him so much as the shallow respectability he finally achieves. Scott repeatedly uses the image of Satan to identify Staunton. The image occurs most importantly, perhaps, when he says to Jeanie: "'Look at me. My head is not horned, my foot is not cloven, my hands are not garnished with talons. . . . Listen to me patiently, and you will find that, when you have heard my counsel, you may go to the seventh heaven with it in your pocket'" (*HML*, p. 349). Jeanie knows better. But the speech reminds us of Jeanie's earlier shock when she thought the devil himself might have spoken in the form of her father. The similarity of spirit in Deans and Staunton is defined by the image. Scott's purpose, however, is to emphasize Staunton's intrinsically greater appetite for the diabolic. For Staunton has just the modish charm and Rousseauistic flair that makes him much more dangerous than a crabby Covenanter shouting political defiance at a conventicle.

For most of the novel, Staunton, whenever he appears before us, is on some sort of generous mission. He is rescuing Wilson from the gallows, or advising Jeanie how she can testify to Effie's advantage, or confessing his sins and asking forgiveness, or seeking to confer the status of gentleman on his semisavage son. This is one of the devices of the novel. We are engaged by Staunton in his pleas for approval, for justification, for forgiveness. Staunton appears before us, in other words, as Jeanie appears before Queen Caroline. In Jeanie's case, however, directness and modesty confirm the justice of her plea. The very elaborateness of Staunton reveals his deviousness. He goes so far as to ask us to take a sprained ankle as the perdurable barrier between himself and a life of probity. It is this contrast with Jeanie, whose search for justice is so spontaneous, that more than anything else convicts Staunton of putting self-interest above the law. The novel is often explicit about this. " 'Tis pity on Measter George,' " says an honest boor, " 'for he has an open hand, and winna let a poor body want an he has it.' " But Scott adds: "The virtue of profuse generosity, by which, indeed, they themselves are most directly advantaged, is readily admitted by the vulgar as a cloak for many sins" (*HML*, p. 370).

If Effie comes to cooperate in Staunton's designs, Madge Wildfire does not. Her life and her ghastly death make the novel's indictment of Staunton—" 'the destroyer at once of her reason and reputation' "—complete. Her last words are: " 'Nurse—nurse, turn my face to the wa' that I may . . . never see mair of a wicked world' " (*HML*, p. 423). Besides being the destroyer of her reason and reputation, Staunton is, in truth, her murderer. She is insane and killed for a witch. Staunton bears the responsibility.

Staunton, as we have seen, will be killed by his son. His son lives in the wild and is, in effect, George Staunton without the mask of respectability. George Staunton has rejected community in his reckless assertion of freedom, and the story of his end is Scott's argument against the autonomy of the self. As Staunton sets out to trace his son, Scott tellingly attributes his motives to "his ancient willfulness of disposition . . . Willful in everything, Sir George's sole desire now was to see this son, even should his recovery bring with it a new series of misfortunes as dreadful as those which followed on his being lost" (*HML*, p. 517). The misfortune this time will be his own death, but it is really death that Staunton has always been seeking. He has negated everything that makes human life possible. The savage son who kills him is the savage self of George Staunton, whose freedom is founded on the denial of the humanity of other people. His rebelliousness is not amenable to the sort of restraints David Deans has accepted. Deans is an evocation of the historical past, and in him Scott reveals how the old spirit of insurrection has yielded to the discovery of community. George Staunton is an evocation of a new spirit of insurrection, one far more dangerous than the old. He cannot be assimilated; he can only be extirpated.

If the meaning of the law has been eroded by oppressive institutions on the one hand and self-idolatry on the other, Jeanie presents the opposite process by which the law's meaning can be reconstituted. She exposes the concrete, lived experience of men in their social and moral relationships, from which law has evolved and to which its abstractions must never blind it. When she finds herself ringed round in her Antigone-like dilemma, Jeanie becomes the most resourceful advocate in the book. *How* she does so is to be seen, again, through the technique of counterplotting. Jeanie's remarkable journey to London in search of justice is arranged so that its narrative structure weaves into the text the configuration of community.

Jeanie's journey begins with a sudden, luminous perception of what she must do: "My sister shall come out in the face of the sun . . . I will go to London, and beg her pardon from the king and queen. If they pardoned Porteous, they may pardon her; if a sister asks a sister's life on her bended knees, they *will* pardon her—they *shall* pardon her—and they will win a thousand hearts by it" (*HML,* p. 267).

This is an act of faith not in the king and queen but in the human content of the law. Jeanie fails to see that the pardon of Porteous was a matter of political expediency because she sees something larger: the foundation of the law in the structure of social life. Jeanie's excursion is not so much a journey out of St. Leonard's to London as a journey down into the communal identity of the nation in which the king and queen indubitably participate. It is essential that Jeanie's journey is financed by the local laird and that her interview with Queen Caroline is arranged by the Duke of Argyle. Jeanie travels, in other words, through a hierarchical order whose merely abstract system of contractual obligation is vivified by her representation of the human purposes it must serve. It is in this sense that she rehabilitates the meaning of the law.

Scott, however, is far from suggesting that Jeanie's break-through is a simple matter of her recognition that she has the right to appeal Effie's case before the queen. Jeanie can effectively represent the human purposes of the law only because her journey takes her through the perilous, thickly textured world of experience that animates, while it tests, her moral imagination. She undergoes symbolic versions of the risks, perplexities, and temptations that elsewhere in the novel result in lawlessness. She comes to embody the conditions that make abstract law incessantly problematical in the individual life. And for this reason she can clarify the image of justice that must always be within our intuitive reach however impossible we find it to externalize the image in law. Jeanie can rehabilitate the law because she knows both the spiritual order that all law must rest on and the fraught human condition that ineluctably taxes the law's power of generalization. Her creative resolution of her Antigone-like situation is achieved as a consequence of both the tragic environment in which she matures and the faith that brings her through it.

Everything about Jeanie's excursion to London mirrors the impaired function of law that is displayed pervasively in the novel from the Porteous riot to the rumors of the '45 we hear at the end. Jeanie is, first of all, acting in revolt. In effect, she overthrows the authority nearest her, her father, who has committed her to his own legal system. At the same time she is symbolically acting on behalf of the murmuring Edinburgh citizens, who feel the immense remoteness of the London government. Her journey itself documents its remoteness. From the beginning, then, Jeanie's movements entail a submerged rebelliousness. But this tinge of rebelliousness allows us to see the sense in which Jeanie sublimates the drive toward self-assertion into a disinterested quest for justice. Again, it can be said that Jeanie takes the law into her own hands, but her manner of doing so completely transmutes the ordinary implications of this act. Jeanie takes the law into her hands in order to discover it rather than defy it. She probes and investigates where the novel's other characters distort and diminish.

Furthermore, Jeanie finds herself constantly undergoing condensed reenactments of the personal trials endured by all those characters in the novel who are endangered by the law. Her passage through England reproduces in her the uncertainties and fears that life in a hostile society has held for her father. She begins to know what it means to be an alien. She experiences the sense of shame that debilitates Effie when she (Jeanie) is found by George Staunton's father in his son's bedroom and taken to be a common slut. She contends, as Effie did, with Staunton's seductiveness as he apologizes for, and half excuses, his behavior. In a clear parallel to the disposition of the Porteous case, she is tempted by expediency when she learns of Staunton's crimes and thus finds herself in a position to trade her information for the pardon she seeks. "In one sense, indeed," Scott writes, "it seemed as if denouncing the guilt of Staunton, the cause of her sister's errors and misfortunes, would have been an act of just, even providential retribution. But Jeanie . . . had to consider not only the general aspect of the proposed action, but its justness and fitness in relation to the actor, before she could be, according to her own phrase, free to enter upon it" (*HML*, p. 367).

Even more excruciatingly, Jeanie relives Effie's ordeal of imprisonment after she is captured by Meg Murdrockson. Similarly, the dispossession and humiliation that Madge Wildfire must accept awaits Jeanie in the Reverend Staunton's church when she is taunted as " 'another Bess of Bedlam.' " Finally, she must plead her case before the queen—the novel being a series of pleas before judges—when her only resource is her ability to project the justice of her case beyond the abstractions of law and the requirements of the political climate.

The tragedy seems to be averted by a *deus ex machina* in the person of the Duke of Argyle. But it is really the formal structure of the counterplot that takes us beyond tragedy. Jeanie *invicta* masters fate by her capacity to act on behalf of the social order and not in violation of it. Her efficacy emerges from what we finally see as the social fullness of her moral nature. She has entered all the troubled corners of her world, and yet has kept her allegiance to the social affections. Having done so, she comes to embody the spirit of community that is radically defined in her rather than radically abrogated for the sake of a merely partial and self-interested view of justice. She is Scott's answer to the Edinburgh mob, to Porteous, to Saddletree, to the embryonic Circumlocution Office, to Deans, and, most of all, to the satanic Staunton. Argyle is only the instrument of her power. Faith in community is its source and the trial of her pilgrimage is its crucible.

The heroine of *The Heart of Mid-Lothian*, like the hero of *Old Mortality*, stands inside the ring of tragedy, but the ring does not close. In *The Bride of Lammermoor* the ring does close as Scott shows us a moderate for whom there is no escape. Though the novel is sometimes characterized as an anomalous excursion by Scott from his usual buoyancy and faith, it makes better sense to read it as a tellingly transformed replica of the novels we have been discussing. In *Old Mortality*, Scott had used as the epigraph for the chapter that gives us our first intimate view of Morton these lines from *Henry IV, Part II*:

> Yea, this man's brow, like to a tragic leaf,
> Foretells the nature of a tragic volume. [*OM*, p. 54]

Morton, however, is able to revise the tragic text of his life, just as Scott's novels try to envision how Scotland may revise the tragic text of her history. In *The Bride of Lammermoor* this revision cannot take place because there is no countertext. The story of community has been edited out. Scott imagines a hero over whom the polarized forces have prevailed—and he imagines a Scotland where the annals of community have been closed.

But narrative structure in *The Bride of Lammermoor* has a pronounced anamnestic quality. Though the annals of community are closed, the plot of the novel establishes a numinous impression of the communal ideal. The factional, politicized world has retained vestiges of the communal order and has learned to pantomime the life founded on the social affections. As a result, the narrative, though not composed of contrapuntal plots, is nevertheless double-edged. A phantasmagoric image of authentic community persists through a whole series of contexts that actually exhibit the conflict of opposing fanaticisms through parodic and perverted enactments of the social will. Scott devised this kind of plot by writing about a period in which we see not revolutionary violence but its sinister aftermath. The swords are sheathed; the masquerade can commence.

Edgar Ravenswood, the novel's hero, is an orphan of history. He has been dislocated by the demise of the old chivalric culture and its entombment in the Revolution Settlement of 1689. He is a more striking figure than Redgauntlet, for it is clear that Redgauntlet has survived too long and has been by-passed by history rather than orphaned by it. But the Master of Ravenswood is young, strong, and capable. Though his emotional and instinctual affiliations are with the old chivalric culture into which he was born, he is not an enemy of ideas. There is an encouraging intellectual lucidity in Ravenswood. He is prepared to accept the progress of culture. Redgauntlet has reached the end of his road, but Ravenswood has reached only a crossroads. With a responsible social environment to support him, he might assume a position of eminence in Scotland. But all roads before him turn out to be blocked.[40]

40. There is considerable disagreement among recent critics about Ravenswood. My own analysis presents yet another view. R. C. Gordon, in *Under Which King?* (Edinburgh and London: Oliver & Boyd, 1969), argues that the novel "offers a very dark answer to those preceding works that depict . . . amiable compromise." I agree with this, but not with Gordon's main point,

The novel had a special appeal for Victorians. John Ruskin, usually an admirer, thought the book overpraised, but Benjamin Jowett and Edward FitzGerald used to reread it frequently and were always much affected by it. Sidney Colvin reports a conversation with Gladstone on the difference between themes inherently tragic and those owing their tragic character mainly to their treatment. "Mr. Gladstone presently, in his most earnest and arresting manner, affirmed that in his judgment no theme was either more tragic in itself or more heightened in effect by its treatment than that of Scott's *Bride of Lammermoor.*" Swinburne compared it, with respect to the "logical and moral certitude" of its structure, to *King Lear* and *The Duchess of Malfi.* Matthew Arnold described Ravenswood as "the most interesting by far of all Scott's heroes." And Thomas Hardy "could not say enough about [the novel's] beautiful symmetry."[41] It is not difficult to tell what these critics had in mind when they praised the book. Edgar Ravenswood projects the life of lost possibilities that the readers of *Maud,* "Childe Roland," and *Wuthering Heights* knew intimately. *The Bride of Lammermoor* is filled with the spirit of that

which is that Scott unleashes his "reactionary despair" in the novel (p. 108), and that Ravenswood is seen as a kind of fated Tory. Still less does it seem to me that the "Master of Ravenswood is Scott's most profound expression of the depths and dangers of selfishness," as Donald Cameron writes in "The Web of Destiny: The Structure of *The Bride of Lammermoor,*" in *Scott's Mind and Art,* ed. Jeffares, p. 202, or that "Ravenswood does not want to live because the world has changed too much for him," as D. D. Devlin would have it (*The Author of Waverley* [London: Macmillan, 1971], p. 110).

41. For the views of Ruskin, Jowett, FitzGerald, and Hardy, see W. M. Parker's "Preface" to *BL,* pp. vii–viii. FitzGerald was perhaps the first to note that Tennyson used the novel in *Maud* (see *The Poems of Tennyson,* ed. Christopher Ricks [London: Longmans, 1969], p. 1038). Hardy's response is discussed in Jane Millgate, "Two Versions of Regional Romance: Scott's *The Bride of Lammermoor* and Hardy's *Tess of the d'Urbervilles,*" *Studies in English Literature,* 17 (1977), 729–38. For Gladstone's remarks, see *Scott: The Critical Heritage,* ed. Hayden, p. 474; for Swinburne, *Swinburne as Critic,* ed. C. K. Hyder (London: Routledge & Kegan Paul, 1972), p. 202; for Arnold, *CPW,* VIII, 198.

curious Victorianized romanticism that had so durable a life later in the century and that seems to have, as its signal characteristic, the apprehension of a diminished future.

One fact that seems to have been overlooked is the special significance of the main character's title. He is called the Master of Ravenswood. "Masters" were the eldest sons of peers. The Act of Union (1707) specifically proscribed them from sitting for shires and boroughs, and even from voting at elections. The reduction of Ravenswood's status is thus foreseen in the way he is addressed. The novel begins with a description of the ruin that has befallen his family. In it Scott alludes to the role that the loss of political power played in bringing about the final result.

> Their house had its revolutions, like all sublunary things; it became greatly declined from its splendour about the middle of the 17th century; and towards the period of the Revolution, the last proprietor of Ravenswood Castle saw himself compelled to part with the ancient family seat, and to remove himself to a lonely and sea-beaten tower, which, situated on the bleak shores between Saint Abb's Head and the village of Eyemouth, looked out on the lonely and boisterous German Ocean. A black domain of wild pasture-land surrounded their new residence, and formed the remains of their property. [*BL,* p. 27]

The final ruin of the family had been brought about by the "legal toils and pecuniary snares" of Sir William Ashton. Ashton attained in Scotland the exalted position of Lord Keeper. He is a new man, a creation of the Whig ascendancy after the revolution. He has the wealth and station of an aristocrat, but nothing of a noble nature. Lady Ashton (who is a Douglas) is more contemptuous of her husband's origins than anyone else in the novel. Scott never explains exactly why she married Sir William, though the usual oligarchical motives are implied. Their marriage is, nevertheless, an important fact. A process of personal corruption is set off by it. Lady Ashton must spend her life preserving her aristocratic dignity from contamination by her husband. The maintenance of her position dictates a magisterial selfishness in everything she does. There is a point to all this, which extends beyond Scott's condemnation of her petty manipulations of power. Lady Ashton is a falsification of the chivalric nobility; she is a warning, as we ultimately see, to Ravenswood.

We first encounter Ravenswood at the funeral of his father. The chivalric tradition is being buried, and Scott carefully indicates that its burial is overdue. The heroic spirit has decayed into loutishness and arrogance. Ravenswood is glad to see the brawling mourners at his father's funeral depart. He is then left alone to contemplate "the tarnished honour and degraded fortunes of his house, the destruction of his own hopes, and the triumph of the family by whom they had been ruined" (*BL,* p. 35). Scott's description summarizes the elements that force Ravenswood's entry into "the mazeway of a culturally disillusioned person."

Ravenswood, of course, falls in love with Lucy, the Ashtons' daughter. But the novel is not a reworking of *Romeo and Juliet.* The echoes from *Hamlet* and *Macbeth* are stronger. We are never allowed to believe that Ravenswood will succeed in marrying Lucy. For one thing, the love story is encased in a great panoply of omen and prophecy that insist on the catastrophic conclusion. Moreover, the love story is clearly subordinated to the story of the Ravenswoods' decline as a family. We are told that a Ravenswood fell at the battle of Flodden (*BL,* p. 256) and we are invited to see the contemporary parallel. A revolution has taken place, and an old culture is being swallowed up. The novel concerns itself with Edgar's unavailing attempts to extricate himself from the ruins of the past and find a way to accommodate himself to the new political and social order.

The action of the novel continually proposes a simple question: How is Edgar Ravenswood to be provisioned? Leslie Stephen was unsympathetic, but not far wrong, when he suggested that *The Bride of Lammermoor* describes the plight of a Scottish gentle-

man who can't invite his friends home to dinner.[42] This is precisely what makes the novel serious and its plot double-edged.
Ravenswood's poverty is a sign of his cultural disenfranchise-
ment. He is, in starkly symbolic terms, deprived of hospitality,
the ancient ceremony that externalizes the significance of the social will.

Many novels of course, deal with the man of good family who
finds himself in embarrassed financial circumstances. But this is
hardly Scott's theme. Indeed, the whole novel develops as a series
of gestures on the part of various persons and parties who wish to
make provision for Ravenswood. Ravenswood is not despised; he
is solicited. Nearly every province of the social order offers a design for his social restoration. It is in this sense that the narrative
recollects the rituals and woven ties of community. The problem,
however, is that the designers are all designing. Every beckoning
to Ravenswood, every gesture of relief and rescue, contains as its
precondition Ravenswood's accession to moral bankruptcy. He is
invited to feast with vultures who pick over the corpse of community.

The parodic distortion of communal allegiance is dramatized in
Caleb Balderstone, the ancient steward of the Ravenswood family. He has been much criticized as a buffoon who spoils the tone
of the novel. He is neither that nor the somewhat exalted figure
made out by R. C. Gordon.[43] Caleb is mortified by the condition
into which the family has fallen. He puts all his energy into sparing his master the social embarrassment of poverty. Once, when a
storm forces Ravenswood to offer the shelter of the Tower to Sir
William and Lucy, Caleb promises the guests an opulent supper.
Shortly thereafter, he makes his apologies to the guests: a bolt of

---

42. "Some Words about Sir Walter Scott," in *Scott: The Critical Heritage,*
p. 449. Stephen sees all of Scott's heroes as "wooden blocks to hang a story
on."
43. *Under Which King?,* p. 103.

lightning has shot down the chimney and turned the roast to a cinder.

Caleb's understanding of economic power derives from the codifications of the feudal order. He behaves as though the rights and privileges of the feudal aristocracy were still of account. When Caleb descends on the village of Wolf's-hope and attempts to levy an assessment for the provisions needed by his master, he is scorned and repudiated. Worse, he is outmaneuvered by the village lawyer, who says, "'As to any threats of stouthrief oppression, by rule of thumb, or *via facti*, as the law termed it, he would have Mr. Balderstone recollect, that new times were not as old times'" (*BL*, p. 134).

The Master of Ravenswood cannot—and does not—expect to be provisioned by an old descendent of the royal purveyors. Caleb is ludicrous because he has pretensions that Edgar Ravenswood has had sense enough to abandon. The thievery, lies, and mock displays of grandeur that Caleb deems necessary are as pathetic in Ravenswood's eyes as they are in ours. Though Ravenswood refuses to claim the antiquated privileges of the chivalric tradition, however, he cannot surrender his temperamental obligation to its high sense of responsibility. Social revolution may have collapsed the fortunes of his family, but it has not liberated the lineal heir from the duty he feels to respect the ideal of civility defined in the chivalric tradition. Ravenswood does not believe in aristocracy; he does believe, however, in dignity, charity, courage, and loyalty.

Ravenswood is somewhat less wary of another scheme that proposes to restore him to the privileges of his birth. He comes perilously close to engaging in a Jacobite plot. "'There is a fate,'" he says, "'watches for us, and we . . . have a stake in the revolution that is now impending, and has already alarmed many a bosom.'" His companion asks: "'What fate—what revolution? . . . We have had one revolution too much already, I think'" (*BL*, p. 95). Ravenswood is not quite sure of this at first. He is tempted by his relative the Marquis of A—— to enlist in the Jacobite cause. The Marquis, as Scott later reveals, intends merely "to take as deep, or as slight an interest in the fortunes of his kinsman, as the progress of his own schemes might require" (*BL,* p. 159). When, toward the end of the novel, a temporary shift in power has brought a Tory government into office, Ravenswood moves into close alliance with the Marquis. At every turn, however, Scott makes it plain that the Marquis is the most perfidious of men. Kinship for him is strictly a matter of political convenience. Ravenswood, desperately reaching for some form of connection, is nearly seduced by the perverse way in which the Marquis disguises his brand of factionalism in meaningless displays of familial affection.

Normally, however, Ravenswood is astutely conscious of factionalism and of its failures. He declares that when he recollects "the times of the first and second Charles, and of the last James," he sees little reason to believe he should draw his sword for the sake of their descendants.

> "I hope to see the day when justice shall be open to Whig and Tory, and when these nick-names shall only be used among coffee-house politicians, as slut and jade are among apple-women, as cant terms of idle spite and rancour."
> "That will not be in our days, Master—the iron has entered too deeply into our sides and our souls."
> "It will be, however, one day. [Men] will not always start at these nick-names. . . . As social life is better protected, its comforts will become too dear to be hazarded without some better reason than speculative politics." [*BL,* p. 98]

Scott's editorializing is never tactful. Ravenswood acquires here the signature of Scott's own hopes. Ravenswood, like Scott, looks forward to the triumph of the social interest. Again like Scott, he refuses to be inspired either by moribund tradition or by revolutionary ideology. Ravenswood sees, then, the conditions that must prevail if Scotland is to have real justice and tranquillity. But, in Schiller's sense, the moral possibility is lacking in the

immediate circumstances of Ravenswood's world. It will make
no provision for him that respects his feeling for the presumptive
life. It refuses to regenerate social connection at the level of the
social affections. And yet Ravenswood must find connection. He
cannot take a mess of shadows for his meat.

There is yet another way. Sir William Ashton will provide for
him. Therein lies the final, irreversible, tragic catastrophe of Edgar Ravenswood. If only Sir William spurned Ravenswood, all
might be well enough. But Ravenswood is tempted into his disastrous romance by Ashton's conciliatory—and conniving—
behavior. In the first place, Sir William is genuinely fond of his
daughter and wishes to make her happy. But, more important,
Sir William sees positive advantages to himself in connecting his
family by marriage to the Ravenswoods. Ashton "was born of
the willow, not of the oak. It had accordingly been [his] policy,
on all occasions, to watch the changes on the political horizon,
and, ere yet the conflict was decided, to negotiate some interest
for himself with the party most likely to prove victorious" (*BL,*
p. 155). And Sir William had this to consider: any lawyer smarter
than himself might figure out for Ravenswood the devious com-
bination of snares and chicanery that he had used to acquire possession of the Ravenswood estates. Since the appearance of a lawyer smarter than himself, or the composition of a court somewhat
less venal than the incumbent privy council, was not improbable,
Ashton could make good use of the additional acquisition from
the Ravenswood family of the Master himself. "'And besides,'
said he to himself, 'it will be an act of generosity to raise up the
heir of this distressed family.'" Nor did he, the parvenu, forget
that "'Lord Ravenswood was an ancient title'" (*BL,* p. 161).
The perversion of the social will evident in Ashton's train of
thought could not be more grotesque.

His are the calculations of the new man who is seeking legitimacy. Sir William Ashton is a projection of the future. The prosperity that would come to the villagers of Wolf's-hope later in

the eighteenth century would bring with it a long line of William
Ashtons. Ashton is not so much base as vacuous. He stands for
nothing and that somehow makes him effective. The most remarkable achievement in Scott's portrayal of him is the complete
compatibility of his nullity and his power. And there is an exten-
sion of this enigma in his facile good nature, which never seems
to be in conflict with his collusive purposes. He is, in fact, meretricious man. The only thing he has is money. Scott leaves us in
no doubt about his origins. In the great castle that once belonged
to Ravenswood

> the pictures of [Ashton's] father and mother were . . . to be
> seen; the latter, sour, shrewish, and solemn, in her black hood
> and close pinners, with a book of devotion in her hand; the for-
> mer, exhibiting beneath a black silk Geneva cowl, or skull-cap,
> which sate as close to the head as if it had been shaven, a pinched,
> peevish, puritanical set of features, terminating in a hungry, red-
> dish, peaked beard, forming on the whole a countenance, in the
> expression of which the hypocrite seemed to contend with the
> miser and the knave. [*BL,* pp. 183–84]

Scott does not use this language in *Old Mortality* or *The Heart of
Mid-Lothian,* though it approximates the language of *Peveril of the
Peak* and *Woodstock.* The difference here is that the puritan has acquired genteel respectability and is fast becoming a Philistine. Edgar Ravenswood cannot accept the provisions of Sir William
Ashton without destroying the only important legacy he has: the
ideal of personal conduct and public virtue that the chivalric tradition has given him.

But Ravenswood is under two influences. He loves Lucy Ashton, and he wants Scotland's future to work out well. Through
the prompting of these influences, he finds himself at last rationalizing his situation:

> If, in reality, this man desires no more than the law allows him—
> if he is willing to adjust even his acknowledged rights upon an

equitable footing, what could be my [late] father's cause of complaint?—what is mine?—Those from whom we won our ancient possessions fell under the sword of my ancestors, and left lands and livings to the conquerors; we sink under the force of the law, now too powerful for the Scottish chivalry. Let us parley with the victors of the day, as if we had been besieged in our fortress, and without hope of relief. [*BL,* pp. 154–55]

Ravenswood is right in one respect; there is no hope of relief. Caleb Balderstone's last stratagem is to fire the fortress as an excuse not to have to receive guests. It is a bleak but eloquent symbol of the chivalric world's demise. But parleying with the victors of the day is equally destructive. If the victors were worthy, if they had any instinct for the true meaning of nobility, if Ravenswood could keep intact the ancient legacy that has made him what he is, then he might parley in relative safety. None of these conditions obtains. Moreover, Ravenswood knows they do not. At bottom, he knows that he cannot treat with the Ashtons without compromising, not so much his family, which had practiced its own form of loutishness, but the authentic virtues of a dying culture that survive only in him and a few like him. He would expose himself to the personal corruption that Lady Ashton freely indulges. He would become the guardian of mediocrity; he would set his seal upon the meretricious future.

The legends, omens, and prophecies that warn Ravenswood against alliance have at their core a moral reality. When Caleb sees the Master in Ashton's company, he says, " 'Your ain conscience tells you it isna for your father's son to be neighbouring wi' the like o' him' " (*BL,* p. 177). Simply put, Ravenswood has to listen to his own conscience. Old Alice, the sibyl in this book, is obviously the very voice of his conscience. At first Ravenswood mistakes Alice's meaning and believes she is charging him with contemplating blood revenge. She corrects him:

"God forbid!" said Alice solemnly; "and therefore I would have you depart these fatal bounds, where your love, as well as your hatred, threatens mischief. . . . I would shield . . . the Ashtons from you, and you from them. . . . You can have nothing— ought to have nothing, in common with them—Begone from among them; and if God has destined vengeance on the oppressor's house, do not you be the instrument." [*BL,* p. 194]

Temporarily, at least, Ravenswood listens to this voice, the voice that denies both revenge and alliance. But he cannot bring himself to surrender Lucy; they are secretly engaged. When Lady Ashton discovers this, she openly humiliates Ravenswood. This is a terrible irony, for she represents precisely the polluted aristocracy to whom the Master would unavoidably link himself should he marry Lucy. At the very moment that he is being insulted by Lady Ashton, old Alice dies—her last prophetic gesture.

In making the arrangements for Alice's funeral, Ravenswood seeks out the village sexton. (The allusions to *Hamlet* and *Macbeth* in this part of the novel are potent.) The sexton, who does not recognize Edgar, has a grudge against the Ravenswoods. " 'I hae seen three generations of them,' " he says, " 'and deil ane to mend other.' " His specific grievance is that he was dragooned by the Master's grandfather into service at Bothwell Bridge, where he sustained an injury that deprived him of his livelihood. This would not have been so terrible, but the Master's father then proceeded to squander the family's wealth, thus bringing general economic depression " 'to huz puir dependent creatures.' " Ravenswood recognizes—and is conscience-striken by—the truth of what the sexton says.

"However," said the sexton, "this young man Edgar is likely to avenge my wrongs on the haill of his kindred."

"Indeed?" said Ravenswood; "why should you suppose so?"

"They say he is about to marry the daughter of Leddy Ashton; and let her leddyship get his head ance under her oxter, and see you if she winna gie his neck a thraw. . . . Sae the warst wish I shall wish the lad is, that he may take his ain creditable gate o't, and ally himsell wi' his father's enemies." [*BL,* pp. 247–49]

The sexton's crafty analysis recapitulates the central theme of the novel. Ravenswood cannot return to his fathers because of the kind of people they became and the disgrace they made of their rank; and he cannot turn to the Ashtons because of the kind of people they are. Edgar Ravenswood would have made a good lord and would not have exploited his "puir dependent creatures." But the sexton doesn't know that. He knows only that he has been the victim of exploitation, and he despises the system of servitude that has left him impoverished: "'Me, that's an auld man, living in yon miserable cabin, that's fitter for the dead than the quick'" (*BL*, p. 249). Edgar Ravenswood has reason enough to feel the force of the sexton's complaint. And if he cannot take the word of Caleb or Alice that his marriage could only destroy him, he might certainly take the word of a man who contemns him.

Ravenswood, however, has engaged himself to Lucy. He cannot break the engagement, nor can he allow it to be broken at the command of Lady Ashton. He bides his time—according to the motto of his family—but no resolution is possible. The crisis comes when Lucy is to be married off to the amiable but inconsequential Bucklaw. Ravenswood tries to prevent the marriage, but cannot. Lucy, desperate to the point of lunacy, tries to kill her husband, and dies herself. Her brother, Sholto, who believes in bravado (and not, as he thinks, in honor), challenges Ravenswood to a duel. Ravenswood, emotionally broken himself, dies before the duel can take place. In the fulfillment of another of the book's prophecies, he is swallowed up in the quicksand not far from Wolf's Crag. No trace remains of him except for an emblematic black plume. He had nothing, he was nothing, he could be nothing. No provision could be made for him.

The Bride of Lammermoor, though it offers occasional reflections of Scott's generally favorable attitude toward the results of the Glorious Revolution and the Act of Union, is very unlike *Rob Roy* and *Redgauntlet.* In those novels Scott concentrates on the tempering of fanaticism and the beginning of an economic prosperity that would give a progressive turn to civilization in Scotland. In *The Bride of Lammermoor*, the revolution creates a menacing aftermath. We see the revolution as essentially a mechanism that has shifted power away from the crude louts of the old nobility and given it to the unctuous louts of the new ignobility. The perspective on the revolution that we get in *The Bride of Lammermoor* does not have its central significance as documentation of some change in Scott's view of the Revolution Settlement. The novel generalizes beyond a specific historical moment in order to explore a tragic territory that the Waverley novels customarily eclipse. Scott is looking at the way in which political revolution and the solutions it reaches can force a devaluation of certain human qualities that are indispensable to man's progress in any age. *The Bride of Lammermoor* records the defeat of community within a framework that has, technically, reconstituted the social order. The reconstitution is factitious. Though the old chivalric order is dead, it acted as a legitimate reference point for a social ethic that bound all "puir dependent creatures." Edgar Ravenswood, who has done with the barbarousness of feudalism, retains what for Scott continued to be meaningful in the chivalric tradition, its feeling for the organic relationships that draw men into union with one another and that spring from the motive of benevolence. All of this is sundered in *The Bride of Lammermoor*. Ravenswood's moderation, integrity, sympathy, and moral idealism are wasted in a world that has been created by political deals and that has learned to maximize the role of force and power within the realm of the social life itself.

Unlike Henry Morton and Jeanie Deans, Edgar Ravenswood finds the image of community deleted, however much he tries to act under its inspiration. He is neither faithless nor cynical; he is anomic. Though he has a social identity, he cannot avow it. Scott saw that revolution might ultimately bring about this condition in his own time. Some of the Victorian admirers of *The Bride of*

Lammermoor may have sensed the book's prophetic quality (as Matthew Arnold certainly did). The novel is as much an elegy for the future as it is a reading of the past. Edgar Ravenswood prefigures the world that Scott feared might be coming, a world in which social membership becomes at best an abstraction and all face-to-face encounters are problematic encounters between derelicts.

To this extent *The Bride of Lammermoor* makes explicit the apprehension that generates the implicit tragic note in all of Scott's fictional studies of revolution. It uses the postrevolutionary situation as the appropriate context in which to depict the life that emerges under the dominion of a politically prescribed order. It is a life with polished surfaces but no depth. This represents the final degradation of the social affections. All human associations are twisted by "legal toils and pecuniary snares," and this is as true of Caleb's mad defense of feudalism as it is of the Ashtons' mastery of philistinism. Only in the plot's parodic recollection of hospitality is the lost life of the social affections faintly visible.

The Bride of Lammermoor thus fetches from the past the story of a historical dead end, a story that Scott could regard as projecting the pattern of an already tangible future. Ravenswood had struggled to surpass his "lonely and sea-beaten tower," situated, typically, between a "bleak shore" of the "lonely German Ocean" and a narrow patch of "black . . . pasture-land." He is inevitably defeated. We know how it will end for Ravenswood, not because of a fanciful prophecy but because he is in quicksand from the beginning. He is one of those for whom, as Herzen would say, there is no way out. The novel cannot plot his survival. It can only dignify his struggle by assimilating it to the *mythos* of tragedy.

But the funereal and elegiac tone of *The Bride of Lammermoor* does not, as I have tried to show, dominate Scott's fiction. Scott ordinarily counterpoints the estranging political order by constructing an antithetical action in which community is bodied forth. This use of narrative is an imaginative reaching out to a dis-

tinction that more and more preoccupied writers from Tolstoy to
Tönnies. It is perhaps the latter's social analysis that best epitomizes the sense of reality that Scott's narrative structures attempt
to illuminate:

> All intimate, private, exclusive living together . . . is understood
> as life in Gemeinschaft. . . . Gesellschaft is public life—it is the
> world itself. In Gemeinschaft . . . one lives from birth on, bound
> to it in weal and woe. One goes into Gesellschaft as one goes into
> a strange country. A young man is warned against bad Gesell-
> schaft, but the expression bad Gemeinschaft violates the meaning
> of the word.[44]

The tragic note in Scott announces this difference. It attempts
to discharge the charisma of revolution by magnifying the moral
distance between *Gesellschaft*, where the designers of revolution
recruit their cadres, and *Gemeinschaft*, where the "good man" re-
cruits his humanity.

44. Ferdinand Tönnies, *Community and Society,* trans. and ed. Charles P.
Loomis (East Lansing: Michigan State University Press, 1957), p. 247.

CHAPTER THREE

Byron: Rebellion
and Revolution

To their earliest readers Byron and Scott represented contrary states of mind. Hazlitt made a point of their differences in *The Spirit of the Age*: "If Sir Walter Scott may be thought by some to have been 'Born universal heir to all humanity,' it is plain Lord Byron can set up no such pretension. He is, in a striking degree, the creature of his own will." Similarly, one young man, a neighbor of Scott's who saw Byron in London, tells us how it all struck a contemporary: " 'How I did stare . . . at Byron's beautiful face, like a spirit's—good or evil. But he was *bitter* —what a contrast to Scott.' "[1]

Yet the bitter Byron and the genial Scott came to regard each other, and each other's works, with great admiration. John Clubbe, who has studied the growth of their friendship in detail, calls attention to the fact that they were both men of the world. This is very likely the key to their personal relationship. Their literary relationship, as Clubbe indicates, is harder to define, mainly because Byron's comments on Scott's work are not detailed.[2] It is

1. William Hazlitt, *The Spirit of the Age* (1825; rpt. London: World's Classics, 1904), p. 92; John Gibson Lockhart, *Memoirs of the Life of Sir Walter Scott* (Edinburgh: Robert Cadell, 1837–38), II, 373.

2. "Byron and Scott," *Texas Studies in Literature and Language,* 15 (1973),

suggestive, however, that Byron avidly read Scott during his years of exile from England. Scott, he said in 1821, "is certainly the most wonderful writer of the day. His novels are a new literature in themselves. . . . I know no reading to which I fall with such alacrity" (*LJ*, V, 167–68). We may imagine that behind this enthusiasm for the novels as a "new literature" lies Byron's fascination with the quality he clearly shared with Scott: a vigorous historical imagination.

It is also possible that Byron responded, especially as an exile, to the spirit of social harmony that Scott could so powerfully evoke. Whether he did so or not, it is important to stress that Byron, for all his bitter alienation, profoundly valued man's social instincts. The author of *Don Juan* rightly protested that he was no misanthrope (*P*, IX, 21). Scott himself recognized this truth about Byron, but the Tory propagandist in him generated a serious misreading of its implications. Basically, Scott was simply not prepared to believe that the poet's "bad metaphysics and worse politics," as he called them, represented the essential Byron. Commenting in an 1816 essay for the *Quarterly Review* on the strife-torn Byron, he expressed the hope that "this darkness of the spirit, this scepticism concerning the existence of worth, of friendship, of sincerity [will not] sink like a gulf between this distinguished poet and society" (*MW*, IV, 396). Scott was on safe ground when he decided there was in Byron no "systematic attachment to a particular creed of politics" (*MW*, IV, 381). But to Scott this could only mean that Byron was a traditionalist, and so he brushed aside "Byron's ridiculous pretence of Republicanism, when he never wrote about the Multitude without expressing or insinuating the very soul of scorn" (*LJ*, II, 376n). And in his eulogy of Byron (*Edinburgh Weekly Journal*, 1827), Scott went so far as to say Lord Byron "would have been found, had a collision

---

67–91. And see the author's supplementary study, "After Missolonghi: Scott on Byron, 1824–32," *Library Chronicle*, 39 (1973), 18–33.

taken place between the aristocratic and democratic parties in the state, exerting all his energies in defense of that to which he naturally belonged" (*MW,* IV, 346).

If the view of Byron as a bitter misanthrope is a distortion, the view of Byron as a disguised reactionary is bizarre. Byron did have a deeply social nature, but he also understood that redemption from bad metaphysics and worse politics did not lie along the road to Scott's peaceable kingdom. He saw plainly enough that the traditional basis of the social order could not accommodate the intellectual and moral freedom he valued so highly. He certainly never thought of fighting a holding action for the sake of aristocratic privileges. Just as there is more to Scott than appears in his Tory diatribes, there is more to Byron than appears either in his bitter face or in his aristocratic bearing.

This is, obviously, to say that Byron was a moderate. But Byron's kind of moderation differs greatly from what is shown in Scott's novels. Scott had made the spirit of moderation a means of release from the tragic environment of revolution. For Byron moderation is not a deliverance but a ceaseless struggle. The danger of self-betrayal is always present. Moderation in Byron does not imply a dissolution of internal turmoil and conflict; it is, rather, the defiant construction of an alternative to the choices polarized in revolution. For this reason Byron, though he undoubtedly appreciated Scott's analysis of revolution, and though he undoubtedly cherished certain aspects of the aristocratic tradition, is finally very far from Scott's way of thinking. He belongs, instead, with Camus. The context for understanding this difference is the tragedy Byron wrote, and the drama he lived, during his years of exile from England.

THE TRIALS OF PROMETHEUS

The tragedy of revolution took its most vigorous hold as a theme in Byron's poetry during roughly the same period that

Scott wrote *Old Mortality, The Heart of Mid-Lothian,* and *The Bride of Lammermoor. Marino Faliero* was composed in 1820, *Cain* and *Sardanapalus* a year later. It should be noted that Byron was working on a draft of *Marino Faliero* as early as February 1817. As these dates indicate, Byron's poetry was open to the same influences that can be observed in Scott's novels: the fall of Napoleon, the growth of counterrevolutionary political power both in Britain and on the Continent, and the subsequent outbreak of political radicalism in Britain and revolutionary violence in Spain, Italy, and Greece.

Byron exiled himself in 1816. While he thus did not witness at firsthand the events that threatened England with revolution, he was personally, if sporadically, in the thick of the Italian revolutionary movement. This is not to say, however, that the political affairs of Italy and later of Greece prevailed upon him as an influence while British politics receded into the background. He watched with great care the progress of revolutionary and quasi-revolutionary actions in both arenas. His diagnosis of the two movements is an important manifestation of his cautious political commitments. For Byron seems to have decided, almost simultaneously, that English radicalism was an inconceivably evil development, while the Italian and Greek revolutions were glorious causes.

This position can be clearly traced in many of the letters Byron wrote in 1820. Early in that year, he learned that his friend John Cam Hobhouse, a supporter of the Westminster Radicals, had been arrested for publishing a pamphlet that denounced the government's repressive Six Acts. Byron was sorry for Hobhouse and glad to hear that he had been released after eleven weeks in Newgate. But the incident apparently solidified in Byron's mind a disapprobation of the radical movement in England that had been growing upon him for some time. During the initial phase of his exile, he occasionally spoke of returning to England to take an active part in an insurrection, though the rhetoric of these refer-

ences made them always a little facetious. By 1819, however, he
was much more subdued when he spoke of such things: "I feel no
love for [England] after the treatment I received before leaving it
. . . but I do not hate it enough to wish to take a part in its ca-
lamities, as on either side harm must be done before good can ac-
crue; revolutions are not to be made with rosewater. My taste for
revolution is abated, with my other passions" (*LJ*, IV, 358). His
reaction to Hobhouse's scrape reveals that the mood of 1819 had
apparently developed into firm resolution. His first question to
Hobhouse was: "Why lend yourself to Hunt and Cobbett, and
the bones of Tom Paine?" (*LBC*, II, 134). This whole "gang,"
together with the Cato Street Conspirators (whose assassination
plot was discovered while Hobhouse was incarcerated), "make
one doubt . . . the virtue of any principle or politics which can be
embraced by similar ragamuffins" (*LBC*, II, 138). For the next
two months Byron returned again and again to the same theme,
which at times he elaborated into an execration of popular democracy. "Pray don't *mistake me*; it is not against the pure principle of reform that I protest, but against low, designing, dirty lev-
ellers, who would pioneer their way to a democratical tyranny"
(*LBC*, II, 148). He hoped that Hobhouse had nothing to do with
the scoundrels who fomented the events that led to the Peterloo
Massacre. "I can understand and enter into the feelings of Mirabeau and La Fayette, but I have no sympathy with Robespierre
and Marat. . . . I do not think the man who would overthrow
all laws should have the benefit of any. . . . I think I have neither
been an illiberal man, nor an unsteady man upon politics; but I
think also that if the Manchester yeomanry had cut down [Ora-
tor] *Hunt only*, they would have done their duty" (*LBC*, II, 143).

One week before writing this letter on Peterloo, Byron was
telling Douglas Kinnaird that the recent insurrection in Spain
(April 1820) was setting "all Italy a constitutioning," and that if
matters grew serious, "I should not like to sit twirling my
thumbs, but perhaps 'take service,' like Duguld Dalgetty [in

Scott's *Legend of Montrose*], on the savage side of the question" (*LBC*, II, 141). Byron's immediate access to the revolutionary societies of the *Carbonari* was provided by the family of his mistress, Teresa Guiccioli, whose father and brother, Pietro, were leaders in the movement. In the summer, Byron met Pietro, whom he liked at once, though he seemed "a little too hot for revolutions."[3] Revolution had broken out in Naples and Byron thought it would soon leave "a calling card" in Ravenna, where he had for some time been living. The Neapolitans, however, proved unequal to their ambitions, and so for the moment Byron could remain an interested onlooker. He did, though, formally attach himself to a branch of the *Carboneri*. There were three branches: *Protettrice* (protectress), the controlling organization; *Speranza* (hope), chiefly composed of educated sympathizers; and *Turba* (mob), a mixture of all sorts, but predominantly the common people. It was in this last group that Byron finally enrolled.

Leslie Marchand, who gives a full account of these activities in his biography of Byron, notices the anomaly produced by Byron's attachment to the *Turba* while he was condemning the Westminster Radicals. The mob, according to Marchand, "seemed more picturesque in a foreign land" (p. 867). The explanation is not quite convincing. Marchand, however, has a much more plausible explanation for the general pattern of Byron's political ambivalences:

> The arrest of Hobhouse had somehow brought to a focus the strange contradictions of Byron's liberal sympathies balanced against his aristocratic pride. This paradox, so frequently noted in him, is partly resolved by a recognition of his eighteenth-century conception of liberalism as a revolt against tyranny which might go even so far as republicanism, but which always envisioned an aristocratic or gentlemanly leadership. This concept involved dis-

3. The remark is cited in Leslie A. Marchand, *Byron: A Biography* (New York: Knopf, 1957), p. 865.

trust of the mob and lack of sympathy for democratic or proletar-
ian, or even middle-class, control or participation in government.
[p. 841]

This view, which is shared by many critics, undoubtedly accounts for Byron's recurrent use of an aristocratic value structure
in order to impose limits on his commitment to revolution.[4] The
trouble with it is that even the most enlightened Whiggism cannot contain the magnitude and passion of Byron's moral revolt
against all forms of oppression. Moreover, as we shall see, Byron
is not at all consistent in his application of enlightened Whiggism
to social crisis. The shifting grounds of his political allegiances
have a meaning that is unfortunately missed by attempts to reconcile Byron's elitism with his liberal sympathies. The major characteristic, as well as the major significance, of Byron's political
temper is precisely his sustained ambivalence and caution, particularly when revolution becomes the chief issue. Fundamentally,
Byron's taste for revolution was in some sense *always* abating.
Even his strongest commitments, as in Italy and Greece, required
a thick apparatus of qualification and rigid distinctions between
the just and unjust uses of political violence. In constructing this
apparatus, Byron was not protecting his elitist tendencies. He
was protecting the integrity of his moral revolt, his right to defy
injustice at the most complex levels of human experience. He realized that political revolution, because it could itself be an injustice, almost inevitably contaminated moral revolt.

From his sense of the incompatibility of moral and political revolt Byron developed a version of the distinction Camus makes

4. David V. Erdman, "Byron and the Genteel Reformers," *PMLA*, 56
(1941), 1065–94, argues that Byron was never a radical and only followed
some members of the Whig aristocracy in their vague sense of the need for reform. For roughly similar comments, see Andrew Rutherford, *Byron: A Critical Study* (Stanford: Stanford University Press, 1961), p. 189, and Carl Wood-
ring, *Politics in English Romantic Poetry* (Cambridge: Harvard University Press,
1970), p. 152.

between rebellion and revolution. Byron cannot be said to have
made the categories of rebellion and revolution completely irreconcilable, as they are in Camus. In Italy and Greece he conceived
of a "right" revolution. Nevertheless, his doubts and resistance
remained. We find him, in the midst of the Italian enterprise, beginning to explore the moral risks of revolution. His instrument
for this exploration was tragic drama. The tragedies dealing with
revolution invariably turn on the protagonist's betrayal of his
conscience, a betrayal that leads from the ethical protest of rebellion to the political violence of revolution. Byron's growing insight into this experience, culminating in *Cain,* is what Camus's
description of the rebel can illuminate.

We can be clearer about the nature of Byron's mature political
judgments by returning to his correspondence during the early
1820s. He had not, in scolding Hobhouse and praising the Ital-
ians, said his last word about revolution. Though he repudiated
English radicalism in 1820, his mood had again altered by 1821.
A journal entry from January of that year indicates the change.
"The *Powers* mean to war with the peoples. The intelligence
seems positive—let it be so—they will be beaten in the end. The
king-times are fast finishing." Yet Byron surrounded this view
with a bleak fatalism that soon became the most distinctive aspect
of his comments on the emerging political crisis. The same passage continues: "There will be blood shed like water, and tears
like mist; but the peoples will conquer in the end. I shall not live
to see it, but I foresee it" (*LJ,* V, 173). He seems half disap-
pointed and half grateful that he will not witness the violent revolution when it comes. Later in the year he developed a similar
prediction in a letter to Hobhouse, whom he was no longer hec-
toring: "Your infamous government will drive all honest men
into the necessity of reversing it. I see nothing left for it but a republic *now*; an opinion which I have held aloof as long as it would
let me. Come it must. . . . It may not be in ten or twenty years,
but it is inevitable, and I am sorry for it." He still despises Hunt

and Waddington as "abominable tyrants" and "low imitations of the Jacobins," and clings to the distinction between a democracy and a republic, but adds, significantly, that "America is a model of force, and freedom, and moderation; [despite] all the coarseness and rudeness of its people" (*LBC*, II, 203–4).

His direct contact with political violence was, in the meantime, serving further to complicate his feelings. All during 1820 the Italian cause seemed lost in uncertainties, but he exempted Italy from his fatalistic mood of the next year as the cause regained vitality. He could say in February 1821 that "it is no great matter, supposing that Italy could be liberated, who or what is sacrificed. It is a grand object—the very *poetry* of politics. Only think—a free Italy!! Why there has been nothing like it since the days of Augustus" (*LJ*, V, 205). Obviously Byron saw the struggle for independence in Italy as wholly different in character from a potential revolution in England. Nevertheless, within little more than a month there was a blow to his Italian expectations that took the bloom of "poetry" off the politics of liberation. At a crucial moment the Neapolitans had surrendered docilely to the advancing Austrians, and Byron saw the grand object of Italian freedom wrecked by the pettiness of squabbling factions. "The present business," he told Thomas Moore, "has been as much a work of treachery as of cowardice" (*LJ*, V, 271). And to Hobhouse he wrote in April that he, as much as anyone, had been taken in by a false show. "Poland and Ireland were Sparta and Spartacus compared to these villains. But there is no room to be sufficiently bilious, not bile enough to spit on them" (*LBC*, II, 169–70). Once more he tried to retrieve the situation by insisting on a distinction: "[do] not blame a whole people for the vices of a province" (*LJ*, V, 272).

He did not intend, when he decided to go to Greece, to be similarly disillusioned. The tone and resonance of his references to the Greek expedition lack the flamboyance of the former *engagé*. "I believed myself on a fool's errand from the outset," he wrote in 1823. "But I like the Cause at least, and will stick by it while it is not degraded [or] dishonoured" (*LJ,* VI, 257). The story of how Byron, once his interest in the Greek revolution took shape, encountered and tried to endure the degradation and dishonoring of the Greek cause is well known. Not long after he arrived at Cephelonia, he imposed an embargo on references to the Greeks until he could find something good to say about them. He came to regard the Greeks as the most dishonest people he had ever known. When he tried strenuously to avoid their factionalism, he discovered that only factions were taken seriously. His task, then, was to make one faction more powerful than all the others in the hope that it could direct the course of the revolution. This very doubtful plan failed, partly because Byron had to spend so much of his time and his gradually decreasing energy dealing with the multitude of corrupt officials who were interested mainly in the funds he controlled.

One inevitably asks why Byron went on with this work, and how he accounted to himself for the incredible ignominy that blackened the whole enterprise. Again, it became for Byron a question of what could be tolerated under a given set of conditions. He knew that the Greeks had indiscriminately massacred the Turks and plundered their property in the early stages of the insurrection, but he fortified himself with the hope that freedom would nurture dignity. William Parry recorded a long conversation in which Byron discussed this development.

> Such acts are the natural consequences of long-suffering, particularly among men who have some traditional knowledge of the high renown of their ancestors; but they have not contributed to soften the Greek character; nor has the plunder of their masters failed to sow for the time the seeds of dissension and ambition among themselves. The insurrection was literally a slave breaking his chains on the head of his oppressor; but in escaping from bondage, the Greeks acted without a plan. There was no system of insurrection organized, and the people, after the first flushing

of their hatred was over, were easily stirred up to animosity
against each other, and they fell under the dominion of some ambitious chiefs. . . . Time will bring [an organized system of gov-
ernment]; for a whole nation can profit by no other teacher.⁵

What Byron told Parry he had inscribed much earlier in his poetry. The "Ode on Venice" (composed in 1818) showed compassion for "the crowd / Maddened with centuries of drought,"
who at last "trample on each other to obtain / The cup which
brings oblivion of a chain / Heavy and sore" (ll. 84–88). He
adopted very much the same perspective on the French Revolution in Canto III of *Childe Harold,* which he wrote and published
in 1816.

> Mankind have felt their strength, and made it felt.
> They might have used it better, but, allured
> By their new vigour, sternly have they dealt
> On one another; Pity ceased to melt
> With her once natural charities. But they,
> Who in Oppression's darkness caved had dwelt,
> They were not eagles, nourished with the day;
> What marvel then, at times, if they mistook their prey?
>
> [III, lxxxiii]

Byron could, by this sociological line of thinking, sanction various revolutionary actions, but his very preoccupation with the
need to exonerate underscores the limits of his assent. Even the
historical determinism that gloomily marks his political thought
in the twenties is an outgrowth of his divided attitude toward
revolution. We can see this in a passage from *Don Juan* written
during the summer of 1822.

> But never mind;—"God save the King!" and *Kings*!
> For if *he* don't, I doubt if *men* will longer—

5. *His Very Self and Voice: Collected Conversations of Lord Byron,* ed. Ernest
J. Lovell (New York: Macmillan, 1954), pp. 517–18.

I think I hear a little bird, who sings
      The people by and by will be the stronger:
The veriest jade will wince whose harness wrings
      So much into the raw as quite to wrong her
Beyond the rules of posting,—and the mob
At last fall sick of imitating Job.

At first it grumbles, then it swears, and then,
      Like David, flings pebbles 'gainst a Giant;
At last it takes to weapons such as men
      Snatch when Depair makes human hearts less pliant.
Then comes "the tug of war";—'t will come again,
      I rather doubt; and I would fain say "fie on't,"
If I had not perceived that Revolution
Alone can save the earth from Hell's pollution.
                                                   [VIII, l–li]

Historical determinism, at least in this case, is not an attempt to legitimize revolution; it is, rather, Byron's sardonic way of absolving himself from having to legitimize it. History will solve Byron's moral problem with revolution by taking the problem out of his hands.

Characteristically, Byron rung a change on this theme a year later when in Canto XV he claimed he was "born for opposition":

      So that I verily believe if they
Who now are basking in their full-blown pride
      Were shaken down, and "dogs had had their day,"
Though at the first I might perchance deride
      Their trouble, I should turn the other way,
And wax an ultra-royalist in Loyalty,
      Because I hate even democratic Royalty.
                                                   [XV, xxii]

Behind the gaity of these lines lies a fatalism that is psychological rather than historical. Byron exchanges an objective for a subjective determinism. The effect, however, is the same. His position ironically releases him from the burden of defining his political tendencies except in the most relativistic terms. The only account he has to give of himself is that he is fated to oppose whatever prevails.

If these reflections of Byron's political consciousness have any common denominator, it is not radicalism, elitism, or enlightened Whiggism, but supreme indifference to doctrinaire positions. Michael G. Cooke, in a fine passage on the *mobilité* of Byron's thought, points out that the diversity of his views is "virtually never a sign of sheer instability, but rather a measure of reluctance to settle prematurely in an intricate field."[6] Byron's elaborate adjustments of his political inclinations constitute just such a response to the moral issues raised by revolution and its allied forms of political violence. His search for justice in revolution came to entail a scrupulous sense of justification, or, conversely, a sardonic and intermittent withdrawal from the dynamics of ethical decision.

All of this could point toward no more than exaggerated symptoms of "middlingness" were it not that Byron's poetic vision is so fundamentally dedicated to the spirit of revolt.[7] He was, after all, the poet who wrote (in 1817) that "the *Prometheus,* if not exactly in my plan, has always been so much in my head, that I can easily conceive its influence over all or any thing that I have written" (*LJ*, IV, 174–75.). And he was the poet who, in his own "Prometheus" (1816), defined revolt as the principle that gives man a significance that "the inexorable Heaven, / And the deaf tyranny of Fate" are always trying to deny. For man in "his sad unallied existence" may oppose to this enforced emptiness his own "Spirit":

6. *The Blind Man Traces the Circle: On the Patterns and Philosophy of Byron's Poetry* (Princeton: Princeton University Press, 1969), pp. 44–45n.
7. See Vincent E. Starzinger, *Middlingness: "Juste Milieu" Political Theory in France and England, 1815–48* (Charlottesville: University Press of Virginia, 1965).

> Which even in torture can descry
> Its own concentered recompense,
> Triumphant when it dares defy.
>   [II, 52–59]

The recompense man creates for himself was always for Byron the
paramount value. His discriminations of revolution are significant, ultimately, not because they allow us to see tensions in his
political creed, but because their cumulative effect is to leave a
vast gulf between the restraint he shows in *all* his political invest-
ments and the fervor of his loyalty to the spirit of Prometheus.

There is a well-known passage in Canto IV of *Childe Harold*
(1818) that suggests that Byron looked beyond both the menace
and promise of revolution in order to identify the pure Promethean spirit.

> But France got drunk with blood to vomit crime;
>   And fatal have her Saturnalia been
>   To Freedom's cause, in every age and clime;
>   Because the deadly days which we have seen,
>   And vile Ambition, that built up between
>   Man and his hopes an adamantine wall,
>   And the base pageant last upon the scene,
>   Are grown the pretext for the eternal thrall
> Which nips Life's tree, and dooms Man's worst—his second fall.
>
> Yet, Freedom! yet thy banner, torn but flying,
>   Streams like the thunder-storm *against* the wind;
>   Thy trumpet voice, though broken now and dying,
>   The loudest still the Tempest leaves behind;
>   Thy tree hath lost its blossoms, and the rind
>   Chopped by the axe, looks rough and little worth,
>   But the sap lasts,—and still the seed we find
>   Sown deep, even in the bosom of the North;
> So shall a better spring less bitter fruit bring forth.
>   [IV, xcvii–xcviii]

Jerome McGann, commenting on these stanzas, notes that
they (and others) have often been taken "as a kind of song before

sunrise, particularly for Italy," and that "Byron's own vigorous involvement in the politics of revolution in Italy and later in Greece have tended to corroborate this view." But McGann rightly argues that Canto IV gives no statement of a political apocalypse, and that, indeed, this notorious revolutionary poem is wholly "lacking in visions of a transformed political order in Italy (or anywhere else)." Canto IV is, rather, a celebration of the individual consciousness. "The poet finds himself able to identify with the most exalted conceptions of his own imagination, and this capacity is presented as the endowment of all men."[8]

This analysis seems to me germane not only to Canto IV of *Childe Harold* but to the theme of revolt in Byron's poetry generally. And it is here that Camus is illuminating. Camus also argues that existential revolt is not to be taken as a song before sunrise. But neither is it "a question of pure and simple negation." Instead, we find in it "a value judgment in the name of which the rebel refuses to approve the condition in which he finds himself" (*TR*, p. 23).[9] This is the "concentered recompense" Byron avows in "Prometheus."

For Camus the machinery of politics smashed the spirit of rebellion by creating, "at the price of crime and murder if necessary, the dominion of man" (*TR*, p. 25). Revolution is the most insidious form of this demand. Once seduced by revolution, the spirit of rebellion rejects "every aspect of servitude [and] attempts to annex all creation. Every time it experiences a setback . . . the political solution, the solution of conquest, is formulated. . . . In principle, the rebel only wanted to conquer his own existence and

8. *Fiery Dust: Byron's Poetic Development* (Chicago: University of Chicago Press, 1968), pp. 133–34.

9. Peter Thorslev, *The Bryonic Hero: Types and Prototypes* (Minneapolis: University of Minnesota Press, 1962), pp. 198–99, and Paul West, *Byron and the Spoiler's Art* (New York: St. Martin's Press, 1960), p. 126, briefly comment on Byron and Camus. Frank McConnell, "Byron's Reductions," *ELH*, 37 (1970), 415–32, reprinted in his Norton Critical Edition of *Byron's Poetry* (New York, 1978) under the title "Byron as Antipoet," argues that Byron lacks Camus's "measured affirmations" (p. 430).

to maintain it in the face of God. But he forgets his origins, and, by the law of spiritual imperialism, he sets out in search of world conquest by way of an infinitely multiplied series of murders" (*TR*, p. 103).

The survival of the authentic spirit of rebellion depends wholly on the rebel's capacity to reject revolution's entanglement in absolutism on the one hand and nihilism on the other. Authentic rebellion acknowledges the inchoate universe and its absurd laws, but it affirms, nevertheless, the reality of the moral self. Rebellion accepts this prodigious tension in the nature of human life and refuses to escape from it either by formulating its own dogmas or by submitting to servitude. In doing so, rebellion asserts that everything is not permitted. "Far from demanding general independence, the rebel wants it to be recognized that freedom has its limits everywhere that a human being is to be found—the limit being precisely the human being's power to rebel" (*TR*, p. 284). Because the rebel is so intensely aware of the moral enslavement that results from both nihilism and absolutism, his assertion of a limit is the only extreme assertion of which he is capable.

Byron shares this perception with Camus. The revolt in his poetry always involves the effort to define a limit. His telling accusation of Napoleon is that he would be "all or nothing" (*Childe Harold*, IV, xcii). And what Byron implies Camus puts explicitly: "One step more and from *All* or *Nothing* we arrive at *Everyone* or *No One*," which is to say that revolt without limits must result either in Caesarism or murder, the czar or the yogi (*TR*, p. 57). In rejecting these alternatives and maintaining the paradox of limited freedom, the rebel acts "in the name of a concept that he has of his own nature" (*TR*, p. 289). This is his humanistic consciousness, which both initiates his rebellion in the absurd universe and checks his will to power. Through this "perpetual state of tension," he begins to exist.

Byron saw this, and saw also that the rebel's great achievement is to lift man out of his terrible isolation. "In our daily trials,"

Camus writes, "rebellion plays the same role as does the '*cogito*' in the realm of thought: it is the first piece of evidence. But this evidence lures the individual from his solitude. It founds its first value on the whole human race. I rebel—therefore we exist" (*TR*, p. 22). Although Byron, whose imagination of revolt was dominated by the model of the individualistic Romantic hero, never says that the "concentered recompense" man creates in revolt dissolves his "sad unallied existence," he clearly understood that the rebel must act on behalf of man's common fate and not merely for his own sake. His dramas on revolution are powerful demonstrations of this point. Indeed, it may be said that Byron's poetry, in its largest frame of reference, is a testament to the same proposition that is central to *The Rebel.* "Every rebel, solely by the movement that sets him in opposition to the oppressor . . . pleads for life, undertakes to struggle against servitude, falsehood, and terror, and affirms, in a flash, that these three afflictions are the cause of silence between men, that they obscure them from one another and prevent them from rediscovering themselves in the only value that can save them from nihilism— the long complicity of men at grips with their destiny" (*TR*, p. 284). Byron acted on this proposition when he rejected the willing servitude of men in all ages—"Rotting from sire to son . . . Proud of their trampled nature" (*Childe Harold*, IV, xciv)—as well as when he rejected nearly every example of the egocentric revolutionary that history has to offer, reserving his favor for George Washington, whom he revered as a veritable Cincinnatus, unstained by any trace of solipsism.[10]

The perspective Camus gives us is a perspective on the tragedy of revolution in Byron. Tragedy arises in Byron's plays about revolution when the hero as rebel, surrounded by willing slaves or absolutist revolutionaries, joins them and so subverts, to use Mc-

10. For Byron on Washington, see *LJ*, V, 462, and his "Ode to Napoleon Buonaparte."

Gann's phrase, "the most exalted conceptions of his own imagination" which are seen as the endowment of all men. The nature of political tragedy in Byron can be defined as a violation of the rebel's exhausting, painful, and yet splendid moderation.

> [Rebellion], in order to remain authentic, must never abandon any of the terms of the contradiction that sustains it. It must be faithful to the *yes* that it contains as well as to the *no* that nihilistic interpretations isolate in rebellion. The logic of the rebel is to want to serve justice so as not to add to the injustice of the human condition, to insist on plain language, so as not to increase the universal falsehood, and to wager, in spite of human misery, for happiness. . . . *The consequence of rebellion . . . is to refuse to legitimize murder because rebellion, in principle, is a protest against death.* [*TR*, p. 285; italics added]

The logic of this protest, it should be remembered, had for Byron a quite contemporary articulation in another "paratragedy" of the age, Shelley's *Prometheus Unbound* (1820). Shelley composed this work, as well as *A Philosophical View of Reform*, only a year or so before Byron was most fully engaged in his political dramas. Camus, I believe, gives us more direct access to the structure of Byron's political thinking than does Shelley, but a comprehensive analysis of Byron and revolution would no doubt find Shelley richly illuminating. As early as 1816, Shelley, having made an extensive study of the French Revolution's failure, recommended that Byron devote himself to an epic poem on the course of the revolution, "the master theme" of the age.[11] This, in fact, is a project informally underlying Shelley's own work of 1819–20. In the *Philosophical View* Shelley supplemented his pamphlet's indictment of oppression by observing that the violence of the French Revolution had been "compensated by a succession of tyrants . . . from Robespierre to Louis 18." He went on to say

---

11. *The Letters of Percy Bysshe Shelley*, ed. F. L. Jones (Oxford: Clarendon Press, 1964), I, 504.

that war either extinguishes "the sentiment of reason and justice" or, perhaps more insidiously, turns it into a mechanical habit that is easily overridden by confidence in brute force. "No false and indirect motive to action can subsist in the mind without weakening the effect of those which are genuine and good."[12] It has long been clear that *Prometheus Unbound* dramatizes the process by which the mythic hero is redeemed from his false motives and prepared for liberation by recognizing that his hatred of Jupiter stems, in effect, from the Jupiter in his own consciousness. Man unbinds himself by learning to love despite the cruel hostility of his material environment. Shelley's Prometheus does so—but only after he senses the real meaning of the prompting that comes to him when he faces the Furies:

> Horrible forms,
> What and who are ye? Never yet there came
> Phantasms so foul through monster-teeming Hell
> From the all-miscreative brain of Jove;
> Whilst I behold such execrable shapes,
> Methinks I grow like what I contemplate.
> [*Prometheus Unbound*, I, 445–50][13]

THE BETRAYALS OF PROMETHEUS

Like Arnold, Byron turned his hand to dramatic tragedy with a specific goal in mind. He wanted to revive, although with modifications, the style and structure of classical Greek tragedy. A letter to publisher John Murray concerning *Sardanapalus* briefly sketches his intention: "My object has been to dramatize, like the Greeks (a modest phrase!), striking passages of history, as they did of history and mythology. You will find all this very *unlike*

12. *The Complete Works of Shelley*, ed. Roger Ingpen and Walter E. Peck (London: Ernest Benn, 1926–30), VII, 54.

13. Cited from *Shelley's Poetry and Prose*, ed. Donald H. Reiman and Sharon B. Powers (New York: Norton, 1977).

Shakespeare and so much the better in one sense, for I look upon him to be the worst of models, though the most extraordinary of writers" (*LJ*, V, 323). These comments directly anticipate the central ideas of Matthew Arnold's 1853 Preface. The comparison completes itself when we remember Byron's interest in the choice of a noble subject. (He told his mistress that love was not a proper subject for tragedy.) In neither Arnold's case nor Byron's is the reversion to Greek models a mere philhellenistic whim. Each saw the drama of his own day as incapable of more than bombast and commonplaces. The drama had lost its moral function and so left unrecorded the tragic experience actually faced by modern men. Byron and Arnold responded to this situation by writing tragedies about revolt. The models of classical tragedy served them by providing a discipline of form in which they could explore with some detachment a tragic action distinctive of their times.

Despite Byron's prescriptions, however, the three plays relevant to our purpose are quite unlike one another in tone, characterization, and dramatic effect. Some of this diversity may be attributed to the deliberately experimental basis of their dramatic construction, but it is mainly a result of the fluidity and enterprise so typical of Byron's restless imagination. One of the ways in which their diversity may be expressed is through the declining historicity (or, alternatively, the expanding mythology) of their subject matter. Byron was careful, for example, to subtitle *Marino Faliero* "an historical tragedy," while subtitling *Cain* "a mystery" (by which he meant a nonhistorical tragedy).[14] Nevertheless, the three works stand related to one another in the steady deepening of their concern with the protagonist who exchanges humanistic rebellion for nihilistic revolution. *Marino Faliero*, the most conventional of the three, depicts a moderate whose moral stature is defined by the ordinary qualities of temperateness and public-

14. Byron identified the term "mystery" as a "tragedy on a sacred subject" (*LJ*, V, 360).

spiritedness. Faliero has the rebel's potential, but the potential is crushed in him by an outbreak of egomania. *Sardanapalus* concerns a much more radical figure who quite appreciates the spirit of rebellion before the threat of revolution makes a reactionary of him. Although Sardanapalus travels from rebellion to reaction, rather than from rebellion to revolution, Camus's analysis remains applicable since its whole point is that revolution is a mimicking of the reactionary world. The archetypal pattern, though, is dramatized in *Cain*. Cain embodies the pure spirit of rebellion. But his existential struggle against a celestial tyranny finally overwhelms him, and in an action that epitomizes the "second and worst fall" he attempts to achieve the dominion of man through murder.

Byron outlined plans for *Marino Faliero* in 1817 but did not follow through with them until three years later. Even then the process of composition was frequently delayed by the daylight passions of Teresa Guiccioli. "The lady," he said, "always apologized for the interruption."[15] Politics intruded upon his work even more insistently than his mistress. His original interest in the fourteenth-century Venetian doge, a prince who led a revolution, was undoubtedly intensified and transformed by the rapidly expanding struggle for Italian independence during the summer of 1820. In August, when he finally sent the play to Murray, he told him that "we are here upon the eve of evolutions and revolutions" (*LJ*, V, 57).

The Risorgimento background of the play has often been discussed, notably by E. D. H. Johnson. Johnson concludes that the historical Marino Faliero was a self-seeking demagogue who aspired to autocratic control of the city, while Byron's protagonist is "a tragic hero who ultimately loses all sense of personal grievance in the higher purpose of freeing the Venetians from an unscrupulous aristocracy."[16] Johnson is also one of the many commentators

15. Marchand, *Byron*, p. 850.
16. "A Political Interpretation of Byron's *Marino Faliero*," *Modern Language Quarterly*, 3 (1942), 420.

who sees in Faliero's evident reluctance to join forces with the contumacious rabble a reflection of Byron's personal contempt for the savagery of popular democracy. Once again, I suggest that this view is reductive, that it fails to respond to the chromatic complexity of Byron's attitude toward revolution. In *Marino Faliero* revolution is treated with ambivalence, but it is an ambivalence that encompasses more than the habitual tensions between aristocrats and democrats. The source of the ambivalence is the congestion of identities in the character of the doge. He has several roles to perform, each of which extends Byron's analysis of revolution.

Byron's original attraction to his subject grew from his fascination with the anomaly of a reigning head of government leading his people in a revolt against his own state (*LJ,* IV, 59). This situation would have appealed to Byron's stubbornly unorthodox view of the functions a ruler might serve. But there are other sides to his characterization of the doge. Most significantly, in the light of Byron's usual practice, the doge is a very old man. The oppositions in the protagonist's identity, mainly conceived as synchronic in Byron's other heroes, are diachronic in Marino Faliero. Faliero has a fatal, anachronistic belief in his personal dedication to disinterested justice. In truth, he has outgrown his best self and during his years as doge he has become almost wholly preoccupied with his official dignity. He will come to collaborate with the revolutionaries under the illusion that he is defending the noble principles of his youth. But by that very collaboration he reveals how much in his life he has already falsified and betrayed. This is not to say that the sordid plutocrats against whom Faliero and the conspirators hope to strike are in any way vindicated by the play. Faliero has not succumbed to their expert treachery, for it is still another facet of the doge's character that he remains perspicacious in regard to the pedigreed forms of political contamination in Venice. What he does not see is his own deterioration. The doge's self-corruption thus exists in ironic relation to both the corruption of the plutocrats and the corruption of the conspirators. The drama maintains its focus on the doge as a man caught between opposing and equally evil political camps. To this extent *Marino Faliero* reproduces Scott's themes. These themes, however, are absorbed by and made subordinate to the drama of Faliero's revolt against himself.

The superannuation of Faliero's heroic self is clear from the beginning. Faliero is outraged because Angiolina, his beautiful young wife, has been gratuitously insulted by a patrician named Michael Steno. Those closest to the doge, including Angiolina, will try to make him regard the case as trivial. Even Steno, when we finally meet him in the fifth act, could not be more gracious and sincere in his apology (V, i, 398–406). But Faliero sees the matter as an affair of state. He is provided some reasonable grounds for his outrage when the council of the Forty returns a very mild judgment against Steno. Faliero interprets this judgment as a manifestation of the Forty's scheme to undermine his authority and reduce him to a figurehead. Though the doge has the wisdom to see through the machinations of the Forty, and though he always proposes to defend the good of the common people, his exorbitant reaction to the insult reveals a sensibility engulfed by vanity. Faliero, despite his haze of self-justifying rhetoric, is a man who has lost the power of soberly discriminating between those things that touch only his pride and those that touch the welfare of the state.

The loss of this power has left Faliero obsessed with the notion that, for all his services to the state, the aristocrats regard him merely as "a pageant":

> This Cap is not the Monarch's crown; these robes
> Might move compassion, like a beggar's rags;
> Nay, more, a beggar's are his own, and these
> But lent to the poor puppet, who must play
> Its part with all its empire in this ermine.
> [I, ii, 412–16]

In a way he does not at all appreciate, he has indeed become a "pageant," a phantom of his former self. And this makes him vulnerable to Israel Bertuccio, chief of the conspirators. Faliero, furious with the patricians, does not perceive that the conspirators have even more reason to prize him as a mere figurehead. Like the peasant leaders who enlist Götz von Berlichingen in their scheme, Bertuccio understands that he can exploit the doge's reputation:

> . . . he is one who may
> Make our assurance doubly sure, according
> His aid; and if reluctant, he no less
> Is in our power: he comes alone with me,
> And cannot 'scape us.
>
> [II, ii, 155–59]

Although it is true that the Forty are undermining the doge's constitutional power and plan to make a figurehead of him, the conspirators are doing no less—and the conspirators succeed because Faliero has already subverted his inner self. We see this most clearly in Faliero's immediate identification with Bertuccio. Bertuccio, a naval officer, initially appeals to the doge for personal reasons: he has been slapped and insulted by a noble. Faliero eagerly accepts Bertuccio's case as an image of his own, thus giving Bertuccio the hold he needs in order to entice the doge into the conspiracy. What the play measures, however, is the extreme degree to which Faliero extends his identification with the conspirators. He assumes to himself not only the injuries they have suffered but the nihilism that, as Byron will indicate, is their ruling intellectual passion. Having hollowed out his inner being in his concern with *amour-propre,* Faliero has exposed himself to the mad venture of trying to ground fulfillment on spiritual emptiness. This is why the play so closely follows the diverse senses in which the doge appears as "pageant."

But Faliero retains stature as a character because part of his nature so obviously struggles against revolutionary nihilism. He is, for example, quite conscious of the social meaning of his action, and he voices this meaning in imagery that recalls Scott:

> Farewell all social memory! all thoughts
> In common! and sweet bonds which link old friendships,
> When the survivors of long years and actions,
> Which now belong to history, soothe the days
> Which yet remain by treasuring each other.
>   [III, ii, 327–31]

Faliero knows that what his new cohorts see as the just retribution of a people against its oppressors can also be seen as a wanton slaughter that will "hew the highest genealogic trees / Down to earth . . . / And crush their blossoms into barrenness" (III, ii, 493–95).

While these last lines reveal to us the doge's buried self, they also project, as does much else in the play, his escalating spiritual confusions. He simply does not understand that he is preparing to attack the genealogy of his own moral nature. Though he says he seeks "no vengeance but redress of law" (I, ii, 114), he ironically confesses to the conspirators that

> the very means I am forced
> By these fell tyrants to adopt is such,
> That I abhor them doubly for the deeds
> Which I must do to pay them back for theirs.
>   [III, i, 114–17]

He, like his companions, secretly justifies the conspiracy on the grounds of private injury. In establishing this emphasis, the play constantly suggests that revolution can occur as revenge writ large. As such, revolution becomes for its personnel the darkest kind of self-injury—the affectation of conscience.

We thus confront Faliero in a conspiracy against himself. This theme is developed through the play's romance elements: its nostalgia for "the times of Truth and Justice" (III, ii, 168), its appeals to the poetic imagination, and, most important, its portrayal of Angiolina.[17]

All the testimony of the play affirms that Faliero, as a younger man, rose to positions of trust because he administered the law equitably and tolerated no curtailments of the people's right. "I can appeal," he says, "to my past government / In many lands and cities." The annals of the state show that he was not an oppressor, but "a man / Feeling and thinking for my fellow men" (III, ii, 182–86). These qualities made him a popular favorite. He was named "Preserver of the City," and at his name "the million's caps were flung / Into the air, and cries from tens of thousands / Rose up, imploring Heaven to send [him] blessings" (IV, ii, 150–54). Such episodes stand prominently among what Faliero calls the "summer shadows rising from the past . . . / Mellowing [my] last hours as the night approaches" (II, i, 458–60). The wrong night is approaching—basically because the meaning of his heroic days has vanished from his moral imagination. Faliero has reduced the significance of "the times of Truth and Justice" to a self-indulgent fantasy and in this spirit he has decided to stake everything on the all or nothing that constitutes the ultimate fantasy of nihilism. Remembering the shadows but not the substance of his past, he says fatefully, "I will be what I should be, or be nothing" (II, i, 453).

Act IV of the play begins with a set piece in which Byron al-

17. Critics have tended to follow E. D. H. Johnson in seeing Faliero as a character with whom Byron basically sympathizes. See, for example, W. Paul Elledge, *Byron and the Dynamics of Mataphor* (Nashville: Vanderbilt University Press, 1968), pp. 97–118, and Thomas Ashton, "*Marino Faliero:* Byron's 'Poetry of Politics,' " *Studies in Romanticism,* 13 (1974), 1–13. But this view is convincingly rejected in G. W. Spence, "The Moral Ambiguity of 'Marino Faliero,' " *AUMLA,* no. 41 (May 1974), 6–18. An analysis of Angiolina quite the opposite of mine is developed in Anne Barton, " 'A Light to Lesson Ages': Byron's Political Plays," in *Byron: A Symposium,* ed. John D. Jump (London: Macmillan, 1975), pp. 148–49.

lows us to see how the aesthetic temperament sharply contrasts with the political temperament that dominates every other scene of the drama. The patrician Lioni, returning from a masked ball, meditates, as Paul Elledge says, on the distinction between the qualities of genuineness and artificiality in a series of figurative contrasts.[18] Lioni's soliloquy leads him to an apprehension of the "false and true enchantments" that forever compete as versions of reality in human experience (IV, i, 63). Their competition is at the heart of what Byron sees as the tragedy of revolution in this play. The relevance of Lioni's soliloquy to the play's revolutionary action is suggested by the light imagery that forms the soliloquy's principal figurative contrast. Lioni compares the masked ball's "dazzling mass of artificial light / Which showed all things, but nothing as they were," with both the moon and the night itself, which together make a "goodlier sight / Than torches glared back by the gaudy glass" (IV, i, 33–34, 69–70). Significantly, when the conspirators first meet, the "atmosphere is thick and dusky" (I, ii, 569–70), and the whole play is set, as G. Wilson Knight says, mostly in half-light.[19] In short, the revolutionary world into which the doge has fallen is a world that avoids the glimpses of the moon. Instead, it imitates the masquerade—the conspirators meet wearing masks—described in Lioni's soliloquy: "false and true enchantments" converge in a context effectively designed to hide their radical differences.

Lioni's discriminations do more than provide a metaphorical commentary on the play's political action. They implicitly challenge the indiscriminate attitudes of the revolution. The manner of the revolution's failure is relevant here. One of the conspirators, Bertram, cannot accept the absolutist temper of his colleagues. "Must all perish in this slaughter?" he asks (III, ii, 275). The conspirators answer: "All! all! / Is this a time to talk of

18. *Byron and the Dynamics of Metaphor,* p. 106.
19. *The Burning Oracle: Studies in the Poetry of Action* (New York: Oxford University Press, 1939), p. 235.

pity?" Bertram, however, resolves to shield Lioni, who has always been kind to him (III, ii, 277–78). Shortly thereafter, as Bertram stammers out his cautions to Lioni, his patron easily detects their true import and immediately foils the conspiracy by having the doge arrested. To the other conspirators, Bertram is no more than a traitor. But Bertram does only what the doge has become incapable of doing. He has distinguished between true and false enchantments. And he has seen that falsehood and terror can but enlarge the masquerade that obscures men from one another.

Angiolina, faultily faultless, splendidly null as a dramatic character, is nevertheless central to our understanding of the doge. She is more than his wife. She is the memoirist of his early manhood. Her father, Faliero's oldest and closest friend, gave Angiolina to him in marriage. Much younger than her husband, she yet knows, partly from her father, partly from her own judgment, the best qualities of the Doge:

> I love all noble qualities which merit
> Love, and I loved my father, who first taught me
> To single out what we should love in others,
> And to subdue all tendency to lend
> The best and purest feelings of our nature
> To baser passions. He bestowed my hand
> Upon Faliero: he had known him noble,
> Brave, generous; rich in all the qualities
> Of soldier, citizen, and friend; in all
> Such have I found him as my father said.
> [II, i, 93–102]

Even more significant, Angiolina is the symbolic expression of Faliero's former self. Unlike some of Byron's women, such as Haideé and Neuha, who embody qualities toward which their lovers grow, Angiolina represents the part of his nature that Faliero has cast away. Her role becomes fundamental when we remember that the occasion of the doge's revolt is Steno's insult. The play redefines this situation by enabling us to see that it is the doge who is dishonoring Angiolina by subduing "the best and purest feelings of [his] nature / To baser passions." Angiolina has, simply, one thing to tell the doge: "Remember what you were" (II, i, 482).

Angiolina's emblematic role makes the tragic position of Faliero manifest. Byron's characterization of Faliero suffers from the awkward and precipitous way in which he changes from an insulted and touchy husband to an aggrieved chief of state, and then to a purposeful but guilt-ridden revolutionary. Actually, these motives are of a piece, and though they are not effectively integrated in the play's formal construction, they are nevertheless thematically unified. Despite his mistakes in proportion, Byron is trying to suggest that each stage in the doge's precipitous development represents a coarsening of his relationship with Angiolina. Faliero begins by interpreting Steno's insult and the court's tame verdict as insults to himself. He has grounds for these conclusions. But he cannot see that the revolution represents a much greater despoiling of Angiolina's finer spirit. He cannot see that it is a conspiracy against his trust. At one point, Faliero recalls the compact he made with Angiolina's father:

> when, oppressed
> With his last malady, he willed our union,
> It was not to repay me, long repaid
> Before by his great loyalty in friendship;
> His object was to place your orphan beauty
> In honourable safety from the perils,
> Which, in this scorpion nest of vice, assail
> A lonely and undowered maid.
> [II, i, 294–301]

Faliero never understands how much these words tell against him. In joining the conspirators, he deserts not his social class but a sacred union that once signified his status as a man. In the context of his revolt against the state, Faliero is a pathetic victim of the dramatic dialectical dance. But in the context of his blindness to the union he desecrates, Faliero appears as the ally of the revolution's relentless negation of conscience.

The nature of his betrayal is defined by the sharp contrast the play creates between the purity of Angiolina and the malignity of the conspirators. The conspirators contend that they are exempted from moral responsibility by the exigencies of revolutionary historicism. As usual, the ground for this supposition is discovered in an absolute value. Bertuccio states the case in terms that are indistinguishable from those used in Nechayev's *Catechism*:

> We must forget all feelings save the *one*,
> We must resign all passions save our purpose,
> We must behold no object save our country,
> And only look on Death as beautiful,
> So that the sacrifice ascend to Heaven,
> And draw down Freedom on her evermore.
> [II, ii, 87–92]

The passage has its reply in Angiolina's earlier comment: "Heaven bids us to forgive our enemies" (II, i, 260).

The conspirators, of course, reject every mode of limitation to their moral privileges. And one of their privileges is the capacity for self-absolution.

> It is the cause, and not our will, which asks
> Such actions from our hands: we'll wash away
> All stains in Freedom's fountain.
> [III, ii, 79–81]

Implicit in this attitude is the assumption of quasi-deific powers, an assumption that always entails, as Dostoevsky shows, the denial of other men's humanity. The doge, in his final crisis of decision, psychologically accommodates himself to this arrogance.

> I will resign a crown, and make the State
> Renew its freedom—but oh! by what means?
> The noble end must justify them. What

> Are a few drops of human blood: 'tis false,
> The blood of tyrants is not human.
>   [IV, ii, 159–63]

The doge has been schooled in the ethics he espouses here by the far less scrupulous men with whom he is in league. Bertuccio is impatient of all scruples. He refuses individuality to the patricians: "All their acts are one— / A single emanation from one body" (III, ii, 285–86). For Calendaro the case against the patricians is sublimely simple: "They cannot co-exist with Venice' freedom" (III, ii, 313). In his bitterness and pain, Faliero accepts Calendaro's philosophy of right. He himself identifies the way in which an absolutist revolution must discount the individuality of men:

> To me, then, these men have no *private* life,
> Nor claim to ties they have cut off from others;
> As Senators for arbitrary acts
> Amenable, I look on them—as such
> Let them be dealt upon.
>   [III, ii, 382–86]

Faliero is not ruthless; he is blind. Again and again he notices the gulf between the enthusiasm of the other conspirators and his own anguished reluctance. He even knows that in the "surpassing massacre" of the senators, "each stab to them will seem my suicide" (III, ii, 472). But he remains unable to perceive the revolution as an action that violates his moral being by refusing to affirm a limit. The dominating imagery of the play is brought to its dramatic climax when he is arrested by a "Signor of the Night." Faliero, unlike Lioni, has used the night, that realm of uncertainty in which man must live and yet find something to live for, as a convenient cover for deception. The true enchantment of the night is the backdrop it makes for the flaming of man's protest against his situation. To this extent, even if the central ambience of the human experience is irreducibly nocturnal, the night may be turned to account in the way it heightens the brilliance of rebellion. But Faliero has used the night's false enchantment: its tempting incentives for deceit and mystification. In short, Faliero willingly cooperates in the falsehood and tyranny that keep men obscure to one another. He acts only for his own sake. The play ends with Faliero's prophecy of Venice's future degeneration: Byron by no means relieves the aristocrats of their responsibility for attempting to perpetuate the masquerade. The play even hints at the coming of the *Carbonari*. But *Marino Faliero* does not in any sense invoke revolution as an adequate solution. It questions the whole enterprise of revolution at the point of its greatest concealments. The plutocratic ambitions of the patricians are known for what they are; and the rationalizations of the conspirators are known for what they are. The doge, however, stands for as well as against the universal death sentence. His great purposes and early dedication to liberal ideals mark his special appreciation of the need for social justice. But he comes to manipulate the conditions of injustice, using the perfect protection of his liberal reputation in order to conceal from himself and from the citizens of Venice his catastrophic denial of conscience. In blinding himself, he blinds the night.

Byron considered *Sardanapalus* his best tragedy, perhaps because it is closest in structure to the remodeled Greek drama that he wanted to write.[20] It is undoubtedly a play of considerable dramatic power, never mired in mere theatricality, and often capable of the true voice of feeling that Byron had made ring across a continent. The play is founded on the legend of a luxurious and pacific ruler (probably a composite of two actual Assyrian kings) by whom Byron had been fascinated even as a schoolboy. Throughout, Byron treats Sardanapalus as a real historical figure, since he

20. See Samuel Chew, *The Dramas of Lord Byron* (Gottingen: Dandenhoed, 1915), pp. 105–6. At several points in this monograph Chew discusses Byron's "imitation" of Greek tragedy.

wished to conjure up an episode in the dismal record of history when peace and pleasure had been the authentically declared objects of government. The refusal of Sardanapalus to make war, to brutalize his subjects, or to persecute his enemies constitutes a compelling form of rebellion. Sardanapalus becomes a rebel, in other words, by spurning the prevailing *nomos* of aggressive empires and attempting to reinstate a lovely world of *physis* as the basis of human life.

These terms may put us in mind of *The Bacchae,* which would, indeed, seem to be a source for the play. Dionysus is among the most important symbolic presences in *Sardanapalus.* At one point Sardanapalus is reminded by his worried military adviser of the exploits of great conquerors, Dionysus among them (for the Greek god is said to have subdued the "golden realm" of India). Sardanapalus replies by lifting his cup to Dionysus:

> of all his conquests a few columns
> Which may be his, and might be mine [remain].
> . . .
> But here—here in this goblet is his title
> To immortality—the immortal grape
> From which he first expressed the soul, and gave
> To gladden that of man, as some atonement
> For the victorious mischiefs he had done.
> [I, ii, 168–77]

This is the god dramatized in *The Bacchae,* which leaves out of account Dionysus' oriental expeditions. Though Byron is known to have read Seneca in preparation for *Sardanapalus,* Euripides must also be credited with some of its inspiration. Essentially, everyone in the play urges Sardanapalus to behave like a Pentheus. But Sardanapalus is Dionysian in many respects. He not only values the condition of peace as a good in itself, he also sees it as a way to generate the life of pleasure. And here our point of reference can shift from Euripides to Wordsworth. Sardanapalus celebrates pleasure as that grand elementary principle which constitutes, as Wordsworth said in the Preface to *Lyrical Ballads,* "the naked and native dignity of man," the principle by which man "knows, and feels, and lives and moves."

This principle is repudiated by every other character in the play. So complete is the isolation of Sardanapalus within the kingdom of his heart's desire that he at last gives it up and adopts both the imagery and action of those who always wanted to confute his wisdom. The pressure that initiates this change comes from a revolutionary movement, though the revolution itself only brings his isolation to its crisis. Sardanapalus suffers from the total failure of anyone, friend or enemy, to comprehend the utopian majesty for which he stands.[21] His life is a burning oracle—a key image from this play—which is obscured by the imperial descriptions of kingship that compete with it and that finally impose on Sardanapalus a distrust of his epicurean ideals.

The beginning of Sardanapalus' isolation can be discovered in his relationship to "the people." He does not fulfill the iconographic function of the traditional king. Like the Duke in *Measure for Measure,* he rarely shows himself "to [his] people's longing; / Leaving [his] subjects' eyes ungratified" (I, ii, 581–82). Moreover, he makes no attempt to extend his empire by war. The result is that the people lose respect for him and are open to the rabble-rousing of Sardanapalus' disaffected satraps. The motive of Sardanapalus' privacy is, of course, his interest in diminishing his people's slavish susceptibility to hero worship. His behavior is a prerepublican discovery of freedom. He is hated for this gesture.

The Chaldean priest Beleses attempts to stimulate and exploit the popular discontent. Beleses is little more than a pseudologist— the term Byron might have used to describe the priestcraft that he saw as so often reducing men to slaves by the tyrannies of dog-

---

21. Throughout, *Sardanapalus* reminds us of Ruskin's assertion that Byron "was the first great Englishman who felt the cruelty of war, and, in its cruelty, its shame" (*The Literary Criticism of John Ruskin,* ed. Harold Bloom [New York: Norton, 1971], p. 229).

matic occultism. As a leader of the revolt, Beleses turns revolution itself into a tyrannizing mystification. He sees the sun as "the burning oracle of all that live," but he assumes exclusively to himself the privilege of reading its messages. His stargazing, beneath its facile romanticism, is limited to veneration of a zodiacal monster, the cosmos that oppresses both nature and man. Sardanapalus, on the other hand, does not indulge himself in the opportunities for deification that the state religion offers him. He conducts what is actually a secular festival in his pavilion of pleasure. The pavilion represents to him all that temple, shrine, and church would deny to human life. As he says, in a passage that sharply counterpoints both the letter and the spirit of the official religion:

> Let the pavilion over the Euphrates
> Be garlanded, and lit, and furnished forth.
>   .   .   .
> A cooling breeze . . . crisps the broad clear river:
> We will embark anon. Fair Nymphs, who deign
> To share the soft hours of Sardanapalus,
> We'll meet again in that the sweetest hour,
> *When we shall gather like the stars above us,*
> *And you will form a heaven bright as theirs.*
>   [I, ii, 1–11; italics added]

Sardanapalus' isolation from the people and from his functionaries is, as I have suggested, a result of his attempt to construct an alternative vision for a world that has been trained to minimize the creativity of the self and to surrender, in spiritual passivity, to a system of cosmic dictatorship. It is, however, the isolation of Sardanapalus from his brother-in-law, Salemenes, and from his Greek mistress, Myrrha, that finally undermines his humanistic rebellion. Salemenes and Myrrha, in their separate ways, both represent the world of *nomos,* the world of law, order, and cultural obligation. They are friends of Sardanapalus, but they are benighted. Unable to appreciate what Sardanapalus is, they annul his grand holiday of the spirit by making him conscious of the phenomena that bind him to his political identity. Myrrha tells him:

> I speak of civic popular love, *self*-love,
> Which means that men are kept in awe and law,
> Yet not oppressed—at least they must not think so,
> Or, if they think so, deem it necessary,
> To ward off worse oppression, their own passions.
> A King of feasts, and flowers, and wine, and revel,
> And love, and mirth, was never King of Glory.
> [I, ii, 537–43]

Salemenes, for his part, defines the inveterate claims of the historical process on anyone who lives in the eye of history. Sardanapalus "must be roused" if only because the blood of Nimrod and Semiramis cannot be allowed to sink in the earth, "and thirteen hundred years / Of Empire [end] like a shepherd's tale" (I, i, 7–8).

Myrrha and Salemenes, though they cooperate in rousing Sardanapalus to action, utterly fail to relieve the king's isolation. Salemenes is far more fundamentally attached to the traditions of the Assyrian empire than Sardanapalus can ever be. And Myrrha, though she loves Sardanapalus, cannot divorce herself from her proud Greek heritage; she is nearly ashamed of her love. In other words, none of the ideologies in the play are compatible with the vision of human purpose that animates Sardanapalus. This point is crucial to the play's political character. Politics is represented as a design for mastery, and the revolution itself is left fundamentally undiscriminated from the political system it pretends to replace. The people are not aroused by a passion for freedom, but by a passion for servitude. Beleses bows to the zodiac. Arbaces, who intends to succeed Sardanapalus as king, joins Beleses in what is essentially a reactionary coup d'état. Myrrha, whose technical position as a slave is not incidental but metaphorically precise, is infatuated by "Glory." Salemenes, for all his generosity and valor, is similarly pledged to "glorious Baal" (I, ii, 112). The isolation of Sardanapalus is a result of the metaphysical rebellion that places him outside the conventional modes of political action and that allows him to see them all as, ultimately, uniform in their given nature. The play shows Sardanapalus' loss of this vantage point, his acceptance of a public and iconographic self. The tragedy is not in the intolerable pressure of his isolation but in his capitulation to the idols of empire. In effect, *Sardanapalus* traces the king's forced retreat from the pavilion that is the symbol of his rebellion to the palace that is the sign of his authority. Salemenes, alerted to the plot against Sardanapalus, urges him to abandon the night's revel. The king replies:

> Forbear the banquet! Not for all the plotters
> That ever shook a kingdom! Let them come,
> And do their worst: I shall not blench for them.
> [I, ii, 308–10]

Sardanapalus finally agrees, however—and he never sees the pavilion again. As he accepts the restrictions of the palace, he says:

> What! am I then cooped?
> Already captive? can I not even breathe
> The breath of heaven?
> [I, ii, 573–75]

The references Sardanapalus makes to his "captivity" point up the ineluctable process by which he forsakes his own freedom. Just moments before his acquiescence in Salemenes' precautionary measures, he had defined the moral basis of his rebellion:

> I hate all pain,
> Given or received; we have enough within us,
> The meanest vassal as the loftiest monarch,
> Not to add to each other's natural burthen
> Of mortal misery, but rather lessen,

> By mild reciprocal alleviation,
> The fatal penalties imposed on life.
>   [I, ii, 348–54]

This is the kind of vision that gives Byron's heroes the identity
Camus ascribes to the genuine rebel. It is ominous, however, that
Sardanapalus can go on to say, even at this point in the play, that
if his people "*would* no more, by their own choice, be human,"
then he must assume the role of Nimrod, his ancestor, and "turn
these realms / To one wide desert chase of brutes" (I, ii, 373–75).
His rebellion cannot be sustained in a world that is uniformly devoted to the suppression of the values rebellion represents.

Salemenes, in a passage already cited, deplores the fading of the
empire, under Sardanapalus, into a mere "shepherd's tale." He
does not see, as the king does, the possibilities of the pastoral
world. Sardanapalus, by the time he has taken arms against the
conspirators, recollects his original purpose in a significant allusion to the pastoral order.

> I thought to have made mine inoffensive rule
> An era of sweet peace 'midst bloody annals,
> A green spot amidst desert centuries,
> On which the Future would turn back and smile,
> And cultivate, or sigh when it could not
> Recall Sardanapalus' golden reign.
> I though to have made my realm a paradise,
> And every moon an epoch of new pleasures.
>   [IV, i, 511–18]

Rebelling against the nightmare of imperial history, Sardanapalus
had dreamed of "The Shepherd Kings of patriarchal times, /
Who knew no brighter gems than summer wreaths, / And none
but tearless triumphs" (I, ii, 560–62).

The pivotal moment for Sardanapalus occurs during the fourth
act when, having energetically accepted his "duty" to fight his
enemies, he is wounded in battle. The wound has made him delir-

ious, and in his sleep he dreams of his ancestors, Nimrod the
Hunter (of men as well as beasts) and loathsome Semiramis, the
warrior-queen who is Sardanapalus' sexual and psychological opposite. He awakens terrorized:

> Hence—hence—
> Old Hunter of the earliest brutes! and ye,
> Who hunted fellow-creatures as if brutes!
> Once bloody mortals—and now bloodier idols,
> If your priests lie not! And thou, ghastly Beldame!
> Dripping with dusky gore, and trampling on
> The carcasses of Inde—away! away!
> Where am I?
>
> [IV, i, 27–34]

When Myrrha comes to him, he tells her that these shades surrounded him in his dreams while he sat hosting a banquet where
he *"deemed himself but guest, / Willing to equal all in social freedom"*
(IV, i, 80–81; italics added). The banquet's celebration of social
freedom indicates that the dream has its emotional origin in Sardanapalus' memory of the world he symbolically constructed in
the pavilion. But in the dream, Nimrod takes the place of his old
friend Zames, while Semiramis occupies Myrrha's accustomed
seat. These visitations from Sardanapalus' subconscious mind
seem to reinforce, at a critical moment, the king's newly discovered capacity for military action. But Nimrod, though outwardly
noble, is a predator among men, and Semiramis is a gruesomely
seductive hag. Though they do strengthen Sardanapalus' growing guilt at having once chosen a voluptuous life over the ma-
rauding rule of a traditional Assyrian monarch, the dream's larger
organization identifies the loss this misplaced guilt has caused.
Baal's avatars have forced themselves into Sardanapalus' dream to
win him from his liberal social purpose. The deadly gaze of Nimrod and the hideous kisses of Semiramis are signs of the black
enchantments that have overpowered the king's humanistic re-

bellion.[22] The dream ends, all too appropriately, in Sardanapalus'
experience of his own death:

> Then—then—a chaos of all loathsome things
> Thronged thick and shapeless: I was dead, yet feeling—
> Buried, and raised again—consumed by worms,
> Purged by the flames, and withered in the air!
>   [IV, i, 159–62]

This nightmare of degeneration does not come to Sardanapalus
because he had "effeminately" renounced a factitious obligation
to his ancestors requiring him to hunt men as beasts. It comes to
him as a rebel who has forsaken the authentic spirit of rebellion
and so become part of the "chaos of all loathsome things."

The dream prepares us for the climax in the fifth act when the
king's imagination undergoes a kind of superfetation that permits
him to give life once more to the spirit of rebellion even though
his self-image as a warrior-king is barely beyond its natal stage.
This process, which once again is subconscious, reverses the
movement of the dream. Sardanapalus enacts a ritual that he intends as the crowning gesture of his recent role as militaristic
king. But the ritual itself takes a form that recalls the world of the
pavilion. When it is clear that his enemies will triumph, we see
the warrior-king immolate himself rather than suffer captivity.
His funeral pyre thus completes the death sequence of the nightmare. It is the culmination of the fate he chose when he turned
against man in order to propitiate the gods of his culture. But the
funeral pyre is more than that. It is, at a distantly stirring level of
consciousness in the king, a reconstructed burning oracle to all

22. Byron's literary source for Nimrod is possibly *Paradise Lost,* XII,
24–63. Milton, like Byron, gives a decisive political meaning to the legend.
The archangel Michael says that "one [Nimrod] shall rise / Of proud ambitious heart, *who not content / With fair equality,* fraternal state, / Will arrogate
dominion undeserv'd / Over his brethren, and quite dispossess / Concord
and law of Nature from the Earth; / Hunting (and Men not Beasts shall be his
game) / With War and hostile snare such as refuse / Subjection to his Empire
tyrannous."

that live. The fire ritualistically reflects the world of the pavilion, for which Sardanapalus, in his final hours, unconsciously yearns. Byron sets up this implication by first giving us a negative demonstration: the apostrophe to the sun that Myrrha utters at the opening of the fifth act. It is a speech that turns the play once more to the imagery of incandescence that has dominated its language from the beginning. The play's subtle treatment of Myrrha achieves remarkable complexity at this point. Throughout, she has been the radiant soul mate of the king—except that her radiance, unlike his, is not informed by any capacity to dwell in the human estate. She seeks the sun because she has a horror of the earth. Her address to the sun is really a ceremony in spiritual cathexis which defines for us the veiled nature of her personal enslavement. In doing so, it also underscores the blighted sense of value she has encouraged in her lover. She asks:

> And can the sun so rise,
> So bright, so rolling back the clouds into
> Vapours more lovely than the unclouded sky,
> With golden pinnacles, and snowy mountains,
> And billows purpler than the Ocean's, making
> In heaven a glorious mockery of the earth,
> So like we almost deem it permanent.
> [V, i, 9–15]

Although Myrrha is sensitive enough to take this vision as an aesthetic consolation created by nature to relieve the "common, heavy, human hours," she does not see that she is paying homage to the dream of transcendence because she does not believe in the immanence of any value. Sardanapalus does, or at any rate once did. A portentous conversation from Act I needs to be juxtaposed with Myrrha's dream of transcendence. It occurs as Sardanapalus is escorting Myrrha to his luxurious enclave:

> *Sar.*   Come Myrrha, let us go on to the Euphrates:
> The hour invites, the galley is prepared,
> And the pavilion, decked for our return,

> In fit adornment for the evening banquet,
> Shall blaze with beauty and with light, *until*
> *It seems unto the stars which are above us*
> *Itself an opposite star*; and we will sit
> Crowned with fresh flowers like—
>
> *Myr.*   Victims.
> *Sar.*   No, like sovereigns.
>
> [I, ii, 552–60; italics added]

For Myrrha the things of this world matter only when they are transfigured by a supernal element. For Sardanapalus the things of this world exist in their own right as the forms out of which man may make "an opposite star." The king's sovereignty is achieved in rebellion, while Myrrha accepts metaphysical victimization. Her unwitting surrender is complete when she concludes her apostrophe by saying that the sun, "the Chaldee's God," is so glorious she could "grow almost a convert to . . . Baal" (V, i, 47–48). Ironically, she is already of Baal's party without knowing it.

With this scene in the background, we can understand more clearly the implications of the funeral pyre with which the play ends. Sardanapalus, realizing he has been defeated, tries to make self-immolation his last act of defiance. To create his ceremonial fire he uses the artifacts of the monarchy itself:

> Let the throne form the *core* of it; I would not
> Leave that, save fraught with fire unquenchable,
> To the new comers.
>
> [V, i, 362–64]

Moreover, in anticipation of a device Byron will use spectacularly in *Cain,* the fire is lit, at Myrrha's suggestion, with a torch taken from Baal's shrine (V, i, 420–21). These details, together with the fact of suicide, give the play's final episode its tragic meaning. The funeral pyre is a structure composed of all those elements that have undermined the king's *révolte.* Myrrha's loyally joining him in death no doubt accentuates the reality of her love, but it is also clear that the pyre would not be complete without her fateful presence among the trappings of monarchy, the instruments of Baal, and the whisperings of the death drive.

Yet the fire cannot fail to remind us of the blazing pavilion and of the "opposite star" that Sardanapalus tried to create. As he makes his final preparations, Sardanapalus says that the light of this

> Most royal of funeral pyres shall be
> Not a mere pillar formed of cloud and flame,
> A beacon in the horizon for a day,
> And then a mount of ashes—but a light
> To lessen ages, rebel nations, and
> Voluptuous princes. Time shall quench full many
> A people's records, and a hero's acts;
> Sweep empire after empire, like this first
> Of empires, into nothing; but even then
> Shall spare this deed of mine, and hold it up
> A problem few dare imitate, and none
> Despise—but, it may be, avoid the life
> Which led to such a consummation.
>
> [V, i, 437–49]

The ironies of the last act lie heavily upon this speech and challenge us by suggesting that the actual lesson to ages and princes is not that their thoughts must be bloody, but rather that Sardanapalus betrayed himself when he defeated the spirit of rebellion.

In this sense, the king's impassioned attempt to make his death a symbol is tragically achieved in the fire's numinous recapturing of his festivals on the Euphrates. And his very turning to the symbolic imagination may be taken as a felt recrudescence of his Promethean self. When Myrrha proposes to him, in a sign of her own continuing benightedness, that they offer one final "libation to the Gods," Sardanapalus replies that his country's tradition is

> To make libations amongst men. I've not
> Forgot the custom; and although alone,
> Will drain one draught in memory of many
> A joyous banquet past.
>
> [V, i, 453–56]

He dies with her, but he does not drink to her. There is something in him that she has not equaled. In the end, he has not equaled it either.

A political interpretation of *Cain* was first suggested by Byron himself. Shortly after writing the play, he described it to Thomas Moore: "You may suppose the small talk which takes place between [Cain] and Lucifer . . . is not quite canonical. The consequence is, that Cain comes back and kills Abel in a fit of dissatisfaction, partly with the politics of Paradise, which has driven them all out of it, and partly because (as is written in Genesis) Abel's sacrifice was the more acceptable to the Deity" (*LJ*, V, 368).

Edward E. Bostetter has made the point that in the play these are finally one and the same reasons. As Bostetter explains, "The politics of Paradise was also the politics of the ruling social order of Byron's day. . . . Byron's 'public' would recognize that Cain's plea is as much political as religious—that it is directed against the politics of Paradise and therefore of western society, against those who rule in the name of God." And Bostetter goes on to describe —accurately, I think—how this background illuminates the relationship between Cain and Abel. "It is the violent rejection of his appeal to reason that arouses Cain to frustrated rage against the obsequious Abel, whose speech and actions are almost a parody of the behaviour of the self-righteous, well-intentioned people who by their blind submission encourage the perpetuation of social tyranny and evil. Ironically, Cain is led into the very violence he has opposed; into adopting the tactics of the tyranny he has defied."[23]

Tragedy in *Cain* is expressed in the irony Bostetter observes. And it is this irony that makes Byron's interpretation of the Genesis story closer in spirit to the tragic action described by Camus

23. "Byron and the Politics of Paradise," *PMLA*, 75 (1960), 574–75. The substance of the essay appears in *The Romantic Ventriloquists* (Seattle: University of Washington Press, 1963), pp. 282–91.

than any other Romantic or Victorian work. In its depiction of a
fratricide standing just outside the locked gates of Eden, *Cain* creates a remarkable image of "Man's worst—his second fall."

The opening of the drama owes a good deal to *Hamlet.* The
family is gathered; the son is sullen. The mother implores him to
compose himself:

> Cain—my son—
> Behold thy father cheerful and resigned—
> And do as he doth.
>
> [I, i, 50–52]

But resignation has no charm for Cain. When Adam and Eve retreat and leave him alone, we learn that his thoughts are suicidal.
These parallels recall Hamlet's preoccupation with the mystery of
death, his sense that he has been stained by the guilt of his parents, his intermittent immunity to the tenderness of those who
truly love him, his compulsion to interrogate the universe, and,
most pointedly, his reluctance to murder. Cain is the Hamlet of
rebels. He struggles to remain a rebel in Camus's sense, to insist
that there is something in him that is superior to the harsh, erratic, and inexplicable justice of Jehovah. But every assertion of
his rebellion produces in him yet another demand for absolute
certainty and final answers. At the crisis, the will to sustain his
rebellion gives way; he murders so that he may contest the politics of Paradise on his own terms. Byron perceives the murder as a
purely revolutionary act.[24]

Cain is not only the first murderer, he is the first alien. He is
the father of separateness. The structure of the drama is domi-

---

24. Leonard Michaels's challenging "absurdist" reading of the play, "Byron's Cain," *PMLA,* 84 (1969), 71–78, regards Cain as essentially an empty
figure who takes a step toward identity by murdering. Michaels at least raises
the right issues about Byron, but his reading is too extreme. Cain takes his
step toward identity in rebellion, but he forsakes his identity in murder and
revolution.

nated by the contrast Byron draws between the significantly different forms of Cain's separateness. His sensitivity to the dismal
present and his inquiring spirit make him conceive of life as already a purgatory and Jehovah as a merely indifferent President of
the Immortals. His rebellion is a reply to the penalty of death that
has been handed down to Adam and his children from on high:

> Here let me die: for to give birth to those
> Who can but suffer many years, and die—
> Methinks is merely propagating Death,
> And multiplying murder.
>
> [II, i, 68–71]

Cain thus expresses the immediate cause of his alienation from the
Old Testament God. Rebellion, Camus says, "in its exalted and
tragic forms is only, and only can be, a prolonged protest against
death, a violent accusation against the universal death penalty"
(*TR*, p. 100). Cain's speech, however, hints at a more desperate
kind of revolt, a revolt against life motivated by the fatal desire
for all or nothing. Cain allows his metaphysical alienation to
breed in him contempt for life, and so he will alienate himself
from the human community. Again, Camus is illuminating:
"Man's solidarity is founded upon rebellion, and rebellion, in its
turn, can only find its justification in this solidarity. We have,
then, the right to say that any rebellion which claims the right to
deny or destroy this solidarity loses simultaneously its right to be
called rebellion and becomes in reality an acquiescence in murder"
(*TR*, p. 22). *Cain* explicates the rebel's tragic loss of solidarity.

The drama differentiates between Cain's related forms of alienation by contrasting the two symbolic settings in which he is presented to us. We see him borne through the cosmos by Lucifer,
who has promised to answer his questions and show him the nature of the universe and the meaning of death. And we see him
with the members of the original human family, dispossessed of
Eden and facing the onset of history and temporality as the the-

ater of human action. Although Cain's journey with Lucifer is presented as a journey through space, it is actually a journey to the abysm of time. This depressing adventure has its structural counterpart in Cain's lugubrious imaginings of the future and of all the misery of man's life to come in the post-Edenic historical world. More subtly, his intellectual partnership with Lucifer, which he forms for the sake of a bewildering glimpse backward into the pre-Adamite millennia, is contrasted to his spiritual and sexual partnership with Adah, which he forms for the sake of life and all that in life remains miraculous and compelling despite the great loss of privilege his parents suffered. In this partnership he might wager for happiness, but his imagination of the historical future is suffocated by his knowledge of the pre-Adamite past.

In the course of Cain's mysterious traveling amid the remnants of prior creations, Lucifer acts as Cain's alter ego. (The criticism that Cain is too much like Lucifer misses the point.) The principal discovery of the journey is the revelation Lucifer provides of the

> Living, high,
> Intelligent, good, great, and glorious things,
> As much superior unto all thy sire
> Adam could e'er have been in Eden, as
> The sixty-thousandth generation shall be,
> In its dull damp degeneracy, to
> Thee and thy son;—and how weak they are, judge
> By thy own flesh.
>
> [II, ii, 67–74]

Cain, whose attraction to Lucifer is stimulated by his Faustian ambition to know the structure of reality and the meaning of death, is overcome by despair and cynicism when he sees what Lucifer has revealed to him: "I am sick of all / That dust has shown me—let me dwell in shadows" (II, ii, 108–9). Mankind seems suddenly dwarfed and enfeebled; Cain's contempt for the inadequacies of mind is grotesquely enlarged. Not even his long intellectual restlessness and brooding sense of cosmic injustice had prepared him to accept the knowledge that humanity is but a minor creation in an ancient universe where even far more splendidly endowed creatures had come to nothing in the struggle for existence. He has on a large scale the experience of Hamlet in the graveyard. The only clarification that takes place for him, as he roams Hades with Lucifer, is in his feeling that the barriers limiting human knowledge and blunting human purpose are thicker than he had ever surmised. Lucifer taunts him:

> Thy human mind hath scarcely grasp to gather
> The little I have shown thee into calm
> And clear thought: and *thou* wouldst go on aspiring
> To the great double Mysteries [of life and death].
> Dust! limit they ambition.
>
> [II, ii, 401–5]

Dominating Cain's gloom, reinforcing it, and embodying its causes is the tyrannical deity who, though being, as Caliban imagines Setebos, subservient to the ultimate Creator, is the power directly responsible for expelling man from paradise and for executing the punishing laws of cosmic destiny against which Cain rebels. It is through Cain's aggrieved resistance to this power that we see the Lucifer-like spirit of the rebel in Cain. But we also see that Cain has taken upon himself not only Lucifer's rebellion but his cynicism, his lethal rationalism, his radical independence, and, compulsively, his desire for self-deification.

The other setting of the play, the world of post-Edenic man, shapes our perception of Cain in just the opposite way. Among the first words we hear from Cain is the declaration that "Life is good" (I, i, 38). And indeed, this conviction must somehow be present in Cain as the motive force of his outrage against the deity who would make life hell. But more and more Cain rejects the natural world as a hoax. Consciousness brings him intimations of disaster. Journeying in the pre-Adamite millennia, Cain seemed courageous in his insistence on knowing the truth. In the human world, however, he seems increasingly a nihilist who dismisses every form of value as a delusion. This development of the drama has its monumental climax in the irony of Cain's fate. What Cain most wanted to learn from Lucifer was the meaning of death, and yet even under Lucifer's metaphysical guidance Cain's quest ended inconclusively. Lucifer evaded the key questions. Yet Cain comes to know, in the natural world, more about the meaning of death than any Lucifer could teach him. Abel is the first man to suffer death, but Cain is the first man to know death. In this bitter fulfillment of Cain's dream of knowledge, we see that Cain had been looking all the while in the wrong place. But we also see the crucial implication that attends Cain's tragic education. It is that the human world is not entirely devoid of moral intelligence; the human community forms man's conscience and ratifies his right to protest the universal death sentence.

The created earth thus supports Cain's original sense that life should have value, though Cain, his imagination darkened by his knowledge, ultimately misses the most important signs. His alter ego in the human world is Adah (a much more credible Angiolina). The preeminent phenomena of the human world are not dust and dying, but fruit and ripening. And in place of the gigantic, dead phantoms that inhabit Hades, there is the child Enoch. Byron does as much as he can to avoid a romantic sentimentalizing of Enoch and so treats the presence of the child as blandly as possible. Nevertheless, Enoch's presence is a critical point. Cain's outraged protestations once go so far as to make him wish the child dead. His immediate recoiling from that thought is an act sponsored by the same sense of value that gives Cain's rebellion its luster. The fruitfulness of the earth, despite the autumnal season, the love of Adah, despite her unphilosophic mind, the promise of Enoch, despite the fact he will grow "spectre-thin and die," all endorse Cain's conviction that man must have some reason to delight in his own existence.

But savage indignation pierces Cain, clouds his vision, and

thwarts the humanistic possibilities of his rebellion. His absolute scorn for God develops into an absolute contempt for man. To modify the language of *Childe Harold,* he who would strike down the Lion is outraged by those who pay the Wolf homage. Adam and Eve, he feels, induced their own thralldom by a failure of nerve. And even if they did offend against an eternal law, he protests, he is not responsible: "they sinned, then *let them* die" (III, i, 75). This sort of reasoning more and more cuts Cain off from the sympathies of membership. And his isolation from his family transforms him into a revolutionary. In attempting to overthrow God, he acts against his brother; he enlarges the reign of death in the world.

From the beginning of the play Byron makes it clear that Cain's anguish threatens to resolve itself into something hard and hateful. His dismay has a sullen aspect.

> My father is
> Tamed down; my mother has forgot the mind
> Which made her thirst for knowledge at the risk
> Of an eternal curse; my brother is
> A watching shepherd boy. . . .
>   .   .   .
> My sister Zillah sings an earlier hymn
> Than the birds' matins; and my Adah—my
> Own and beloved—she, too, understands not
> The mind which overwhelms me.
>   [I, i, 176–86]

Whether Adah understands Cain's overburdened mind is, finally, irrelevant; she understands something else. When Lucifer tempts Cain with his promise of knowledge, Adah tries to make him resist: "Oh, Cain! choose love" (I, i, 428). But Cain's shrouded imagination turns him to Lucifer. His choice is not rendered as implicitly self-defeating, but the choice is ominous nonetheless because it represents Cain's first major affirmation of his separateness. The cosmic tour, which formidably increases his negative knowledge, leaves him, when he returns to earth, far less able to identify with the human moment than he had ever been, and much more remote from Adah's kind of courage and faith. Just as Cain too readily imitated the treacherous qualities of his satanic alter ego, so we find him too readily abandoning the saving qualities of Adah, his best self. Adah can say, "where'er thou art, I feel not / The want of this so much regretted Eden" (III, i, 39–40), but Cain looks upon a conditional paradise as an absurdity. The alarming danger of his metaphysical discontent and increasing withdrawal from Adam's family is apparent in his perplexed rejection of his son, in whom he sees "The germs of an eternal misery."

> better 'twere
> I snatch'd him in his sleep, and dash'd him 'gainst
> The rocks,
>
> [III, i, 124–26]

This violence prefigures the play's climax. The war Cain made against the absolute power of God has become a war against the limited power of man. Cain does not, of course, dash his child against the rocks. But in the very imagery of his outburst there is a prologue to the crime he is about to commit, when, judging his brother to be oblivious of his servility, Cain smashes the life out of him.

Abel, who is beyond question servile, comes to Cain to entreat him to make a sacrifice to "the Most High." Cain is too exhausted to resist. The altars are built and dressed and ignited with a brand. In a spirit that momentarily permits him to transcend mere servility, Abel prays to the Lord of light, acknowledging that all things in the world serve some "good end / Of thine omnipotent benevolence" (III, i, 234–35). Cain, on the other hand, makes his prayer a challenge and a question.

> If thou must be induced with altars,
> And softened with a sacrifice, receive them!
>
> [III, i, 253–54]

In his worship Cain deliberately refuses to make a blood sacrifice. He offers to the Lord only the "sweet and blooming fruits of earth." From Abel's altar a column of bright flame leaps toward heaven, while a sudden whirlwind scatters Cain's fruits upon the earth. Abel implores him to make another sacrifice "before it is too late." This for Cain is the terminal provocation. His reply is a simple but explosive utterance in which rebellion changes into revolution at one breath:

> I will build no more altars,
> Nor suffer any.
>
> [III, i, 288–89]

His achievement as a rebel is to build no more altars. But it is a revolutionary who refuses to suffer any. Cain's rationalism has moved him from disgust to the threshold of murder. The self-abasement of Abel, and before him Adam, has no doubt maximized Cain's impressions of the celestial tyranny and become a tyranny in itself (with implicit reference to the spirit-destroying orthodoxies of nineteenth-century bourgeois society). And yet Cain's impending murder of Abel is, as Camus would say, the outgrowth of "a misguided intelligence that prefers, to the suffering imposed by a limited situation, the dark victory in which heaven and earth are annihilated" (*TR*, p. 7).

It is important to remember that Cain's violence is directed against God. His specific purpose is to cast down the blood-stained altar and cast out the unappeasable deity whose rule is a corruption of creation and whose authority is founded on an unlimited right to punish man.

> Give way! this bloody record
> Shall not stand in the sun, to shame creation!
>
> [III, i, 303–4]

Cain, in this moment, stands at the edge of revolutionary nihilism. His first victim will be his brother. Cain will leave his own bloody record to shame creation. The Bible does not specify how Cain slew Abel, but Byron's stage direction is excruciatingly explicit: Cain strikes "him with a brand, on the temples, which he snatches from the altar." Nothing in the play crystallizes so well as this the tragic theme of the rebel's fall into revolution. And as though to render the full measure of the catastrophe, Byron allows us to see Cain instantly offering to God the blood of his brother. As he strikes, his words are:

> Then take thy life unto thy God,
> Since he loves lives.
> [III, i, 316–17]

Language and gesture coalesce at this point to make history out of myth and myth out of history. Few things even in Byron achieve such intense irony. Revolutions, at their center of moral paradox, have, as it were, lived up to this mythic moment by reestablishing, in the name of freedom, blood worship, and by continuing, in the name of fraternity, to slay their victims with instruments snatched from the altars of the gods they have routed. This is what the tragic vision of *Cain* seeks to illuminate. The theme is spelled out in Camus's own commentary on the Cain myth.

> He [Cain] rebelled in the name of the identity of man with man and he sacrifices this identity by consecrating the differences in blood. His only existence, in the midst of suffering and oppression, was contained in this identity. The same movement, which intended to affirm him, thus brings an end to his existence. He can claim that some, or even almost all, are with him. But if one single human being is missing in the irreplaceable world of fraternity, then this world is immediately depopulated. [*TR*, pp. 281–82]

Rebellion becomes revolution, and for Cain alienation becomes exile. It is Eve who banishes him, replaying, without understanding, a scene she knows well.

> May every element shun or change to him!
> May he live in the pangs which others die with!
> And Death itself wax something worse than Death
> To him who first acquainted him with man.
>   [III, i, 434–37]

He does, however, go into the wilderness with Adah, the redemptive possibility in his life. Adah has never been servile, but she has been content with all of paradise that we shall ever know. She understands that we reach nihilism when we refuse love, and she does not refuse Cain her love. She persists in trying to release him from his separateness: "Now, Cain! I will divide thy burden with" (III, i, 551).

The point of these analyses of tragedy and revolution in Byron has not been to make Byron a precursor of Camus. To do so would be both to distort Camus and to patronize Byron. They are writers who differ in many ways. Byron was not writing with the example of Stalin before him; Camus was not writing with the modern democratic state virtually unformed and unknown. Byron is less Pascalian than Camus, less politically oriented, of much greater subtlety as an imaginative writer, closer to the development of the Romantic consciousness, and still intrigued by a hierarchically ordered culture that externalized its notions of excellence in an aristocracy. The analyses instead propose to supply a set of distinctions to describe the senses in which Byron confronted the tragedy of revolution with something finer to support him than an array of naive and partisan loyalties. If Wordsworth can be said to have withdrawn from an explicitly political mode of revolutionary aspiration in order to dedicate himself to a revolutionary reappraisal of the common things of this world, Byron can be said to have subordinated the executive action of revolution in order to grasp its relation to the larger drama of man's search for his Promethean identity. He did so because he wanted to preserve the inspiration of the genuine Promethean spirit. His effort brought him to the paradox Camus calls rebellion. Rebellion, also, is one of the things of this world. Just as the miraculous ordinary became Wordsworth's means of sanctifying the human realm, so rebellion became Byron's means. Byron looked away from the injustice and inanition of the hostile cosmos to see the arc earth makes against the sky, its steady flowing back into itself, its indispensable assertion of a limit.

The failure of this perception is tragic. E. D. Hirsch has suggested that "in all Byron's poetry the periodic recurrence of a Fall is predicated on the periodic recurrence of a Redemption."[25] The comment certainly isolates the largest rhythms of Byron's poetry, although Hirsch does not account for the fact of recurrence. Unlike Dickens, whose works strain toward a redemption that is complete, Byron, in constructing his basic myth, confronts us with redemptions that fail. And it is from this condition that the tragic vision emerges in Byron's poetry generally. Redemption fails us because we so often convert the process of redemption into a resumption of the fall. An invisible hand plays some part in the process, but, in the final analysis, Byron is more concerned with the part played by man. Thus the pervasive presence of the French Revolution in his work (counterpointed by the myth of Washington). For the French Revolution produced a monumental example of the emergence of tragedy in the interval between conception and act. Byron's work has multiple examples of the widening of this interval until all relationship between conception and act is lost, but the major instance is revolution, because Byron saw how effective revolution can be at concealing the gulf between its ends and its means. Revolution often pretends to remain faithful to the idea of freedom by making freedom virtually

25. "Byron and the Terrestrial Paradise," in *From Sensibility to Romanticism,* ed. F. W. Hilles and Harold Bloom (New York: Oxford University Press, 1965), p. 473.

equivalent to redemption—for which it will risk everything. Rebellion, however, insists on a limited freedom and attempts to fill
up the interval between idea and act with conscience. In Byron's
world (the Washington myth aside) this attempt is almost always
defeated. Man's search for freedom becomes again and again
either a masked tyranny or a naked exploitation. The tragic in
Byron is, then, a resource for moral definition. It names the point
at which man becomes a collaborator in the renewal of his fall.
Byron's tragedies are not about the ruins of paradise; they are
about the ruins of rebellion.

CHAPTER FOUR

Carlyle: The True Man's Tragedy

It was Carlyle, not Byron, who risked a certain indulgence in the nihilistic character of revolution. But Carlyle's position in this matter must be understood in the context of his complex development. He is exceptionally easy to distort. His career is so polymorphic, his attitudes at a given moment so frequently tentative (often despite their strident expression), and his capacity for self-criticism sometimes so inert and sometimes so active that his separate works yield only partial portraits. If Carlyle took the risk I have ascribed to him, he also took precautions. And when he saw the precautions failing, he again modified his view of revolution and tried to restructure the nature of his prophecy. Through all of these shifts, however, one point remained constant: he consistently identified revolution as a tragic action. We can always hear in his discussions of revolution the echo of this remark: "Unhappy age, to which this sad task of Revolution was appointed, and could not longer be delayed. As to myself I look forward to it with the sorrowfullest interest."[1] The hint of paradox in this statement anticipates the major function of tragedy in Carlyle's analyses of revolution.

1. *Letters of Thomas Carlyle to John Stuart Mill, John Sterling, and Robert Browning*, ed. Alexander Carlyle (London: Fisher Unwin, 1923), p. 50.

187

Carlyle both abhorred and honored the spirit of revolution. Its disorder was despicable; its potential for spiritual and social renovation was inspiring. Tragedy in Carlyle is a means of maintaining the violent dualism of this view. He uses tragedy as an enabling device, a sort of protective armor that allows him to cultivate revolution and repudiate it too. For various reasons Carlyle found that he had to do both and that the *mythos* of tragedy, always receptive to the demands of paradox and ambivalence, would serve his purposes. Tragedy gave Carlyle access to a complex political wisdom in which he tried to instruct his world.

We shall be concerned with Carlyle's politics only as they relate directly to the problem of revolution, my main assumption being that his view of revolution is the touchstone of his political thought. One issue that can unduly complicate any discussion of Carlyle and revolution ought to be disposed of immediately. Carlyle sometimes did, and sometimes did not, openly advocate the use of revolutionary violence. Mainly he did not. Often he said he expected a revolution in England or outright anarchy in Europe, but even on such occasions he tended to allow two hundred years for the political questions to be debated. The issue is really irrelevant. Carlyle's literary treatment of revolution is what matters. In his re-creations of revolutionary experience he often enough gives his moral support to the grim necessity of revolution.

The substantive issues are much more subtle; it may be useful to summarize them here. The second and third sections of this chapter explore *The French Revolution* and *Heroes and Hero-Worship* respectively. *The French Revolution* is Carlyle's most radical and disturbing book. Under the aegis of tragedy, it uses the negative content of revolution to purge the world of its sick fantasies. *Heroes and Hero-Worship,* though it never wholly subdues the intermittent ferocity of the later Carlyle, is basically a retreat from the harsh prophecies of *The French Revolution.* It is a work motivated by Carlyle's grief for a world threatened by endless reigns of terror. The modern hero is sent to protect men against the negative content of revolution.

The first section of the chapter is less easy to summarize because it deals with a variety of published works and private writings that bear on the formation of Carlyle's role as a political prophet, and it necessarily involves a cluster of related questions. The principal question—the question Carlyle asked himself—has to do with whether a prophet ought even to address himself to political matters. Though it was undoubtedly the political crises of 1829–32 that encouraged Carlyle to throw the mantle of prophecy about his shoulders, he was for many reasons reluctant to equip the prophet with a political vision. Crucially, the idea of tragedy emerges in this period to shield his entry into the political realm. The first section, then, considers both Carlyle's development in the early thirties and the specific nature of tragic experience as he conceived of it. The section goes on to consider Carlyle's relation to Scott and Byron. Finally, it discusses Book III of *Sartor Resartus* as Carlyle's first attempt to render the tragedy of revolution, a task he undertook even before he had learned to live with his political consciousness.

THE DILEMMA OF THE PROPHET
AND THE IDEA OF TRAGEDY

Any discussion of Carlyle must to some extent take his style into account. Two aspects of Carlyle's art have an important bearing on the subject at hand. One is a specific motif of Carlyle's rhetoric that we will have several occasions to observe. The other concerns a much more general and formative principle of style that is central to Carlyle's preoccupation with revolution.

Carlyle is perhaps more responsible than any other British writer for extending the meaning of "tragedy" beyond its conventional description of a dramatic form to a moral description of life. His broad usage of the word—the *Oxford English Dictionary* cites him for "tragicality"—is one of the most distinctive elements of his rhetoric. But while in effect he expanded the semantic base of the word, he kept a quite special emphasis on its signification of literary form. Indeed, he frequently adverts to the idea of literary genres as a way of distinguishing strands of reality. In a typical passage, he describes actual experience as a "thing of multifarious tragic and epic meanings. . . . A many voiced tragedy and epos, yet with broad-based comic and grotesque accompaniment; done by actors *not* in buskins (*WTC*, **XXIX**, 258). As this passage suggests, Carlyle exploited the idea of genre by intimating, on the one hand, that there are separable and ideal structures, and, on the other, that life is a conflation of the distinct realities that literary forms abstract from experience. Carlyle seldom, however, imagines the conflation as a random mingling. The imagery is usually charged with classical notions pertaining to the principle of literary decorum and the proper ordering of genres. Epic takes precedence over tragedy, tragedy over comedy, comedy over farce. In fact, the rhetoric of genres, when Carlyle employs it as a criticism of life, usually nullifies all the surface implications of random conflation by repeatedly stressing just two kinds of juncture. A passage from *Frederick the Great* illustrates one of these junctures, the strange but meaningful juxtaposition of dissimilar genres: "Something of Farce will often enough, in this irreverent world, intrude itself on the most solemn Tragedy" (*WTC*, **XIX**, 293). The other kind of juncture is the close affinity of two allied forms, epic and tragedy. Their contiguity, as we shall see, is extremely important in Carlyle's description of revolution. At the moment we may ask why Carlyle so often alluded to the symbolic structures of literature. It seems evident that they offered themselves as emblems of an old idea of order in a world of vertiginous change. They were of ancient authority. Even in the nineteenth century, while literary practice was dissolving the old notions of literary form, the traditional idea of the genres maintained the status of an immutable hierarchy. A classically based system of education fostered this attitude. Carlyle could play on his readers' assumptions by treating poetic categories in just the way Kenneth Burke has suggested that they might be treated: as "major psychological devices whereby the mind equips itself to name and confront its situation."[2]

It was an ominous situation Carlyle found himself confronting. Having abandoned in the late twenties the pedestrian obligations of reviewer, translator, and editor, he began devising an art through which he could speak as a seer, a social visionary. His duty was to make sense of an epoch that was remarkable for its incoherence. As a minimal qualification, the seer had to be free of commonplaces and conventional wisdom. Carlyle made his claim to this qualification in an act that boldly defined his radical perspective: he insisted on the *veracity* of the French Revolution. It was, he proclaimed, an oracle to the age. Any truth-telling and truth-seeking prophet had to be in possession of its manifold meanings. As Carlyle remarked to Froude, "I could not have known what to make of this world at all if it had not been for the French Revolution."[3] His style itself vividly demonstrates how he used the fact of revolution as the engine of his prophecy. He enacts a revolution in his style and so makes his style a witness to his consummate appreciation of the fact. He himself said as much when he called his history of the French Revolution "a wild savage Book, itself a kind of French Revolution."[4] This is just what

2. *Attitudes toward History*, 2d ed. (1959; rpt. Boston: Beacon Press, 1961), p. 99.
3. James Anthony Froude, *Thomas Carlyle: A History of the First Forty Years of His Life* (1882; rpt. New York: Scribner's, 1906), II, 15.
4. *New Letters of Thomas Carlyle*, ed. Alexander Carlyle (London: Bodley Head, 1904), I, 50. For a more complex and indispensable account, see Carlyle's description of his style in a letter to Emerson (August 12, 1834), in *The Correspondence of Emerson and Carlyle*, ed. Joseph Slater (New York: Columbia University Press, 1964), pp. 103–4. See also George Levine, "The Use and Abuse of Carlylese," in *The Art of Victorian Prose*, ed. George Levine and Wil-

Carlyle wanted: an art built by illuviation, an art whose energies and materials had been leached out of the most significant event in modern history.

But the event, even for the prophet, was full of ambiguity. Carlyle had his conflict with each kind of content in revolution. He applauded liberal democracy, but only because it was self-annihilating; he hankered after the apocalypse of the imagination (Burke's phrase) but distrusted the aesthetic realm and would not mount any unbridled Pegasus; he would permit revolution to shoot Niagara, but he would also demand that the fall be broken —and, prodigiously, reversed. And so Carlyle contentiously abraded the patron of his muse. In a sense that is not true of Scott, Byron, or Arnold, Carlyle was committed to the idea of revolution as the generative principle of his work and the inspiritor of his authorial voice. He needed to be both inspired and intimidated by revolution and he used it both to inspire and to intimidate his audience.

The full significance of these points should become clear as we see Carlyle, in the early thirties, moving from detachment to commitment. As a sort of leitmotif for this period, we might apply to Carlyle the comment that M. H. Abrams makes about Keats in *Hyperion*: "By demonstrating his readiness and capacity to endure the burden of the tragic knowledge that human growth and creativity entail correspondent loss and suffering, [he] has established his identity as a poet and defined the kind of poet that he is."[5] Before Carlyle could establish his identity as a social visionary, he had to resolve for himself whether it was even possible for a visionary to be embroiled in political matters. He dealt with this

---

liam Madden (New York: Oxford University Press, 1968), p. 104. G. B. Tennyson has skillfully analyzed the forging of Carlyle's style in *"Sartor" Called "Resartus"* (Princeton: Princeton University Press, 1965). See especially pp. 259–73 on Carlyle's inventiveness with language.

5. *Natural Supernaturalism: Tradition and Revolution in Romantic Literature* (New York: Norton, 1971), p. 128.

issue by accepting his descent into the political world as a result of the tragic knowledge with which his prophetic imagination had burdened him. "Reform," he would always say, "is not joyous but grievous" (*WTC,* XXIX, 304). We have already seen how Scott and Byron sought to protect themselves from the grime of political conflict. Later in the century, Matthew Arnold would cite Carlyle's immersion in politics as a notorious violation of disinterestedness.[6] The charge Arnold would make, of course, was that Carlyle had compromised himself as a writer by advancing a political polemic. This is precisely what Carlyle knew he must avoid. It was an especially severe problem for him, since he had originally developed his literary vocation under the influence of German transcendentalism, which had given him a very exalted idea of Schiller and Goethe as modern seers. "The genuine interpreter of the Invisible," Carlyle said in his 1831 essay on Schiller, "has to struggle from the littleness and obstruction of an Actual world, into the freedom and infinitude of an Ideal" (*WTC,* XXVII, 172). And even as late as 1838, when his struggle with the dream of detachment was really long since over, Carlyle could say of Goethe that "he never took part in the political troubles of his time. . . . He did right not to meddle in these miserable disputes. To expect this of his genius would be like asking the moon to come out of the heavens, and become a mere street torch."[7]

As early as 1829 Carlyle's antipolitical stance began to shift. His journal in that year registers the attitude that would come to dominate his sense of the prophet's fate: "Politics are not our Life

6. *The Complete Prose Works of Matthew Arnold,* ed. R. H. Super (Ann Arbor: University of Michigan Press, 1960–77), III, 275. Arnold had *Latter-Day Pamphlets* in mind. In his essay "Politics and the Poet's Role," John Lucas discusses the parallel examples of Tennyson and Browning anxiously fencing themselves off from politics: *Literature and Politics in the Nineteenth Century,* ed. John Lucas (London: Methuen, 1971).

7. *Lectures on the History of Literature Delivered by Thomas Carlyle, April to July 1838,* ed. J. Reay Greene (London: Ellis & Elvey, 1892), p. 209.

(which is the practice and contemplation of Goodness), but only the *house* wherein that Life is led. Sad duty that lies on us to *parget* and continually repair our houses: saddest of all when it becomes our *sole* duty" (*TNB*, p. 141). Carlyle is not referring to duty in any impersonal way. He had recently completed "Signs of the Times," the essay that marks his first attempt to assess the political climate of the age. It is true that the essay minimizes the value of political action, but it still casts a fascinated glance at the turbulence of the time. "Doubtless this age is advancing. Its very unrest, its ceaseless activity, its discontent contains matter of promise" (*WTC*, XXVII, 80). This, of course, represents something less than a political position, and yet it is for Carlyle a distinct move toward the development of a political consciousness. The immediate background is the volcanic condition of both Britain and Europe as the century's fourth decade began. It is not quite true that Carlyle was awakened from his slumbers by such issues as the repeal of the Test Act or by the imminent outbreak of revolution all over the continent. Carlyle never slumbered. But he was moved by the crisis of reform and revolution to assess what the signs of the times meant to his destiny as a writer. During the next eighteen months, as his journal shows, he found that no simply contemplative position would be available to him. Toward the end of 1830, he wrote:

> The Whigs in office, and Baron Brougham Lord Chancellor! Hay-stacks and corn-stacks burning all over the South and Middle of England! Where will it end? Revolution on the back of Revolution for a century yet?   [*TNB*, p. 178]

And in February 1831 he waited anxiously in Craigenputtock, just as Scott waited at Abbotsford, for the fateful news from London.

> All Europe is in a state of disturbance, of Revolution. About this very time they may be debating the question of British 'Reform'

in London: the Parliament opened last week, our news of it expected on Wednesday. The times are big with change. Will *one* century of constant fluctuation serve us, or shall we need two? . . . The whole frame of society is rotten, and must go for fuelwood, and *where* is the new frame to come from? I know not, and no man knows. [*TNB*, pp. 183–84]

The Reform Bill was defeated on March 22, the bitter election was contested, the Second Bill was passed by the Commons in September, and was thrown out by the Lords on October 8. Two days later Carlyle wrote:

> Meanwhile *what* were the true duty of a man; were it to stand utterly aloof from Politics . . . or is not perhaps the very want of this time, an infinite want of Governors? . . . Canst *thou* in any measure spread abroad Reverence over the hearts of men? . . . Is it to be done by Art?

And the next day, less ambiguously:

> Vain hope to make mankind happy by Politics! [*TNB*, pp. 203–5]

The Third Reform Bill was passed by the Commons in March 1832, the familiar and dramatic struggle to defeat it was again mounted, and finally Lord Grey was recalled on May 17 with the king's promise to create new peers. On May 16 Carlyle had written: "The only Reform is in *thyself*. Know this O Politician, and be moderately political." But he also continued by saying:

> For me I have never yet done any one political act. . . . My case is this: I comport myself wholly like an alien. . . . When the time comes, should it ever come, that I can do *any good* in. . . coming forward, then let me not hang back. Meanwhile pay thy taxes to his Majesty and the rest, so long as they can force thee; the instant they can*not* force thee, that instant cease to pay. This has been my political principle for many a year. [*TNB*, pp. 274–75]

In August he returned to the question as to a persistent ache:

> Politics confuse me—what my duties are therein? As yet I have
> *stood apart,* and till quite new aspects of the matter turn up, shall
> continue to do so. The battle is not between Tory and Radical (that
> is but like other battles); but between believer and nonbeliever.[8]

Here the ambivalence is tormenting. Carlyle insists on defining
the problem in spiritual terms, but in a way that shows he is no
longer very confident that the spiritual battle can be separated
from the political context. The journal is only reflecting what
had already taken place. Much of Carlyle's work since 1829 had
gravitated toward the idea of revolution. Although he continued
to manifest and to record in his journal an emotional attachment
to the seer unbesmirched by the "miserable disputes" of the political world, he could not play the part of quietist. Perhaps it is his
April 1833 letter to John Stuart Mill, in which he describes his
age as one to which the sad task of revolution has been appointed,
that we can see him, at last, explicitly forsaking the dream of detachment: "Out upon it! One cannot look at it without a mixture of horror and contempt. I declare my prayer was that I
should hide altogether from hearing of it; but that may not be.[9]

In print, he had not only by this point already surrendered his
detachment, he had written what amounts to an analysis of his
plight in the generally ignored essay on the "Corn-Law Rhymes"
of Ebenezer Elliott that he published in July 1832.[10] It is in this es-

---

8. Froude, *Thomas Carlyle: First Forty Years,* II, 249.
9. *Letters of Carlyle to Mill.* Cf. Carlyle in 1843: "It was John Sterling, I
think, that first told me my nature was Political; it is strange enough how, beyond expectation, that oracle is verifying itself" (*New Letters,* I, 282). The
cool shoulder Carlyle gave politics has recently been discussed in Philip Rosenberg, *The Seventh Hero: Thomas Carlyle and the Theory of Radical Activism*
(Cambridge: Harvard University Press, 1974), pp. 15–44. Although our discussions overlap to some extent, I find myself unable to see the pre-Marxian
Carlyle Rosenberg sees.

say that Carlyle arms himself with the tragic vision. One can detect the advance that the essay makes by noticing its treatment of Robert Burns. Elliott is likened to Burns because of his background as a laborer and an uneducated man. Five years earlier, when Carlyle wrote his major essay on Burns, he was careful to point out that "meteors of French Politics [rose] before him, but these were not *his* stars." Thus he disposed of Burns's political consciousness (*WTC*, XXVI, 304). No mention is now made of Burns's putative political chastity. For it is specifically Elliott's political voice that catches Carlyle's ear.

> *He has turned, as all thinkers up to a very high and rare order in these days must do, into Politics*; is a Reformer, at least a stern Complainer, Radical to the core: his poetic melody takes an elegiaco-tragical character. . . . Not yet as a rebel against anything does he stand; but . . . not far from rebelling against much; with sorrowful appealing dew, yet also with incipient lightning, in his eyes. . . . Nevertheless, under all disguises of the Radical, the Poet is still recognisable: a certain music breathes through all dissonances, as the prophecy and ground-tone of returning harmony. [*WTC*, XXVIII, 148; italics added]

The passage directs us toward a compromise where the tensions exhibited in Carlyle's journal entries are, if not resolved, at least brought under aesthetic control. The poet must deal in politics, if the burden of the times forces him to do so, but the elegiaco-tragical character of his work can testify to his earnestness and ennoble his purpose.

The place beyond tragedy that Carlyle leaves for the singer of "a very high and rare order" is fundamentally important. Given

10. Emery Neff seems alone in noticing that the essay "reveals Carlyle half-consciously taking stock of his own qualifications as a social prophet" (*Carlyle* [London: Allen & Unwin, 1932], p. 153). Rosenberg argues that Carlyle's intention in the essay seems to be to "depoliticize" Elliott, which is surely not the case (*Seventh Hero*, p. 30).

the background of the journal, we can assume that Carlyle himself aspired to the sublimity of that position. Yet all the signs of the times were pressing him on toward a position that would embrace both politics and prophecy. In its substructure, "Corn-Law Rhymes" can be seen as an essay that tries to keep some continuity between the "rare genius" and the "radical poet." The whole essay depends on its various reiterations of the distinction in purpose that separates these types. Carlyle's point in making the distinction is not to emphasize the separation. Instead of postulating an interstellar distance between the order of the rare genius and the order of the radical poet, he is able to see their spheres as contiguous. There is a clear border between them, but it is a border, not a barrier. This means that the radical poet can work in a vicinity that is dignified by its proximity to the empyrean. The essay keeps asserting this point in various ways; it is a concept of poetic activity that derives, ultimately, from Carlyle's assumptions about the relative intimacy between epic and tragedy. They are intimate because both are inspired by the same lofty vision, which sees Time reposing on Eternity. It is a vision that seeks to reveal what Carlyle often called "the innermost heart of Nature" for the sake of an integrated harmonious culture. But epic means the *achievement* of this vision; tragedy means a failed effort to achieve it. Epic for Carlyle can include tragedy, but always transcends it. Tragedy, on the other hand, can envision sublimity, but must stress some element of defeat or destruction.

The prose-poem with which the essay begins unmistakably echoes these assumptions (commonplace in Carlyle's time), distanced though they are by its tone.

> The Works of this Corn-Law Rhymer we might liken . . . to some little fraction of a rainbow: hues of joy and harmony, painted out of troublous tears. No round full bow, indeed; gloriously spanning the heavens; shone on by the full sun; and, with seven-stripped, gold-crimson border (as is in some sort the office of Poetry) dividing Black from Brilliant: not such; alas, still far

from it! Yet, in very truth, a little prismatic blush, glowing genuinely among the wet clouds; which proceeds, if you will, from a
sun cloud-hidden, yet indicates that a sun does shine, and above
these vapours, a whole azure vault and celestial firmament stretch
serene. [*WTC,* XXVIII, 137]

Later in the essay Carlyle proceeds to make explicit what he
sees as the relationship between epic and tragedy. "So our Corn-
Law Rhymer plays his part. In this wise does he indite and act his
Drama of Life, which for him is all-too Domestic-Tragical"
(*WTC,* XXVIII, 157). But even the Corn-Law Rhymer, "in his
humble chant of the Village Patriarch," reveals something that is,
"in its nature and unconscious tendency, Epic. . . . What we
might call an inarticulate, half-audible Epic!" It is the story not of
Arms and the Man but of Tools and the Man, "the true Epic of
our Time,—were the genius but arrived that could sing it"
(*WTC,* XXVIII, 161–62). This genius is, clearly, the thinker of
"a high and rare order" who may stand clear of the meteors. But
the essay has by now legitimized the tragic position by understanding its proximity to epic. And so, at the conclusion, Carlyle
can project, through his treatment of Elliott, his own intense effort to locate the role of the prophet in an anarchic age.

> He takes amiss that some friends have admonished him to quit
> Politics: we will not repeat that admonition. Let him, on this as
> on all other matters, take solemn counsel with his Socrates-
> Demon; such as dwells in every mortal; such as he is a happy
> mortal who can hear the voice of, follow the behests of, like an
> unalterable law. At the same time, we could truly wish to see
> such a mind as his engaged rather in considering what, in his own
> sphere, could be *done,* than what, in his or other spheres, ought to
> be *destroyed.* [*WTC,* XXVIII, 165–66]

The Socrates-Demon in Carlyle's breast persuaded him that his
"coming forward" to address the political realm would not sub-
vert his moral authority. Not as long as he could present himself
as a writer whose residual appreciation of the sublime (and really

apolitical) epic order could be ratified by his tragic utterance.

The Elliott essay formally concludes Carlyle's search for a principle that would justify the prophet's active scrutiny of the political world. And not only does it find that principle in the model of tragedy, it also implicitly identifies the essential nature of tragedy. Tragedy is the fate of the true man in combat with false circumstance. Everywhere in Carlyle's work this classic, rooted attitude of the Romantic mind manifests itself. In a general and perhaps even nebulous sense, Carlyle sees tragedy as the condition inflicted on all mortals by their passage through the temporal world.

> The life of every man . . . the life of even the meanest man, it were good to remember, is a Poem, perfect in all manner of Aristotelian requisites; with its Will-strength (*Willenkraft*) and warfare against Fate, its elegy and battle-singing, courage marred by crime, everywhere the two tragic elements of Pity and Fear; above all, with supernatural machinery enough,—for was not the man *born* out of NONENTITY; did he not *die,* and miraculously vanishing return thither? The most indubitable Poem. [*WTC,* XXVIII, 249]

Carlyle frequently writes in this way, vaguely illuming the immortal world that is man's true home.

It is when Carlyle refines his sense of the tragic to represent the uniquely grievous conditions of modern history that tragedy becomes vital to his prophetic attitude. If all human life is a deprivation, life in early Victorian England is subject to a special falsification. In "The Diamond Necklace" (February 1837) Carlyle gives his clearest account of the tragic situation in his time. We face, he says, the spectacle of the human spirit reduced to a waxwork. Man has all but renounced the character of Man; only in rare moments is his human voice audible from within the mummy wrappings of Gigman and Gentleman.

> The high-born (highest-born, for he came out of Heaven) lies drowning in the despicablest puddles; the priceless gift of Life . . .

we see slowly strangled out of him by innumerable packthreads; and there remains of the glorious Possibility, which we fondly named Man, nothing but an inanimate mass of foul loss and disappointment, which we wrap in shrouds and bury underground, —surely with well-merited tears. To the Thinker here lies Tragedy enough; the epitome and marrow of all Tragedy whatsoever. [*WTC,* XXVIII, 324-25]

This is, undoubtedly, the essence of tragedy for Carlyle. All of his disparate remarks on tragedy as *mythos* suggest that tragedy is the shriveling of "glorious possibility." The wing trailing in the mud; the shadow of a magnitude—these constitute the appropriate emblems of tragedy in the Carlylean schema.[11] Many men, perhaps even most men, squander their chances for a meaningful life. But there are others, true men, to whom a sad task is appointed. For them, what Yeats calls a Body of Fate inevitably frustrates and complicates the exploratory process of mortal existence. Under these circumstances man as a glorious possibility is subjected to a loss of destiny because of the hostile environment to which he has been exposed. Life becomes labyrinthine; exploration never leads to discovery. A man's exploration may be sincere, his struggle heroic, but his passage may remain forever blocked by the cruel contrivances of the mud gods. On the other hand, he may actually find a promising avenue of escape but die on the threshold of liberation, spiritually exhausted by his efforts and not quite in possession of reality. Various versions of these defeats are strewn through Carlyle's work. For example, in "Characteristics" the true man is simply "the youth" (a significant stress) virginally confronting the *Zeitgeist*'s display of a barren past and a blank future.

The sum of man's misery is even this, that he feel himself crushed under the Juggernaut wheels, and know that Juggernaut is no divinity, but a dead mechanical idol. Now this is specially the

11. Carlyle toned down but never abandoned the attitude he expressed in

misery which has fallen on man in our Era. Belief, Faith has well-nigh vanished from the world. The youth on awakening in this wondrous Universe no longer finds a competent theory of its wonders. . . . The old ideal of Mankind has grown obsolete, and the new is still invisible to us, and we grope after it in darkness, one clutching this phantom, another that.   [*WTC*, XXVIII, 29]

A somewhat different example is Carlyle's friend Edward Irving, who was goaded by the age into self-destructive activities. Carlyle wrote that in Irving's life we see "enacted the old Tragedy . . . of *The Messenger of Truth in the Age of Shams.*" Irving, who "might have been so many things," left his native Scotland to pursue a public purpose in London. He was devastated by this attempt to strive with "Tithe Controversy, Encyclopedism, Catholic Rents, Philantropism, and the Revolution of Three Days." Carlyle acknowledges that Irving allowed himself to be duped, but his emphasis falls on the ease with which the age can pervert the best motives of men by intoxicating them with its "foul incense" (*WTC*, XXVIII, 320–21).

The most intensely tragic case of all, however, is that of the man who understands his destiny, who is not trapped in the labyrinth of unworkable possibilities, but who is fated to mount toward his destiny on heaps of rubble, ashes, and ruin. His proper labor is the labor of destruction (whereas the proper labor of the epic hero is creation). Since he has desolating work to do, he can but be desolate himself. "It is not a light matter when the just man can recognise in the powers set over him no longer anything that is divine; when resistance against such becomes a deeper law than obedience to them; when the just man sees himself in the tragical position of a stirrer-up of strife! Rebel without due and

---

his 1827 essay on Richter: "For the great law of culture is: Let each become all that he was created capable of being; expand, if possible, to his full growth; resisting all impediments, casting off all foreign, especially all noxious adhesions; and show himself in his own shape and stature, be these what they may" (*WTC*, XXVI, 19).

most due cause, is the ugliest of words; the first rebel was Satan"
(*WTC,* XXIX, 189).

All of these figures are masks of Carlyle himself. The gravest
mask is that of the rebel (or heroic radical poet), who is a dramatic embodiment of the prophet with a political mind. He is
very far from Camus's rebel and very far from Byron's. Not only
is he fated to destroy gross evils, he cannot allow even bare ruined
choirs to stand. His spiritual energy, which in a less hostile environment he would dedicate solely to glorious possibilities, must
be concentrated in a work of extirpation. The explicit note of
tragedy that marks his life is sometimes the only sign he can offer
of his deep longing for harmony, community, and the simple
practice and contemplation of goodness. In this sense, Carlyle's
use of tragedy is, rather traditionally, a paradoxical revelation of
man's highest nature through an account of sublime failure. Karl
Jaspers's summary of this view applies directly to Carlyle: What
we essentially learn "from tragic knowledge . . . is what makes
man suffer and what makes him fail, what he takes upon himself
in the face of which realities, and in what manner or form he sac-
rifices his existence."[12]

In the same month (May 1832) that Carlyle composed "Corn-
Law Rhymes," he began his long essay "Goethe's Works." The
essay presents to us yet again the proposition that "no man is his
political constitution" and that "a nobler task than . . . *house-
pargeting* and smoke-doctoring" is exemplified in Goethe (*WTC,*
XXVII, 442). Carlyle almost seems to be apologizing for the road
taken in his essay on Elliott. The essay continues to suggest, however, that the joy of Goethe's "political practice, or rather no-
practice," remains exasperatingly out of reach.

There is another issue raised by the Goethe essay. Perhaps more
than any other single factor, it was the example of Goethe that

---

12. *Tragedy Is Not Enough*, trans. H. A. T. Reiche et al. (Boston: Beacon
Press, 1952), p. 56.

put Carlyle so much in awe of the serenely disengaged poet, and consequently so much in doubt as to his own justification in developing a political voice. But Carlyle did not take all his cues from Goethe. Other writers provided him with other ways of assessing his situation. Scott and Byron were two of the most important. When he was young they made a blaze in his imagination. "Read *all* Scott's Novels at odd hours," he told his brother in 1822, "and Byron's poetry—and Shakespeare—and Pope—and the like. These things are of the very highest value" (*CL,* II, 137). When he matured, he withdrew from their influence. He did not, however, withdraw from them negligently and indifferently. He discovered aspects of his own message by repudiating theirs.

The general nature of his repudiation is familiar. Carlyle's essay on Scott (January 1838) is well known and his remarks on Byron have been gathered and analyzed in C. R. Sanders's important and influential essay.[13] But something remains to be said about Carlyle's response to Scott and Byron as a significant pair. Not only do they represent the failure of possibilities, they also, in their failures, clarified for Carlyle the burden of his own position. The shades of Scott and Byron, Carlyle suggested, inhabit two of the chief hells of modern history. Carlyle himself had to descend into the third hell, revolution, in order to find an exit leading to new belief and activity.

By 1827, Carlyle, who had been sniping at Byron for several years, was prepared to define his mature judgment. In the "State of German Literature" he said that Byron "loved truth in his inmost heart, and would have discovered at last that his Corsairs and Harolds were not true. It was otherwise appointed. But with

13. "The Byron Closed in *Sartor Resartus,*" *Studies in Romanticism,* 3 (1963), 77–108. Morse Peckham makes some use of Scott and Byron in his remarks on Carlyle in *Beyond the Tragic Vision* (New York: Braziller, 1962), pp. 177–95. There are few useful remarks in H. J. C. Grierson's "Scott and Carlyle," *Essays and Addresses* (London: Chatto & Windus, 1940), pp. 27–54.

one man all hope does not die" (*WTC,* XXVI, 69). Concurrently, though Carlyle still read Scott, he was doing so with less and less fervor. Late in 1826, punning magnificently, he called him "the great *Restaurateur* of Europe" (*TNB,* p. 71). He does not openly discuss Scott in the "State of German Literature," but when he argues for the greatness of Goethe because Goethe addresses the real world and not "periods of Chivalry," it is clear that he is thinking of Scott (*WTC,* XXVI, 59). Moreover, the essay explicates Fichte's conception of the highest kind of literary genius as opposed to the useful "hodman." The very month that the essay was published, Carlyle was calling Scott "a sufficient 'hodman' " whose hod "is filled with good gingerbread."[14]

Thus Carlyle closed his Byron *and* his Scott at the same time. But it is important to keep in mind the qualifications he made in each case. As Sanders says, "not all of Byron was shut out," and the same thing may be said of Scott.[15] Scott's case is complicated somewhat by two events that occurred just as Carlyle was turning his back on the Wizard of the North. In December 1826, Carlyle had been eagerly awaiting the publication of Scott's *Life of Napoleon.* It would be, he reported, "the great work of the winter" (*CL,* IV, 164). Publication was delayed until July 1827. Carlyle had not read it by the time he composed the "State of German Literature," and his anticipation of something quite wonderful from Scott may have deterred him from attacking Scott openly in the essay. Then, in February 1828, Goethe dispatched to Carlyle two medals that he wished Carlyle to present to Scott. Goethe's gift was inspired by a presentation copy of the *Life,* which he had read with the deepest admiration. Elated, Carlyle wrote to Scott asking permission to present the gift in person and so serve as ambassador "between two Kings of Poetry" (*CL,* IV, 354). Scott never answered Carlyle's letter, "perhaps because

---

14. *CL,* IV, 271; and see the editors' note on the same page (n. 8).
15. "Byron Closed," p. 104.

he was a busy or uncourteous man" (*CL*, IV, 382–83). During this inauspicious time Carlyle read the *Life*. His first allusion to it in print comes, appropriately enough, in his "Goethe," published in the *Foreign Review* for July 1828. It is a minor but slurring reference (*WTC*, XXVI, 229).

The timing of these incidents is what matters most. Carlyle, at the zenith of his dedication to German Romanticism, saw in Scott and Byron a pattern of achievement and impotence. This impression lasted, even when Carlyle substantially moderated his idealism. Whatever he was to become as a writer, however much he had to alter his commitments, he knew that his path led away from Scott and Byron. *Sartor Resartus* helped to create a generation of anti-Byronists. *The French Revolution* was written in direct opposition to Scott's history.[16]

Their example, however, was not simply negative. Scott and Byron represented to Carlyle distinct and major phases of the spiritual history of modern Europe. They established the frame of reference within which Carlyle defined the necessity of action. This point can best be shown in a passage from an essay published in 1827, the pivotal year. Carlyle used the passage several times; it is much expanded in his 1838 essay on Scott. (And the passage later influenced Arnold.) Inevitably, Carlyle is discussing Goethe. *Götz von Berlichingen* and *Werter,* though noble specimens of a youthful talent, are not, he says,

> so much distinguished by their intrinsic merits as by their splendid fortune. . . . Sir Walter Scott's first literary enterprise was a translation of *Götz von Berlichingen*: and if genius could be communicated like instruction, we might call this work of Goethe's the prime cause of . . . all that has followed from the same creative hand. Truly, a grain of seed that has lighted in the right soil!

16. Neff notes this point (*Carlyle*, p. 175). Some of the larger historiographical issues between Scott and Carlyle are discussed in Hedva Ben-Israel, *English Historians on the French Revolution* (Cambridge: The University Press, 1968), pp. 119–26.

. . . It may be sufficient to observe of *Berlichingen* and *Werter,* that they stand prominent among the causes, or, at the least, among the signals, of a great change in modern Literature. The former directed men's attention with a new force to the picturesque effects of the Past; and the latter, for the first time, attempted the more accurate delineation of a class of feelings, deeply important to modern minds; but for which our elder poetry offered no exponent, and perhaps could offer none, because they are feelings that arise from passion incapable of being converted into action, and belong chiefly to an age as indolent, cultivated and unbelieving as our own.   [*WTC,* XXIII, 15-16]

Carlyle interpolated this passage into his *Foreign Review* essay on Goethe of the next year. There the implied connection between *Werter* and Byron is made explicit. Carlyle indicates the root source of his inexorable revolt against Byron by arguing that the lament of Byron, like the lament of Werter, takes hold— temporarily—of all Europe. But "it prescribes no remedy; *for that was a far different, far harder enterprise, to which other years and a higher culture were required*" (*WTC,* XXVI, 218; italics added). This is one of Carlyle's earliest and most significant applications of historicism, and its purpose is transparent. It endows Carlyle's times (and Carlyle himself) with the signal quality absent in Byron: a creative purpose.

A similar point is made about Scott. The 1838 essay on Scott, written only months after the publication of *The French Revolution,* credits Scott with carrying "several things to their ultimatum and crisis, so that change became inevitable" (*WTC,* XXIX, 77). The nature of this change is explained in Carlyle's expanded version of the original passage on Götzism and Werterism. The passage remains substantially the same up to the point where Scott is pictured as the "right soil" for the transplantation of Goethe's manner in *Götz.* Then Carlyle breaks off verbatim quotation and loosely intercalates the remainder of the passage with the next few paragraphs. Scott is to be seen as the genius of a "languid age without either faith or scepticism"; it could effect nothing and so whiled away its life with "an affectionate half-regretful looking-back into the Past." The age then turned to Byron; "here, if no cure for its miserable paralysis and languor, was at least an indignant statement of the misery; an indignant Ernulphus' curse read over it. . . . Half-regretful lookings into the Past gave place, in many quarters, to Ernulphus' cursings of the Present" (*WTC,* XXIX, 58–59). Carlyle sees *both* styles as expressive of those feelings deeply interesting to modern minds: "*passion incapable of being converted into action*" (*WTC,* XXIX, 59; Carlyle's italics).

Scott and Byron epitomize the demonstrably inadequate responses of modern man to the age of skepticism. Each performs a service, however, by bringing a major phase of the modern disease to its ultimatum and crisis. Carlyle is the direct heir of Scott and Byron. He had to do what they could not do: he had to act. The nature of his action is, of course, implied by the Meisterism with which Goethe cured Götzism and Werterism. But the Scott essay also alludes to France, which, "busy with its Revolution and Napoleon, had little leisure . . . for Götzism or Werterism" (*WTC,* XXIX, 58). And, as it happened, Carlyle busied himself in the same way. The dead ends of Scott's nostalgia and Byron's self-consciousness prepared Carlyle for his descent into the hell of revolution—where, at least, a world of action was discoverable.

Scott and Byron were not contemptible to Carlyle. They were tragic figures beset, as he said of Scott, by "waste Ruin's havoc" (*WTC,* XXIX, 85). In 1828, while proposing that modern man must emerge from "doubt and discontent into freedom, belief and clear activity," Carlyle called Byron "almost the only man we saw faithfully and manfully struggling, to the end, in this cause; and he died while the victory was still doubtful, or at best, only beginning to be gained" (*WTC,* XXVI, 243). And of Scott he wrote: "Walter Scott, one of the gifted of the world, whom his admirers call the most gifted, must kill himself that he may be a country gentleman. . . . It is one of the strangest, most tragical histories ever enacted under this sun" (*WTC,* XXIX, 72). The defeat of possibility in these men, the shipwreck of their genius in the early phases of modernity, illuminated for Carlyle the phase of history in which he was to encounter his own fate. Scott and Byron were Carlyle's step-brothers.

Sartor Resartus disdains nostalgic lookings into the past, and though it surely execrates the present, it turns with hope toward the lively future. *Sartor* is Carlyle's answer to Scott and Byron. As such, the book is comic in its aspiration as well as comic in its style. But the tragic themes appear nonetheless. As Carlyle knew very well, the future had to be earned.

Sartor behaves like a book about fragmentation.[17] Narratively and imagistically it spreads before us the tattered rags of self and society. In keeping with this procedure, it professes its own incompleteness by several times referring to a further installment of Teufelsdröckh's teachings to be called *On the Palingenesia, or Newbirth of Society*. This being the fictional case, *Sartor Resartus* may be read as a work that is leading up to the rediscovery or reformulation of social order. The book's narrative method amounts to a political statement. Carlyle is gingerly but deliberately aligning the resurrection of the spirit with the reconstitution of the body politic. Moreover, the political matter of the book is not simply recessive. Just as *Sartor* is, finally, a densely organized work that transcends fragmentation through powerful demonstrations of its internal order, so also does it spell out the substance of Palingenesia, the missing volume notwithstanding. It does so structurally. "The Newbirth of Society" is articulated not as an idea but as an event. The event occurs in the act of reading, or rather courageously enduring, *Sartor Resartus*. In this sense, Carlyle is saying that those who read may run.[18] They have new life and the clues to social order. They form a brotherhood. And, as with Carlyle him-

17. See G. B. Tennyson, *"Sartor" Called "Resartus,"* pp. 223–31, and Leonard Dean, "Irrational Form in *Sartor Resartus*," *Texas Studies in Literature and Language*, 5 (1963), 438–51.

18. The image of the reader is discussed more generally in Jerry Allen Dib-

self, the badge of brotherhood is their tragic knowledge.

The unfolding of this development is clearest in "Circumspective" (Book III, Chapter ix), which follows immediately upon the mystic lecture, "Natural Supernaturalism." The Editor begins the chapter by asking "the so momentous question":

> Have many British Readers actually arrived with us at the new promised country; is the Philosophy of Clothes now at last opening around them? . . . Can many readers discern, as through a glass darkly, in huge wavering outlines, some primeval rudiments of Man's Being . . . ? In a word, do we at length stand safe in the far region of Poetic Creation and Palingenesia, where the Phoenix Death-Birth of Human Society, and all Human Things, appears possible, is seen to be inevitable?

The Editor answers his own question by doubting that many have completed the journey without accident. But those who have, the "happy few," shall labor in the "highest work of Palingenesia," building new bridges, while "the most have recoiled, and stand gazing afar off, in unsympathetic astonishment, at our career" (*WTC*, I, 213–14).

The select few upon whom the many gaze constitute a transfigured society. In "Farewell" the Editor specifically identifies the very important sense in which the *Clothes* volume, by gathering readers to whom it is legible, *performs* palingenesis, thereby obviating the need for a treatise on the subject.

> What of the awestruck Wakeful who find [existence] a Reality? Should not these unite . . . ? —In which case were this enormous Clothes-Volume properly an enormous Pitchpan, which our Teufelsdröckh in his lone watchtower had kindled, that it might flame far and wide through the Night, and many a disconsolately wandering spirit be guided thither to a Brother's bosom! [*WTC*, I, 235]

---

ble, "Carlyle's 'British Reader' and the Structure of *Sartor Resartus*," *Texas Studies in Literature and Language*, 16 (1974), 293–304.

What is legible is combustible; language becomes an action. But it must be observed that the action reverberates in a symbolic zone that is by now very familiar to us. It is the place of wanderers, the limited clearing in historical time where the age's derelicts have gathered. They are happy only because they are wakeful, not because they have reached any consummation. There is no May dance at the base of Teufelsdröckh's tower. The derelicts are a chorus of tragedians. This would *not* be the case if the derelict-readers were united only in the sorrow of their dispossession. But by this point the burden of dispossession has been eased for them in the embryonic community they form. It is the sad task of revolution, the inevitable next phase of palingenesis, that defines their tragic identity. Teufelsdröckh has already stated what is for Carlyle the basic tragic perception in his world: "Painful for man is . . . rebellious Independence, when it has become inevitable" (*WTC*, I, 200). He who reads discovers, and accepts, this pain.

Albert LaValley has made the central point: in *Sartor* "the sense of fatality engulfing society, ready to doom it, is kept alive and emphasized." He goes on to say, with the last chapters of *Sartor* in mind, that "the celebration of society's regeneration in 'Signs of the Times' and 'Characteristics' has disappeared. If society is to purge itself, it will be through revolution, for Teufelsdröckh has, after a week of silence, been propelled back into the social dimension by the Parisian Three Days, the Revolution of 1830."[19]

Although *Sartor* remains a gospel of hope, hope is chastened by the tragic vision in just the same way that the Everlasting Yea is rooted in and chastened by its opposite. One does not exist without the other. Book III reiterates at the level of public prophecy the sore trials of modern reality that Teufelsdröckh experienced privately. The private experience ended in baptism. The public

19. *Carlyle and the Idea of the Modern* (New Haven: Yale University Press, 1968), p. 104. The tone of the book seems less threatening to George Levine (*The Boundaries of Fiction: Carlyle, Macaulay, Newman* [Princeton: Princeton University Press, 1968], pp. 32–33).

experience ends in revolution, the new social sacrament. Teufelsdröckh knows the efficacy of the sacrament because he knows the
agonistic nature of all renewal. Tragedy authorizes hope. This is
understood by those who gather at Teufelsdröckh's tower.

The structural event is reinforced by a good deal of explicit
commentary, especially in Book III, which establishes the protective function of the tragic vision. The "wakeful" reader is en-
treated by this commentary to cherish the heretical and rebellious
Teufelsdröckh because he proves his sincerity by his tragic de-
meanor. The reader is tutored in this respect by the Editor, who
has himself drawn close to Teufelsdröckh out of a sense of tragic
identification. At a more remote level, the relationship between
the Editor and Teufelsdröckh echoes the dialogue Carlyle conducted with himself in his journal over the danger of politics to
prophecy and which he resolved, as we have seen, by highlighting the sorrowful, appealing countenance of the prophet who
must speak out.

Teufelsdröckh is, insouciantly, a sansculotte. The term captures and perfectly amalgamates his political and visionary identities. Carlyle repeatedly draws attention to this particular synergy.
In "The Everlasting No," for example, Teufelsdröckh is abruptly
transported to "the French Capital or Suburbs," a locale that cli-
mactically defines the intersection of his spiritual grief and social
alienation. The Editor, however, begins by attempting to deflect
attention from Teufelsdröckh's political significance. His "practical tendency," we are told, is "towards a certain prospective, and
for the present quite speculative Radicalism" (WTC, I, 10). Even
by Book III the Editor confesses that of all the provinces of Teufelsdröckh's world "there is none he walks in with such astonishment, hesitation, and even pain, as in the Political." Nevertheless,
the Editor acknowledges "that, looking into this man, we discern a deep, silent slow-burning, inextinguishable Radicalism,
such as fills us with shuddering admiration" (WTC, I, 199).
Radicalism in Teufelsdröckh always implies much more than po-

litical consciousness, but it includes political consciousness as one of its integral features. As the Editor has more and more come to participate in Teufelsdröckh's social vision, he has increasingly responded to the clothes-philosopher's "characteristic vehemence" as a *cri de coeur*. He has, in other words, seen that Teufelsdröckh's Radicalism has no vainglorious ideology in it, but is the utterance of a "much-suffering" man who is fated to be a "much-inflicting" man (*WTC*, I, 234). What Teufelsdröckh inflicts on his world is the tragedy of revolution. For Teufelsdröckh "would consent, with a tragic solemnity, that the monster UTILITARIA, held back, indeed, and moderated by nose-rings, halters, foot-shackles, and every conceivable modification of rope, should go forth to do her work;—to tread down old ruinous Palaces and Temples with her broad hoof, till the whole were trodden down, that new and better might be built" (*WTC*, I, 88). This passage is from the chapter on "The Phoenix," where the derelict-reader is inducted into the mysteries of palingenesis. There is, however, no mystery here. "The Phoenix" candidly envisions the overwhelming of the old order through destructive means. All the modifications of rope and foot shackles will not modify, for Teufelsdröckh's followers, the moral violence of "fierce Transition's blood-red morn." As Teufelsdröckh says: "When the Phoenix is fanning her funeral pyre, will there not be sparks flying! . . . Still also have we to fear that incautious beards will get singed" (*WTC*, I, 188–89).[20]

There is compensation for the harsh truths of "The Phoenix" in the chapters "Organic Filaments" and "Natural Supernaturalism," but the explicit commentary on the social crisis awaiting the world is trenchantly renewed in "The Dandiacal Body." It is at this point in *Sartor Resartus* that Carlyle offers his quite particular version of the cataclysm produced by polarization. Teufels-

---

20. On these issues, R. D. McMaster, "Criticism of Civilization in the Structure of *Sartor Resartus*," *UTQ*, 37 (1968), 268–80, is helpful.

dröckh sees in England the emergence of two sects that form two nations, the privileged (Dandies) and the impoverished (Drudges).

> To the eye of the political Seer, their mutual relation, pregnant with the elements of discord and hostility, is far from consoling. . . . In their roots and subterranean ramifications, they extend through the entire structure of Society, and work unweariedly in the secret depths of English national Existence; striving to separate and isolate it into two contradictory, uncommunicating masses. . . . It seems probable that the two Sects will one day part England between them; each recruiting itself from the intermediate ranks, till there be none left to enlist on either side. Those Dandiacal Manicheans, with the host of Dandyising Christians, will form one body; the Drudges, gathering round them whosoever is Drudgical, be he Christian or Infidel Pagan; sweeping-up likewise all manner of Utilitarians, Radicals, refractory Potwallopers, and so forth, into their general mass, will form another. . . . Thus daily is the intermediate land crumbling-in . . . till now there is but a foot-plank, a mere film of Land between them; this too is washed away: and then—we have the true Hell of Waters, and Noah's Deluge is outdeluged! [*WTC*, I, 227–28]

The situation imagined here is not a deadlock but the defeat of all possibility. It is a world divested even of wanderers. Most important, it is a world divested even of revolution. This is what distinguishes Carlyle's rendering of polarization. Other writers portray unmitigated division as the precondition of revolution. But Carlyle, through Teufelsdröckh, hints at something worse than the tragedy of revolution. The true hell of waters comes when revolution itself is blocked. Polarization destroys the dynamic of change: "and then—What then? The Earth is but shivered . . . by that Doom's-thunderpeal; the Sun misses one of his Planets in Space, and thenceforth there are no eclipses of the Moon" (*WTC*, I, 228–29). The escalation of social disorder into cosmic holocaust represents a stage beyond tragedy where all hope of renewal is voided. It is Carlyle's way of explicating what is everywhere implicit in *Sartor*'s treatment of revolution: revolution is a cathartic process. In place of revolution, there is only extinction.

By focusing in this way on the problem of revolution, Carlyle, even before he had entirely quelled the apolitical voice within him, had successfully reached the shores of political prophecy. Revolution in *Sartor* is exempted from the blustering logomachy of ordinary politics. It is ritualized as a new revelation of the sacred. If it is tragic, it is, like tragedy, cathartic. And so, embedding in the revolutionary process the spiritual catharsis of tragedy, and thus compensating for the viciousness of modern revolt, Carlyle found a protective shelter for the prophet who would, alas, have to do much more than pay his taxes.

TRANSCENDENTAL DESPAIR:
THE FRENCH REVOLUTION

There are two much-quoted descriptions of *The French Revolution*. Mill began his review of it by saying that "this is not so much a history, as an epic poem." Froude, a long while later, responded: "It is rather an Aeschylean drama composed of facts literally true, in which the Furies are seen once more walking on this prosaic earth and shaking their serpent hair."[21] Froude is more accurate. The French Revolution did not achieve epic harmony as a political event, and it does not do so in Carlyle's symbolic retelling either. The work is addressed to Carlyle's own

21. Mill's review of *The French Revolution* is reprinted in *Thomas Carlyle: The Critical Heritage*, ed. Jules Paul Seigel (London: Routledge & Kegan Paul, 1971), p. 53. The reply is in James Anthony Froude, *Thomas Carlyle: A History of His Life in London* (1884; rpt. New York: Scribner's, 1910), I, 76. La-Valley has clearly demonstrated Carlyle's use of epic elements, but he acknowledges that the "epic legacy" is strangely misshapen as Carlyle finds himself "uncomfortable with the heritage of the Revolution, an upheaval which has resulted not in a new version of the stable social order of feudal Christianity but the dislocated, relative, and complex world of the modern spirit" (*Carlyle and the Idea of the Modern*, p. 126).

world and it attempts to discover a new social order. The discovery, indeed, is made; but how forbidding it is we shall see. As a history, the book rests on the negative content of revolution; its essential purpose is to redefine, radically, the meaning of hope in a transitional age. This theme is made quite explicit.

> Hope deferred maketh the heart sick. And yet, as we said, Hope is but deferred; not abolished, not abolishable. It is very notable, and touching, how this same Hope does still light onwards the French Nation through all its wild destinies. For we shall find Hope shining, be it for fond invitation, be it for anger and menace; as a mild heavenly light it shone; as a red conflagration it shines: burning sulphurous-blue, through darkest regions of Terror, it still shines; and goes not out at all, since Desperation itself is a kind of Hope. Thus is our Era still to be named of Hope, though in the saddest sense,—when there is nothing left but Hope. [*WTC*, II, 59]

The book insists on this point and on the tragic action it specifies. It is through the idea of tragedy that Carlyle explains the strange metamorphosis of hope upon which his analysis of the revolution depends. Strikingly, we are given a development that first envisions a tragedy based on the revolution's positive content, moves, after a fashion, toward a tragic action that responds to its latent content, and at last wrests hope from despair by siphoning energy from the revolution's negative content. These phases are shaped by the central, governing feature of the book's design. Carlyle's history is divided into three parts: "The Bastille," "The Constitution," and "The Guillotine." At the exact midpoint of the book—that is, halfway through "The Constitution"—occurs the death of Mirabeau. Carlyle sees Mirabeau as a political figure, but he also sees him as a man inspired by a poetic consciousness. In Mirabeau's death we witness the loss of imagination in the revolution. It is the great crisis of the whole book, and it organizes the events preceding it and following it. For before Mirabeau's death we have been shown that the *philosophes* cannot make their revolution through reason work. And after Mirabeau's death, the irrational force of the Jacobins is unleashed. Representing Nature's savage assertion against a life founded on lies, the Jacobins emerge to establish the primitive rights of "Reality." ("The Guillotine" is the climax of this process.) Thus the book's three principal stages come to this: the galling of the *philosophes*; the death of Mirabeau; the violence of the sansculottes. Each is represented as, in its own way, a tragic event, though clearly Carlyle looks constantly to the last stage, which he calls "transcendental despair." Transcendental despair brings a ferocious kind of catharsis where hope is reborn not so much out of pity and fear as out of blind terror.

There is nothing implausible in finding that Carlyle uses a narrative design that matches the general scheme of revolutionary content discussed earlier in this study. Carlyle was imbued with the idea of revolution; his art was its mirror. But it is important, of course, to see that his understanding of tragedy in *The French Revolution* is stamped by his own characteristic emphases. As a visionary historian, he comes bearing the tragic knowledge that reform is grievous—even for orators in the National Assembly. As a poet, he sees a tragic situation when the creative man is strangled by innumerable "packthreads." And, as a political thinker, he stresses that the greatest catastrophe lies in the fact that men have been forced to rebel by the fiats of history and by the dictates of their own alienated nature. There is, as well, a certain degree of resemblance between the phases of the Revolution as Carlyle discerns them and the stages of modern history defined in his essay on Scott. The world of the *ancien régime* is historically analogous to the void in which Scott worked, where several things had to be carried to their ultimatum and crisis. "The Constitution" is a version of the labyrinth in which seekers of the new world wander without discovery and can only curse the present. "The Guillotine" is the hell of radical action.

"The Bastille" begins with a survey of the void, the decadent

age in which no ideal could grow or prosper. Belief and loyalty
had passed away. "All Solemnity has become Pageantry; and the
Creed of persons in authority has become one of two things: an
Imbecility or a Macchiavelism" (sic) (*WTC*, II, 10). The leaders
of France try to support their false position by loans and *lettres de
cachet*, but they cannot overcome their nullity. The historic meeting of the Estates General becomes an occasion for Carlyle to review the injustice of the traditional arrangements in French society. Later, when the Third Estate summarily converts itself into
the National Assembly, the journey out of the void has begun.

The crisis of July 14 is now predictable. Carlyle, in this part of
the book, engages our sympathy for men who have taken upon
themselves the grief of revolution. "O poor mortals, how ye
make this Earth bitter for each other; this fearful and wonderful
Life fearful and horrible; and Satan has his place in all hearts! Such
agonies and ragings and wailings ye have, and have had, in all
times:—to be buried all, in so deep silence; and the salt sea is not
swoln with your tears" (*WTC*, II, 183). The tone that one hears
in this passage has been carefully built up over two chapters
(Book V, Chapters iv and v). These chapters take us to the night
of July 13. "Under all roofs of this distracted City is the nodus of
a drama, not untragical, crowding towards solution. The bus-
tlings and preparings, the tremors and menaces; the tears that fell
from old eyes! This day, my sons, ye shall quit you like men"
(*WTC*, II, 186).

The fall of the Bastille is the solution, however, of only an in-
termediate drama. A larger drama begins, or rather, the issues in
the larger drama suddenly emerge. What is happening is "surely
a great Phenomenon: nay it is a *transcendental* one, overstepping
all rules and experience; the crowning Phenomenon of our Modern Time" (*WTC*, II, 212). The taking of the Bastille proved
that the "age of Conventionalities" was over, that mere formulas
would not do. For long years it had seemed "as if no Reality any
longer existed . . . and men were buckram masks that went

about becking and grimacing." Then, "on a sudden, the Earth yawns asunder, and amid Tartarean smoke, and glare of fierce brightness, rises SANSCULOTTISM, many-headed, fire-breathing, and asks: What think ye of *me?* Well may the buckram masks start together terror-struck. . . . *Wo also to many a one who is not wholly buckram, but partly real and human"* (*WTC,* 212–13; italics added). Carlyle has brought before us, not Teufelsdröckh but the sansculotte with blood on his hands, and he has named him the singular reality of the modern world. This is the sort of "fact" that matters to the visionary historian. It is in itself a tragic fact, and it points toward other, not less tragic facts. One such fact, guardedly hinted at, is the woe in store for those who are partly real and human (mainly, the moderates).

The way in which Carlyle will finally judge these facts (particularly in "The Guillotine") is unobtrusively decided in the very next paragraph. "Truth of any kind breeds ever new and better truth; thus hard granite rock will crumble down into soil, under the blessed skyey influences; and cover itself with verdure, with fruitage and umbrage. But as for Falsehood . . . what can it, or what should it do but . . . decompose itself, gently or even violently, and return to the Father of it,—too probably in flames of fire" (*WTC,* II, 213). This is the bedrock of moral consciousness in *The French Revolution,* which one may dismiss as grotesquely expedient or accept as a tragic vision. For it is clearly the function of tragedy in this book to hallow "truth of any kind," making it palatable until some sweeter truth can be raised by the blessed skyey influences.

At this point in "The Bastille" the awesome difficulty of climbing completely out of the void is stressed. Hannah Arendt's analysis of the revolutionary's dilemma is apposite: "If foundation was the aim and end of revolution, then the revolutionary spirit was not merely the spirit of beginning something new but of starting something permanent and enduring. . . . From which it seems to follow that nothing threatens the very achievements of revolution more dangerously and acutely than the spirit which brought them about."[22] This is precisely what Carlyle calls "the question of questions . . . for rebellers and abolishers" (*WTC*, II, 215). In "The Bastille" this question illuminates the inevitable collapse of the moderate party that tried to lead the revolution. For the moderates were the prisoners of the freedom they celebrated. Carlyle carefully builds up the tensions that began to debilitate the philosophical seekers of freedom, once they called revolution to their assistance. They became figures in the dramatic dialectical dance.

> The Revolution is finished, then? Mayor Bailly and all respectable friends of Freedom would fain think so . . . ? Which last, however, is precisely the doubtful thing, or even the not doubtful. Unhappy Friends of Freedom; consolidating a Revolution! They must sit at work there, their pavilion spread on very Chaos; between two hostile worlds, the Upper Court-world, the nether Sansculottic one; and beaten on by both, toil, painfully, perilously, —doing, in sad literal earnest, "the impossible." [*WTC*, II, 234]

"The Bastille" concludes with the insurrection of the "maenad-led" mob in early October and the retrieval of Louis from Versailles. These events show the impossibility of consolidating the revolution. The king and the people had scores to settle.

"The Constitution" summarizes the fruitless labor of rationalizing the revolution to which the friends of freedom were condemned. All the while, Carlyle reminds us, sansculottism was maturing. "Thus if the sceptre is departing from Louis, it is only that, in other forms, other sceptres, were it even pike-sceptres, may bear sway" (*WTC*, III, 2). No one yet takes the sansculottes seriously, except Mirabeau, who begins "to discern clearly whither all this is tending." The passive point of view is that of the moderate patriots who believe the Constitution will march—

_____

22. *On Revolution*, 2d ed. (1965; rpt. Harmondsworth: Penguin Books, 1973), p. 232.

once it gets legs to stand on. The active point of view, however, is the visionary's who knows that "dark is the way of the Eternal as mirrored in this world of Time: God's way is in the sea, and his path in the great deep" (*WTC*, III, 5, 6).[23]

So the National Assembly plays at making miracles while Louis commences his forty-one months of ever increasing danger in the Tuileries and the sansculottes grow from kittens into tigers. The miracle sought by the National Assembly would have been wrought "successfully, had there been any heaven-scaling Prometheus among them; not successfully, since there was none" (*WTC*, III, 5). The problems are massive. A civil constitution for the clergy must be worked out, the provinces of France must be united, royalists must be watched, traitors arrested, food found, and the angry kings of Europe kept in their place. "Such things has an august National Assembly to hear of, as it goes on regenerating France. Sad and stern: but what remedy"? As always, the remedy is Hope. "O blessed Hope, sole boon of man: whereby, on his strait prisonwalls, are painted beautiful far-stretching landscapes; and into the night of very Death is shed holiest dawn" (*WTC*, III, 12, 34).

Carlyle, at this point, drops even the narrowest account of the political maneuvering and debate in Paris, and grandly mines a once familiar political vocabulary for its special metaphorical meanings. Whole chapters are developed around such terms as "symbolic representation" and "federation" as Carlyle suggests the profound social and spiritual implications of what the world stares at in perplexity. These implications plainly resolve themselves into a single significance: the enormity of attempting to replace the religious *Thou shalt* with the secular *I will*. This is a leap toward anarchy made in the guise of government. "With noise

23. There is a much more rigorous treatment of Carlyle's handling of point of view in H. M. Leicester, Jr., "The Dialectic of Romantic Historiography: Prospect and Retrospect in 'The French Revolution,'" *Victorian Studies*, 15 (1971), 5–17.

and glare, or noiselessly and unnoted, a whole Old System of things is vanishing piecemeal: the morrow thou shalt look, and it is not" (*WTC,* III, 106-7).

As the relative ineffectuality of the unvisionary legislators becomes apparent, the strength of the clubs grows. Jacobins, Cordeliers, and Feuillants breed and multiply. The clubs are actually cells shaping a new organic structure to replace the old one that has vanished and the theoretical one that arrived stillborn. Although there are many clubs, only one carries the right genetic code. "All clubs . . . fail, one after another. . . . Jacobinism alone has gone down to the deep subterranean lake of waters" (*WTC,* III, 111).

By the end of 1790 France had reached a state of "clangour and clamour, debate, repentance,—evaporation. Things ripen towards downright incompatibility" (*WTC,* III, 115). Only one man could have saved France from the agony of inconclusiveness. But Mirabeau died in the spring of 1791. From the beginning, Mirabeau is made a hero. Carlyle gives little space in *The French Revolution* to Mirabeau's bizarre career prior to 1789, and, although he alludes to his "questionable" nature on several occasions, we are given few details of his disreputable background. He is introduced mysteriously: "Count Mirabeau, who has got his matrimonial and other Lawsuits huddled up, better or worse; and works now in the dimmest element in Berlin . . . scents or descries richer quarry from afar. He, like an eagle or vulture, or mixture of both, preens his wings for flight homewards" (*WTC,* II, 70).

But Mirabeau found that the nobles would not have him as one of theirs, and so he "stalks forth into the third Estate." In order to ingratiate himself with his prospective constituency (at least as rumor would have it), he opened a cloth shop in Marseilles, and "became a furnishing tailor." Carlyle remarks that "even the fable that he did so, is to us always among the pleasant memorabilities of this era" (*WTC,* II, 125).

Carlyle 223

Once established, Mirabeau is no longer eagle or vulture: Carlyle begins to see him as the Lion. It is occasionally assumed that Carlyle made so much of Mirabeau only because there was no other great man to admire.[24] There is no question that he is less than a perfect hero for Carlyle, but that Carlyle genuinely esteemed him is clear both from the history and from passages in his other works. In the "Six Lectures on Revolutions in Modern Europe" (1839, unpublished but reported in *The Examiner*), Carlyle was emphatic in his estimate:

> The "strongest man" of the eighteenth century was Mirabeau, "a very lion for strength,—unsubdueable—who could not be beaten down by difficulty or disaster, but would always rise again: *an instinctive man*,—better than a premeditative; your professional benefactor of mankind being always a questionable person." Mirabeau would have been the Cromwell of the French Revolution, had he lived. "A gigantic heathen was he, who had swallowed all formulas; a man whom we must not love, whom we cannot hate, and can only lament over, and wonder at."[25]

This is the Mirabeau who commands Carlyle's allegiance in *The French Revolution*, the Mirabeau who says, "The National Assembly? *C'est moi.*"

Carlyle sees Mirabeau's death as climactic because without him France could not easily escape from the labyrinth of its own making. The alternatives facing it were "slow-pining chronic dissolution and new organisation; or a swift decisive one; the agonies spread over years, or concentrated into an hour. With a Mirabeau for Minister of Governor, the latter had been the choice; with no Mirabeau for Governor, it will naturally be the former" (*WTC*, III, 79). Mirabeau was composed of a rare union, "the glorious

24. This is the view of Alfred Cobban in *Aspects of the French Revolution* (1968; rpt. London: Paladin, 1971), p. 245, and it is shared by B. H. Lehman, *Carlyle's Theory of the Hero* (Durham, N.C.: Duke University Press, 1928).
25. R. H. Shepherd, ed., *Memoirs of the Life and Writings of Thomas Carlyle* (London: W. H. Allen, 1881), I, 210.

faculty of self-help" combined miraculously with "the glorious natural gift of *fellowship.*" This makes him "a born king of men. . . . A man not with *logic-spectacles*; but with an *eye*" (*WTC,* II, 140). As the miasma of constitution making spreads over France, Mirabeau tries to effect a compromise with Louis (for which he will later be vilified) and to reconcile all of the conflicting parties by the force of his indomitable will. Carlyle makes a brilliant portrait of Mirabeau commanding France to stand back from the abyss.

> What can murmurs and clamours, from Left or from Right, do to this man; like Teneriffe or Atlas unremoved? With clear thought; with strong bass voice, though at first low, uncertain, he claims audience, sways the storm of men: anon the sound of him waxes, softens: he rises into far-sounding melody of strength, triumphant, which subdues all hearts; his rude seamed face, desolate, fire-scathed, becomes fire-lit, and radiates: once again men feel, in these beggarly ages, what is the potency and omnipotency of man's word on the souls of men. "I will triumph, or be torn in fragments," he was once heard to say. "Silence," he cries now, in strong word of command, in imperial consciousness of strength, "Silence the thirty voices, *Silence aux trente voix!*"—and Robespierre and the Thirty Voices die into mutterings; and the Law is once more as Mirabeau would have it. [*WTC,* III, 131]

And yet it is ordained that as France "waxes ever more acrid, feversick: towards the final outburst of dissolution and delirium," Mirabeau is enfeebled by disease. The most significant aspect of Carlyle's treatment of Mirabeau is revealed in his portrait of the Lion's final days. We have seen that Carlyle put the moderate friends of freedom in a blind alley between court and mob, where they could, pathetically, do nothing. Mirabeau comes to be the Atlas, or the almost "heaven-scaling Prometheus," who could enter this symbolic space and break the politics of polarization. Death, however, overtakes him. Carlyle replaces the pathos of impossibility with the tragedy of defeated possibility.

To us, endeavouring to cast his horoscope, it of course remains doubly vague. There is one Herculean Man; in internecine duel with him, there is Monster after Monster. Emigrant Noblesse return, sword on thigh, vaunting of their Loyalty never sullied; descending from the air, like Harpy-swarms with ferocity, with obscene greed. Earthward there is the Typhon of Anarchy, Political, Religious; sprawling hundred-headed, say with Twenty-five million heads; wide as the area of France; fierce as Frenzy; strong in very Hunger. [*WTC,* III, 137]

Whatever the future might have been, the terrible fact is that Mirabeau's strength is at last exhausted, and "King Mirabeau is now the lost King":

Be it that his falls and follies are manifold,—as himself often lamented even with tears. Alas, is not the Life of every such man already a poetic Tragedy . . . full of the elements of Pity and Fear? This brother man, if not Epic for us, is Tragic; if not great, is large. . . . Here then the wild Gabriel Honoré drops from the tissue of our History; not without a tragic farewell. [*WTC,* III, 147]

Mirabeau's death constitutes the major tragedy of *The French Revolution.* His immense significance is that he represented a "Reality" in his personal being. Translated into more conventional terms, this means that Mirabeau was an insightful man, that he came to the truth of things by a process of creative thought. His attributes made him that specially honored figure in Carlyle: a tailor. There is a fundamentally important point here. A certain kind of intellectual cultivation, learned in the established modes of civilized life, and known to us as enlightenment, had proclaimed itself a power, but shown itself to be effete. It could not make the constitution march because, at bottom, its habits of thought had grown mechanistic. Mirabeau transcended the mechanistic; he thought symbolically. However, he did not push so far beyond the modes of civilized life as to become a person separated from personality. He did not dwell in caverns measureless to man. Before Mirabeau, thought was pale. After Mirabeau, thought became demonic and its own scourge. Some of the later leaders of the revolution, according to Carlyle's pregnant terms, had personality and meant something real. But Mirabeau was different even from these. As Carlyle put it in his 1837 essay, Mirabeau had a genius equal to Napoleon's, "*but a much humaner genius, almost a poetic one*" (*WTC*, XXVIII, 412; italics added). This quality is brought forth in *The French Revolution* as Mirabeau's capacity for "fellowship." Unlike the philosophes, his genius was dynamic. Unlike the sansculottes, he was not estranged from the moral tradition of civility.

This is why "one can say that, had Mirabeau lived, the History of France and of the World had been different" (*WTC*, III, 138). Carlyle's account uses every suggestive detail he can find to establish the idea that, given time to do his work, Mirabeau might have turned from monolithic political action and secured the New Era on the basis of new spiritual insight. With Mirabeau gone, personality and mind disappear, and the impersonal force of pre-rational Nature, working through the sansculottes, arises in a maelstrom of murder.

The second half of "The Constitution" traces the total disintegration of the constitutionalist movement. The death of the real king, Mirabeau, persuades the false king, Louis, to flee. After his capture at Varennes an empty constitution is accepted. The National Assembly gives way to the Legislative Assembly, and then, while France fights off the First Coalition, the empty constitution expires. The cataclysm of August 10 (1792) ends with the emergence of the Paris Commune and the Jacobin clubs as the effective source of government in France. The way is open for the September Massacres. As Carlyle points out, the history of the Legislative Assembly had been "a series of sputters and quarrels; true desire to do [its] function, fatal impossibility to do it" (*WTC*, III, 209). The testing of possibilities is over; there remains no way out of the labyrinth except through the self-consummation of anarchy. "So, then, the Constitution is over? Forever and a day! Gone is that wonder of the Universe; First biennial Parliament, water-logged, waits only till the Convention come; and then will sink to endless depths. One can guess the silent rage of Old-Constituents, Constitution-builders, extinct Feuillants, men who thought the Constitution would march" (*WTC,* III, 307). Appropriately, Carlyle concludes "The Constitution" with the flight of Lafayette to Holland. The Hero of Two Worlds, the paragon of reason and moderation, hurries into exile on his gleaming white horse as the black demons of the Terror take their seats.

"The Guillotine" opens with the deadly work of the Septemberers. They are distinguished by their "lucency" (Scott would have said lunacy). But theirs is "lucency of the Nether-fire sort; very different from that of our Bastille Heroes, who shone, disputable by no Friend of Freedom, as in Heavenly light-radiance: to such phasis of the business have we advanced since then" (*WTC,* IV, 41). In their lucency, a truth is finally perceived: "The Nation is for the present, figuratively speaking, *naked:* it has no rule or vesture; but is naked,—a Sansculottic nation" (*WTC,* IV, 67). "The Guillotine" is written in defense of nakedness and the rights of reality, even if it must be the reality of the netherworld. This section may be read as standing in every point opposed to Camus's criticism of revolution. It accepts, as the passage just quoted shows, the betrayal of the original spirit of rebellion; it refuses to acknowledge a limit to murder; and it implicitly takes comfort in the fact that revolution ends by reinforcing the power of the state (*TR,* p. 177). "As no external force, Royal or other, now remains which could control this Movement, the Movement . . . must work and welter, not as a Regularity but as a Chaos; destructive and self-destructive; always till something that *has* order arise . . . Which something . . . will not be a Formula . . . but a Reality, probably with a sword in its hand" (*WTC,* IV, 114–15).

The tragic experience of "The Guillotine" is a corollary of its moral paradoxes. Freedom *from* revolution must now be the end and aim of the revolutionaries. The guillotining of Prometheus becomes an act of liberation. The revolution must learn to eat its children. Carlyle accepts these paradoxes and contradictions as adjuncts of the eternal mystery that reconciles freedom and necessity. Under the guidance of that mystery, the visionary historian calmly comprehends what the world gapes at in horror. Between the mystery and the horror Carlyle interposes his sense of tragedy, his sense that men were only carrying out "one of the sorrowfullest tasks poor Humanity has" (*WTC,* IV, 91).

This is by no means to suggest that "The Guillotine" is a lament. Carlyle continually reminds us that while we may shriek, the sansculottes acted. Nevertheless, Carlyle appeals to the tragic spirit as a way of mitigating the horror that he says we must condone:

> For a man, once committed headlong to republican or any other Transcendentalism . . . becomes as it were enveloped in an ambient atmosphere of Transcendentalism and Delirium; *his individual self is lost in something that is not himself.* . . . He, the hapless incarnated Fanaticism, goes his road; no man can help him, he himself least of all. *It is a wonderful, tragical predicament;*—such as human language, unused to deal with these things, being contrived for the uses of common life, struggles to shadow out in figures. [*WTC,* IV, 121–22; italics added]

Tragic experience of this kind is, to say the least, a very long way from the experience of a Mirabeau or the experience of any of Carlyle's messengers of truth in the age of shams. It is the tragedy of historical determinism that sanctions the loss of personal conscience in the interests of a renovated universe. It resolves for Carlyle the moral problem posed by Camus: "Revolution is an attempt to conquer a new existence, by action that recognizes no moral strictures. That is why it is condemned to live only for history and in a reign of terror" (*TR,* p. 250). By converting the reign of terror into a tragedy that preempts the moral will, Carlyle legitimizes its violence and exculpates its cosmic indifference to "common life."

In effect, the visionary historian has discovered the tragedy of transcendental despair, and in doing so has found an exit from hell. This is what "The Guillotine" tries to "shadow out in figures." Ordinary human speech and reason are incapable of identifying the "grand product of Nature" that the revolution has at last made manifest. "Now surely not realisation, of Christianity or of aught earthly, do we discern in this Reign of Terror, in this French Revolution of which it is the consummating." For the grand product of Nature comes not to "range itself under old recorded Laws of Nature at all, but to disclose new ones." There has been an oath taken that hypocrisies and lies shall perish, and perish they must. This is the first of the new laws and the foundation of all others. The men of the revolution must remain dedicated to their oath or else no rehabilitation of the universe will take place.

> The fulfillment of this Oath; that is to say, the black desperate battle of Men against their whole Condition and Environment,—a battle, alas, withal against the Sin and Darkness that was in themselves as in others: this is the Reign of Terror. Transcendental despair was the purport of it, though not consciously so. False hopes, of Fraternity, Political Millennium, and what not, we have always seen: but the unseen heart of the whole, the transcendental despair, was not false; neither has it been of no effect. Despair, pushed far enough, completes the circle, so to speak; and becomes a kind of genuine productive hope again. [*WTC*, IV, 204–5]

In the end, then, extremism, if not a virtue, is at least its own reward. Hope springs from the infernal. This is a climax beyond the drama of tragic possibilities. At a point outside the purview of conventional morality, the search for new order, consistently inspired by hope, abruptly ends, and is replaced by the dictatorship of despair. Transcendental despair is in the nature of an absolute, a compelling, imperious command to order. For Carlyle, a whiff of grapeshot clears the head. "The Revolution, then, is verily devouring its own children? All Anarchy, by the nature of it, is not only destructive but self-destructive" (*WTC*, IV, 254).

The difference between *The French Revolution* and *Sartor Resartus* is that *The French Revolution* counts heavily, even programmatically, on the negative content of revolution. Both books declare that ash will fertilize. But in *Sartor*, this doctrine is leavened by the visionary's very reluctance to address the political world, by his extensive exploration of "natural supernaturalism," and, perhaps, most of all, by his use of the comic vision to distance himself from the certainty of his postulates. *The French Revolution*, while it firmly places political action in a secondary and intermediary role, relies on the self-consummation of democratic politics as the indispensable prelude to the rebirth of spiritual purpose in the Western world. Unnatural supernaturalism is its tautological gospel. Transcendental despair, figured as a tragic action, is its answer to two centuries of constitution writers who had tried to define the means by which the state might keep itself intact while giving some scope to the freedom of the individual. What the law fails to control, a dose of nihilism will.

And yet *The French Revolution* is not a brutal book. As a work of art it is surely the equal of *Sartor Resartus*, though it has until recently been extravagantly neglected. What commends *The French Revolution* to us is not its desperate remedies, but its brilliantly particularized study of man in the throes of incomprehensible struggle. Several times I have contrasted Carlyle and Camus. They may also be compared. In his essay "Create Dangerously" Camus writes: "The prophet, whether religious or political, can judge absolutely and, as is known, is not chary of doing so. But the artist cannot . . . The aim of art . . . is not to legislate or reign supreme, but rather to understand first of all . . . No work of genius has ever been based on hatred and contempt. This is why the artist . . . absolves instead of condemning. Instead of being a judge, he is a justifier. He is the perpetual advocate of the living creature, because it is alive."[26] In *The French Revolution*, Carlyle the prophet judges absolutely, but Carlyle the artist advocates the living creature. Because his art is so deeply informed by the phenomenon of revolution and because he committed himself so decisively to a polemical purpose, prophecy and art cannot, in Carlyle, be easily separated. But they can be so far separated, in *The French Revolution*, as to make it perfectly obvious that there is a Carlyle whose heart is on the side of light, not lightning.

THE LIMITS OF DESPAIR: ON HEROES AND HERO-WORSHIP

On Heroes and Hero-Worship is usually associated with Carlyle's densely political works: *Chartism, Past and Present,* "Dr. Francia," the 1848 letters on Ireland, "Occasional Discourse on the Nigger Question," *Latter-Day Pamphlets*, and "Shooting Niagara." Authoritarianism is the common denominator of these works. But *Heroes* is really a book about revolution. Though it does raise the question of how men should be ruled, its principal political object is to revoke the dictatorship of despair. It does so by finding in the modern hero a figure who, while quite imperfect and quite without absolute powers, can rescue man from the Moloch of revolutionary nihilism.

The place of *Heroes* among Carlyle's works on revolution is suggested by several relevant dates. *The French Revolution* was published in 1837. Two years later, in April 1839, Carlyle gave his "Six Lectures on Revolutions in Modern Europe." The lectures on heroes and hero worship were offered the next spring and were published a year later in the form we now have them.

---

26. *Resistance, Rebellion, and Death*, trans. Justin O'Brien (1960; rpt. New York: Modern Library, 1963), p. 204.

This sequence draws *Heroes* into the compass of Carlyle's work in the thirties. Some of the early foreshadowings of the main idea also suggest that the hero is preeminently an eidolon conjured up by Carlyle's meditation on the problem of revolution. "The Death of Goethe" (1832) exclaims against the ultimate inefficacy of revolutions: "these were but spasmodic convulsions of the death-sick time. . . . The real new era was when a Wise Man came into the world" (*WTC*, XXVII, 379). *Sartor Resartus* defines hero worship as "the corner-stone of living rock, whereon all Politics for the remotest time may stand" (*WTC*, I, 200). Finally, in both *The French Revolution* and the 1837 essay on Mirabeau, Carlyle attributes to Mirabeau the "faculty of king," which the *sine qua non* of the hero. Mirabeau is, in fact, the first fully drawn Carlylean hero.

The form of *Heroes* is strictly governed by its relation to the phenomenon of revolution. The whole series of lectures leads up to "The Hero as King," which is subtitled "Modern Revolutionism." This lecture presents the hero in his most basic form. And, though Carlyle gives the hero diverse historical guises, there is a broader division in the book than the six chapters would indicate. The heroes represent, by emphatic contrast, either politically stable or revolutionary ages.[27] The first three types of hero, in their roles of divinity, prophet, and poet, belong to a nearly inconceivable expanse of history reaching from primitive times to the Renaissance. The remaining three are confined to the rebellious epoch that began with the Reformation. The French Revolution itself is "properly the third and final act of Protestantism" (*WTC*, V, 237). Carlyle seems to take this division of the six heroes into two basic types as a natural dichotomy:

27. John Lindberg, "The Decadence of Style: Symbolic Structure in Carlyle's Later Prose," *Studies in Scottish Literature*, 1 (1964), 183–95, discusses the book's movement "from feudalism to revolution," which is not quite accurate; Robert A. Donovan, "Carlyle and the Climate of Hero-Worship," *UTQ*, 42 (1973), 136, notes the "destructive or revolutionary role of the hero."

Thus, then, as we have seen Great Men, in various situations, building-up Religions, heroic Forms of human Existence in this world, Theories of Life worthy to be sung by a Dante, Practices of Life by a Shakspeare,—we are now to see the reverse process; which also is necessary, which also may be carried-on in the Heroic manner. . . . The mild shining of the Poet's light has to give place to the fierce lightning of the Reformer. . . . Doubtless it were finer, could we go along always in the way of *music* . . . Or failing this . . . how good it were could we get . . . *peaceable* Priests, reforming from day to day . . . But it is not so; even this latter has not yet been realised. Alas, the battling Reformer too is, from time to time, a needful and inevitable phenomenon. [*WTC*, V, 116–17][28]

There is throughout Carlyle a fairly consistent use of reversal as a principle of unification (e.g., in his notion that comedy is "inverse sublimity"). *Heroes* finds its essential organization in the reversed "heroisms" that dialectically connect religion and revolution. The hero in religious ages reveals that "a thousandfold hidden beauty and divineness dwells in all Nature" (*WTC*, V, 111). The hero in revolutionary ages reminds us that we live in a fallen world. This rather stark (and reductive) contrast, not a full-blown philosophy of history, is at the thematic center of *Heroes and Hero-Worship*. *Heroes* is a tract for revolutionary times.

The modern hero's quasi-mystical function in limiting chaos is emphasized at the outset. Carlyle regards hero worship in the way that Blake regarded the material creation: as a merciful interposition that halts the fall of man.

In times of unbelief, which soon have to become times of revolution, much down-rushing, sorrowful decay and ruin is visible to everybody. For myself, in these days, I seem to see in this indestructibility of Hero-worship the everlasting adamant lower than

28. This passage is from the beginning of Carlyle's discussion of "The Hero as Priest," and he is, of course, thinking mainly of the Priest as Reformer. But the language of the whole discussion clearly divides *all* the remaining types of the hero from the early religious world and places them in an epoch of continual rebellion that began in the sixteenth century.

which the confused wreck of ordinary things cannot fall. The confused wreck of things crumbling and even crashing and tumbling all round us in these revolutionary ages, will get down so far; *no* farther. It is an eternal corner-stone, from which they can begin to build themselves up again. That man, in some sense or other worships Heroes; that we all of us reverence and must ever reverence Great Men: this is, to me, the living rock amid all rushings-down whatsoever;—the one fixed point in modern revolutionary history, otherwise as if bottomless and shoreless. [*WTC*, V, 15]

But though these remarks would seem to equip society with an invincible protector against tragic fate, the modern hero himself is most often a tragic figure. The specific action that halts chaos is the loyalty ("hero-worship") that the confused multitude feels for the charismatic man. The hero, however, has no personal immunity. Most often, in fact, he is not only enmeshed in the revolutionary process, he is actually a perpetrator of revolution. Unlike the heroes of religious ages, the latter-day heroes do not serve to freshen the faith of man. They work amid ruins in an effort to make a new faith possible.

Such a view puts the hero in an equivocal position that Carlyle instinctively characterizes as tragic. The disparity between what the modern hero achieves for his world and what happens in his own life can be enormous. This disparity throws into relief the essential difference between *Heroes* and *The French Revolution*. Prophecy in *The French Revolution* proclaims that chaos will be limited by homeostasis: blind self-preservation will exert its force. In *Heroes*, Carlyle reclaims the creativity of the self. Personality reenters the equation in resistance to the notion that we are to be saved by transcendental despair. Indeed, we are to be saved neither by demons nor by angels. Relief comes in the form of a man who concentrates in his own being many of the highest attributes of human nature. It is true that Carlyle festoons the hero with semidivine powers, and it is also true that his allegiance to the hero often betrays a contempt for the unenlightened masses.

The main point, however, remains: the heroes are men, not Molochs. In the tragic acts of their lives, they express their compassion; they acknowledge the humanity of other men.

Perhaps the hero as man of letters (Dr. Johnson, Rousseau, and Burns) most significantly illustrates Carlyle's preeminent interest in the human face of the hero. The eighteenth-century men of letters are hardly demigods. On the contrary, they are distinguished by nothing so much as by their vulnerability and mortality. They lived, Carlyle says, in an age of spiritual paralysis, and could not unfold themselves into clearness. "It is . . . the *Tombs* of three Literary Heroes that I have to show you" (*WTC*, V, 158).

The hero as man of letters is a sort of unacknowledged legislator waiting to serve the European world by guiding it through the upheavals of history. "Try these men: they are of all others the best worth trying." Carlyle argues that "there is no kind of government, constitution, revolution," or other social apparatus so promising as that which would place the man of intellect at the top of affairs: "this is the aim of all constitutions and revolutions, if they have any aim" (*WTC*, V, 169). The implication here is that when the modern world has tired of its chaos and spiritual paralysis, it may turn to the man of letters for Promethean relief. In other words, Carlyle substitutes the reign of letters for the reign of terror, and in doing so he reanimates the latent content of revolution as a potential field of discovery for the men of his own time. Meanwhile, the actual experience of the man of letters (Carlyle himself being the templet) is obnoxious. "He wanders like a wild Ishmaelite, in a world of which he is as the spiritual light" (*WTC*, V, 159).[29]

The abstract potential of the man of letters and his actual situation are kept distinct from one another by the device of historical

29. See David J. DeLaura, "Ishmael as Prophet: *Heroes and Hero-Worship* and the Self-Expressive Basis of Carlyle's Art," *Texas Studies in Literature and Language*, 11 (1969), 705–32. DeLaura sees the fundamental unity of the book as given in the ways in which the various heroes become occasions for

plotting. Carlyle uses the eighteenth century as a dark age, a period when "the very possibility of Heroism had been, as it were, formally abnegated in the minds of all" (*WTC,* V, 170). This perspective allows him to see an elevated and efficacious function for the man of letters in the later, nineteenth-century stage of modernity when the world is thirsting for renewal. Even so, Carlyle's preoccupation is with the estrangement of the man of letters. Though the other modern heroes are also tragic figures, the heroism of the man of letters is almost *exclusively* a matter of his tragic being. All through the essay we see this implication as the raw, untransmuted datum on which Carlyle founds his sense of the writer's fate in the modern world. It is as though he had no real confidence that the man of letters would ever be acknowledged, revolution or no, and he mourns the world's relentless derogation of its willing and able benefactors.

Samuel Johnson becomes the "great mournful Johnson [who] guided his difficult confused existence wisely." Rousseau is a "most pregnant spectacle. Banished into Paris garrets, in the gloomy company of his own Thoughts and Necessities . . . driven from post to pillar; fretted, exasperated till the heart of him went mad, he had grown to feel deeply that the world was not his friend" (*WTC,* V, 187). Rousseau could only *misguide* men. Finally, Burns had to labor under every disadvantage to make his voice known. But, "spite of his tragical history, he is not a mourning man" (*WTC,* V, 190). Startlingly, he resembles Mirabeau. "Burns too could have governed, debated in National Assemblies." The world, however, really had no use for Burns. "The Life of Burns is what we may call a great tragic sincerity" (*WTC,* V, 191–92). These figures are all made tragic by the revolution's dormant stage, which, in various ways, blocked their growth.

Carlyle's exploration of his own identity. This leads to a discussion of Carlyle's "various modes of self-presentation," from which I have profited a great deal. The simpler unity of *Heroes* that I have argued for I would apply only to the manifest structure of the book.

The priest-heroes (Luther and Knox) are in some respects even more equivocal figures than the men of letters. Basically peace-loving, they are temperamentally inclined to live out of the world in serene contemplation of God's holiness. Both priest-heroes, however, are compelled to rise up against the sham that the church made of man's religious life. The European world asked Luther: "Am I to sink ever lower into falsehood, stagnant putrescence, loathsome accursed death"? Luther could not "desert us," even though great wars, contentions, and disunion followed out of his Reformation. But Carlyle, in one of the book's most telling statements, maintains that "the controversy did not get to fighting so long as [Luther] was there. To me it is proof of his greatness in all senses, this fact. How seldom do we find a man that has stirred-up some vast commotion, who does not himself perish, swept-away in it. Such is the usual course of revolutionists" (*WTC,* V, 135–38). To us the point is that Luther has the hero's power of checking the violence of revolution. But, again, in his personal life tragedy presides. "In the eyes especially there is a wild silent sorrow; an unnameable melancholy, the element of all gentle and fine affections; giving to the rest the true stamp of nobleness. Laughter was in this Luther, as we said; but tears also were there. Tears also were appointed him; tears and hard toil. The basis of his life was Sadness, Earnestness" (*WTC,* V, 142).

Knox is similarly presented as a man who both took upon himself the burden of revolution and, at the same time, provided the world with an escape from interminable disorder. "Tumult was not his element; it was the tragic feature of his life that he was forced to dwell so much in that" (*WTC,* V, 150). Out of the tumult, however, he brought "a believing Nation." It was not "a smooth business; but it was welcome surely, and cheap at any price." Carlyle, proleptically, credits Knox with sparing Britain the horror of social revolution. The real faith that he brought to the nation stabilized its life and thus defanged its later political turmoil. "How many earnest rugged Cromwells, Knoxes, poor

Peasant Covenanters, wrestling, battling for very life, in rough
miry places, have to struggle, and suffer, and fall, greatly cen-
sured, *bemired*,—before a beautiful Revolution of Eighty-eight
can step-over them in official pumps and silk-stockings, with universal three-times-three" (*WTC,* V, 146).

The reference to Cromwell brings us to the subject of the final
lecture: the hero as king. The focus for the essay is "modern revolutionism," the fully realized form of the phenomenon that has
dominated modern history and that has been the central circumstance shaping the heroisms of both priest and man of letters. The
hero as king is the consummate form of the heroic type. "The
Commander over Men; he to whose will our wills are to be subordinated, and loyally surrender themselves, and find their welfare in doing so, may be reckoned the most important of Great
Men. He is practically the summary for us of *all* the various figures of Heroism" (*WTC,* V, 196). However, the organization of
On Heroes and Hero-Worship, as well as the other lectures on heroes since the Renaissance, has notified us not to expect what this
statement might otherwise suggest, that Carlyle's examples will
illustrate lives of unequivocally triumphant personal endeavor. By
the essay's fourth paragraph, we are already reminded that "ideals
can never be completely embodied in practice. Ideals must ever lie
a very great way off; and we will right thankfully content ourselves with any not intolerable approximation thereto" (*WTC,*
V, 197). This warning is critical since Carlyle, rather than creating a historical superman in "The Hero as King," is preparing his
analysis of "the rugged outcast," Oliver Cromwell, his largest
and most significant tragic figure.

Cromwell appears in tandem with Napoleon, and though they
would therefore seem to be spiritual kin, Carlyle is fundamentally
divided in his attitude toward them. The division of attitude is itself a manifestation of the role of tragedy in Carlyle's treatment of
revolution. Cromwell is a sainted hero for Carlyle, Napoleon a
man whom Carlyle must struggle to admire. Cromwell searches

painfully for the new order that will return man to his true self; Napoleon produces a new order by administrative fiat. Cromwell remains within the complex structure of Carlyle's meditation on the problem of revolution; Napoleon is simply a commander over men, a genius of the force whose spirit dominates the egregious *Latter-Day Pamphlets.* Cromwell alone appreciates the tragic nature of revolution; he alone has the capacity to sympathize with those who wrestle with its terrible mysteries. He is appointed to bring an end to nightmare, while Napoleon simply brings an end to political disorganization. Napoleon becomes a vain and ambitious man, pitifully grounded at St. Helena and offended that the world did not wish to become his pedestal (*WTC,* V, 243). Cromwell, on the other hand, laments the sad task that has been appointed to him, and he wishes nothing for himself. Carlyle could not refuse to admire Napoleon if only because Napoleon appealed to his developing taste for men who could efficiently deal with public chaos. But Napoleon only ruled; he did not understand. Cromwell ruled and understood. The sign of his understanding is his tragic vision, a quality Carlyle never attributes to Napoleon.

In a letter of 1840 to Thomas Erskine, Carlyle wrote that he had "got lately . . . to fancy that I see in Cromwell one of the greatest tragic souls we have ever had in this kindred of ours."[30] "The Hero as King" and, later, *Oliver Cromwell's Letters and Speeches* (1845) are developments of this perspective. At the time Carlyle was writing, Cromwell was almost universally regarded as a fanatic and opportunist. Carlyle's effort was "to pluck-up the great History of Oliver . . . like drowned Honour by the locks" (*WTC,* VIII, 2) and ascertain Cromwell's continuing significance for Englishmen. He intended, moreover, to make Cromwell not just palatable, but appealing. The first of these purposes Carlyle pursues by showing that Cromwell comprehended the

---

30. Froude, *Thomas Carlyle: Life in London,* I, 169.

logos of revolution, which the "vulpine" nature of modern skepticism has completely distorted. Skepticism, by growing hypercritical in its revolt against shams, has ended in intellectual and moral paralysis. "Of all dupes," Carlyle says in "The Hero as King," there is none "so fatally situated as he who lives in undue terror of being duped" (*WTC,* V, 216). Cromwell, on the other hand, accepted the burden of revolution without allowing it to deprive him of his sense of spiritual purpose. The core of his understanding is his firm belief that revolution "is but the *transition* from false to true. Considered as the whole truth, it is false altogether" (*WTC,* V, 203). But Cromwell's understanding is not conveyed to us by a simple polemic. Instead, Carlyle surrounds Cromwell with a tragic aura that functions complexly to dramatize "the deeper insight he had" (*WTC,* V, 220). Intrinsically, tragedy represents in Cromwell "a weight of meaning, a terror and a splendour as of Heaven itself" (*WTC,* V, 223) which he was fated to realize within the context of revolutionary chaos. Extrinsically, it awakens for Carlyle's own world a current of feeling and responsiveness long since frozen by the tradition of "vulpine" intellect. What Carlyle essentially means by the "worship" we owe Cromwell is not "worship" at all, but tragic sympathy. The combined effect of these functions creates the fullest development of what *Heroes* actually seeks: a reversal of the transcendental despair inflicted on men by modern revolution.

Carlyle takes the occasion of this lecture to restate what was for him the most grievous of tragic possibilities:

> May we not say . . . while so many of our late Heroes have worked rather as revolutionary men, that nevertheless every Great Man, every genuine man, is by the nature of him a son of Order, not of Disorder? It is a tragical position for a true man to work in revolutions. He seems an anarchist; and indeed a painful element of anarchy does encumber him at every step,—him to whose soul anarchy is hostile, hateful . . . We are all born enemies of Disorder: it is tragical for us all to be concerned in image-

breaking and down-pulling; for the Great Man . . . it is doubly
tragical. [*WTC,* V, 203–4]

How little this applies to Napoleon is apparent in almost everything Carlyle says about him (and he spends less than one-fifth of
the lecture on Napoleon). "I find in him no such *sincerity* as in
Cromwell; only a far inferior sort" (*WTC,* V, 237). Napoleon
did have a certain ineradicable feeling for reality, and from this he
derived the power to rule. But, in Carlyle's eyes, he became an
apostate "from his old faith in Facts" (*WTC,* V, 241).

The "worship" we may owe such a man is implicitly of a very
narrow kind. Cromwell, on the other hand, "stood bare, not
cased in euphemistic coat-of-mail; he grappled like a giant, face to
face, with the naked truth of things! That, after all, is the sort of
man for one" (*WTC,* V, 209). This sense of personal attraction is
an effect of Cromwell's human regard. "Consider him. An outer
hell of chaotic confusion . . . yet a clear determinate man's-
energy working in the heart of that." What we are asked to appreciate in Cromwell (and this is true of all Carlyle's essentially
tragic figures) is "the depth and tenderness of his wild affections:
the quantity of *sympathy* he had with things" (*WTC,* V, 217).
Mirabeau, as we have already seen, resembles Cromwell.[31]

Cromwell is the true man working in revolution, committing
great reserves of his energy and authority to a process of destruction, but all the while faithfully advancing the spiritual catharsis
that is the revolution's hidden purpose. His "glorious
possibility" is sacrificed to the selfless object that inspires him,
and by virtue of this tragic effort, the revolution retained amid its
weltering ruins the stamp of a worthy purpose. "Poor Cromwell,
—great Cromwell! The inarticulate Prophet . . . struggling to
utter himself, with his savage depth . . . among the elegant Eu-
phemisms, dainty little Falklands, didactic Chillingworths, diplo-
matic Clarendons" on the one side, and the "dreadfully dull," if

31. Shepherd, ed., *Memoirs,* I, 210.

honorable, Hampdens, Eliots, and Pyms on the other (*WTC,* V, 209, 217). All through Carlyle's analysis we can see that Cromwell's greater wisdom is *articulated for him* by the tragic spirit that accompanies and gives a somber strength to his momentous labors. "Sorrow-stricken, half-distracted; the wild element of mournful *black* enveloping him,—wide as the world. It is the character of a prophetic man; a man with his whole soul *seeing,* and struggling to see" (*WTC,* V, 217–18).

One detail tells us, perhaps, more about Cromwell's tragic significance than any other. He is out of place in the time scheme of *Heroes.* Carlyle reserves him for the lecture that, according to the book's general design, is specifically to deal with the contemporary world. It is clear that Carlyle regards Cromwell as the symbolic hero needed by the nineteenth century. And it is also clear that the historical gap between the seventeenth and nineteenth centuries is to be bridged through one's ability to appreciate how much Cromwell's sufferings reflect the sufferings of nineteenth-century man.

"Modern Revolutionism" is the term that binds Carlyle's audience to Cromwell. With the vulpine intellect souring all spiritual activity, revolution's gravest danger for men in the nineteenth century is the likelihood that it will be regarded as "the whole truth," a consummate verification of skepticism's exclusive privileges in the contemporary world. As I have suggested, the tragic emotion evoked by Cromwell becomes a source of liberation from the deadness induced by the critical mind. This is the sense in which Cromwell is Carlyle's largest example of the hero functioning to limit the catastrophe of revolution. By inspiring a deep stirring of sensibility, specifically a tragic emotion, he releases man from his moral atrophy. "Truly it is a sad thing for a people, as for a man, to fall into Skepticism, into dilettantism, insincerity; not to know a Sincerity when they see it. For this world, and for all worlds, what curse is so fatal? The heart lying dead, the eye cannot see" (*WTC,* V, 215–16). Cromwell's mission to the nineteenth century, and indeed the mission of all Carlyle's tragic heroes, is to make the believing heart feel again. In *Heroes,* this is the equivalent to an everlasting yea—though it must be an uncapitalized version, so to speak, for the later Carlyle. And it must be achieved (such are the conditions of the modern age) in and through the revolutionary process, however much that process seems devoted to the purposes of godless men.

For 150 years Cromwell had been vilified, but Carlyle turns the tradition of obloquy on itself by making it enhance Cromwell's tragic stature. The total effect of Carlyle's portrait, far from compelling mindless prostration before a demigod, is rather to create a means of identification with a true man who, obligated to perpetrate disorder, nevertheless believed "the world does exist; the world has truth in it" (*WTC,* V, 216). Cromwell thus represents a foundation for hope that can be grasped and nurtured by other true men before the only kind of hope left is that strange, subrational, and terrible discipline in which the sansculottes once tutored the world.

Later, Carlyle would amplify his account of Cromwell in his edition of the *Letters and Speeches.* This work completes his effort in *Heroes* to put Cromwell vividly before Victorian England by allowing him to become "tragically audible across the centuries" (*WTC,* VIII, 114). To deal with this work would be only to repeat what has already been said here. One passage in it, however, makes an apt summary for our discussion of Carlyle. Carlyle is speaking of Cromwell's fighting in the Puritan revolution as a "god-intoxicated" man:

> I have asked myself, If anywhere in Modern European History, or even in ancient Asiatic, there was found a man practicing this mean World's affairs with a heart more filled by the Idea of the Highest? Bathed in the Eternal Splendours,—it is so he walks our dim Earth: this man is one of the few. He is projected with a ter-

rible force out of the Eternities, and in the Times and their arenas
there is nothing that can withstand him. It is great;—to us it is
tragic; a thing that should strike us dumb!   [*WTC,* VII, 174–75]

The rhetoric of this passage catches and mingles, if we allow
for just a little overreading, a number of the themes that have
been of major concern to us. It describes, once again, the true
man in combat with false circumstances, and it suggests that
though such a man must find his glorious possibility deprived of
epic fulfillment and achievement, the magnificence of his combat
can be authenticated in the tragic mode. That the figure described
is revolutionary, and yet one still filled by the idea of the "Highest," may be taken as both consolation and catharsis. Historical
anarchy and despair have their limits, for, as Cromwell illustrates, the revolutionary event, once set in motion, need not necessarily obliterate all consciousness of the spiritual self. (The
passage continues: "My brave one, thy old noble Prophecy *is* divine . . . and shall, though in wider ways than thou supposest,
be fulfilled.")

The passage does not define the spiritual self, and this is also
characteristic of Carlyle. Once he had written *Sartor,* he would
never go so far as to say that a specifically religious culture, attached to a personal God, would arise from the ashes of revolution. He didn't believe it. He preferred to dwell on the dynamics
of revolution, its excesses and grievousness, its necessity, its pur-
gations, its counterforce in the inspired if begrimed hero, in
short, its tragic *mythos.* He did so because as long as the world remained in a revolutionary attitude, the perspective of spiritual in-
determinacy could be used pertinently and creatively to expose
the nature of historical crisis in the modern age. Tragedy gave
this position the redeeming benefits of sobriety, earnestness, and
sincerity. Indeed, for Carlyle the tragic position was really his
only alternative to "silence," which, in his usage, is an awesome
but at the same time desperate last resort by which beleaguered
man may hope to possess his being.

Finally, the same passage intones the Caesarism, or rather the Napoleonism, that more and more suited Carlyle's disposition when his capacity for sheer exasperation exceeded his capacity for the sense of tragedy. "There is nothing that can withstand him." The phrase is jolting rather than engaging. It represents the Napoleonism that comes when Carlyle retreats from the tragic imagination. His Napoleonism, in fact, became a melodramatic and disillusioned straining after the old apolitical posture of his younger years, for it incites in Carlyle the image of a world where politics disappears in the still homogeneity of one man's rule. Carlyle was easily tempted by such a tame resolution to the world's historical nightmare. But he wrote with genuine compassion and extraordinary power when, under the sway of tragedy, he could treat the political realm as a match treats a flint.

CHAPTER FIVE

Arnold: Tragic Vision and the Third Host

Matthew Arnold's provocative 1853 Preface, his lonely pride in *Merope*, and his urgent defense of the classical tradition have made it seem that he would accept as tragedy only the high, stately form that many critics associate exclusively with Greek and Shakespearean drama. The most commonly accepted characteristics of tragedy in the classical sense are that it sees a local disorder in relation to a cosmic scheme, that it dwells upon a conflict that is noble and significant, that the central figure in the conflict represents humanity in general, and that his struggle is carried out in both pride and humility, in guilt and innocence against powers that shake his world to its foundations. Arnold's 1853 Preface, based as it is on Aristotle's *Poetics*, reflects some of these ideas and would thus seem to take its place as a Victorian protest against the Romantic valorizations of tragedy that announce themselves in the works of Scott, Byron, and Carlyle. Arnold, in other words, appears to anticipate the arguments of such critics as Joseph Wood Krutch and George Steiner, who believe that the emergence of modern skepticism, the Romantic ego, the scientific habit of mind, and the democratic spirit has been deeply injurious to the Greek and Shakespearean tragic vision.[1] One might

1. George Steiner, *The Death of Tragedy* (New York: Knopf, 1961), and

even presume that Arnold differs from such critics only in his belief that the classical vision can be revived—his own failure to revive it being simply an ironic blow to the Olympian prescriptions
he hands down in the Preface.

   None of this is really true. The 1853 Preface is itself inspired by
the Romantic tradition of tragedy that we have been discussing.
It will be remembered, for example, that in the Preface Arnold
quotes Schiller's comment that "all art is dedicated to Joy"
(*CPW*, I, 2). Although he applied this remark to the idea of cathartic pleasure that readers have long associated, under Aristotle's guidance, with the effect of tragedy, there are many reasons
to think that Arnold was contemplating joy of an entirely different kind. The Preface dwells more on the Hellenic ideal than on
the nature of tragedy, and soon replaces the principle of catharsis
with an argument for the power of Greek poetry *in general* to
bring composure to the soul. This is a transformation effected by
Arnold's aesthetic temperament. William A. Madden has com-
mented suggestively on the link between Arnold's aestheticism
and his devotion to Greece: "In great poetry the terror of life as
hell was ameliorated [for Arnold] and converted into delight by
the 'disinterested' poetic power which, inspired by the Muse,
converted the spectacle of life into matter for delight by organiz-
ing experience in beautiful language. This was the consummation
towards which Arnold's poetry and criticism reached out, the
transfiguration of reality by the 'Greek spirit.' "[2] Arnold's response to Greece is the response of Goethe, a response deriving ultimately from Johann Winckelmann, who had declared that in
Greece tragedy had been banished or, where not banished, transfigured by beauty.[3]

Joseph Wood Krutch, *The Modern Temper* (New York: Harcourt, Brace,
1929).

   2. *Matthew Arnold: A Study of the Aesthetic Temperament in Victorian En-*
gland (Bloomington: Indiana University Press, 1967), p. 185.

   3. See E. M. Butler, *The Tyranny of Greece over Germany* (Cambridge:

The 1853 Preface, then, can be read as an essay almost completely in consonance with the Romantic tradition because its fervent critical motive is not to define tragedy but to privilege it. While Arnold does identify in the essay some formal properties of tragic literature, his latent concern is with the grandeur of tragedy:

> The terrible old mythic story on which the drama was founded stood, before he entered the theatre, traced in its bare outlines upon the spectator's mind; it stood in his memory, as a group of statuary, faintly seen, at the end of a long and dark vista: then came the poet, embodying outlines, developing situations, not a word wasted, not a sentiment capriciously thrown in: stroke upon stroke, the drama proceeded: the light deepened upon the group; more and more it revealed itself to the riveted gaze of the spectator: until, at last, when the final words were spoken, it stood before him in broad sunlight, a model of immortal beauty.
> [*CPW*, I, 6]

For the actual *content* of tragedy in Arnold we must look to other formulations. His tragic vision is rendered most concisely in the famous lines that image man as "Wandering between two worlds, one dead, / The other powerless to be born."[4] This predicament, which is paradigmatic for all the writers we have discussed, is offered as the hallmark of tragic experience in Arnold's 1877 essay on Lord Falkland. "Falkland" quite clearly identifies Arnold's sense of tragedy as a response to revolution. The tragic sense he develops in the essay appears as the informing vision of *Empedocles on Etna*, *Balder Dead*, the planned drama on Lucretius, and, perhaps most tellingly, in *Merope* itself, the work he composed to exemplify the doctrines of the 1853 Preface.

The University Press, 1935), p. 97. Warren Anderson finds little of the Greek tragic vision in Arnold (*Matthew Arnold and the Classical Tradition* [Ann Arbor: University of Michigan Press, 1965], p. 252).

4. "Stanzas from the Grand Chartreuse" (ll. 85–86). Arnold's poetry is quoted from *The Poetical Works of Matthew Arnold*, ed. C. B. Tinker and H. F. Lowry (London: Oxford University Press, 1950).

THE THIRD HOST

Arnold wrote the 1853 Preface ostensibly to explain why he was omitting *Empedocles on Etna*, published a year earlier, from a new edition of his *Poems*. It has several times been pointed out that the Preface is, consequently, paradoxical because the poem itself rejects the figure of Empedocles for much the same reasons as those given in the Preface.[5] The Preface keeps turning out to be a highly ironical text when it is looked at in the light of Arnold's declared intentions. Its irony becomes even more elaborate when it is realized that Arnold's subtextual espousal of Romantic tragedy is woven into an essay that quietly skirmishes with Scott, Byron, and Carlyle.

We must, initially, go a long way from the 1853 Preface to see why and how Scott, Byron, and Carlyle are implicated in it. In January 1878 Arnold published "A French Critic on Goethe" (later collected in *Mixed Essays*). The essay contains the following passage: "We all remember how Mr. Carlyle has taught us to see in *Götz* and *Werther* the double source from which have flowed those two mighty streams,—the literature of feudalism and romance, represented for us by Scott, and the literature of emotion and passion, represented for us by Byron" (*CPW*, VIII, 257–58). Arnold is here reflecting what sounds very much like a major locus in the evolution of his thought about the literary tradition he inherited. We have already seen how Carlyle kept addressing Scott's "Götzism" and Byron's "Werterism" in order to clarify his own mission as a writer. What we can now observe is the way Arnold assimilated Carlyle's account of "Götzism" and "Werterism" into his own search for an adequate poetic, a search that entailed, moreover, his dissatisfaction with "Carlyleanism."

When, twenty-five years earlier, Arnold explained his rejection of *Empedocles*, he wrote:

5. The point is made by Madden in *Matthew Arnold*, p. 101, and by A.

What then are the situations, from the representation of which, though accurate, no poetical enjoyment can be derived? They are those in which the suffering finds no vent in action; in which a continuous state of mental distress is prolonged, unrelieved by incident, hope, or resistance; in which there is everything to be endured, nothing to be done. In such situations there is inevitably something morbid, in the description of them something monotonous. When they occur in actual life, they are painful, not tragic; the representation of them in poetry is painful also. [CPW, I, 2–3]

There can be little doubt that these reflections derive directly from Carlyle's description of the "Götzism" practiced by Scott and the "Werterism" practiced by Byron as styles that signify "a class of feelings deeply important to modern minds; feelings which arise from *passion incapable of being converted into action*" (*WTC*, XXIX, 59).[6] By echoing the passage Arnold is implying that Carlyle himself had not advanced beyond the paralysis he saw in Scott and Byron. Indeed, Arnold was one of the many mid-Victorians who shared Arthur Hugh Clough's sense that "Carlyle led us out into the wilderness and left us there."[7] It was as recently as 1849, for example, that Arnold was speaking of "moral desperadoes like Carlyle," though he had once regarded Carlyle as "the beloved man."[8]

Into the writing of the 1853 Preface there thus entered Arnold's phylogenic version of Romanticism, which he found originally in Carlyle and had extended to include Carlyle himself. He wanted

---

Dwight Culler in *Imaginative Reason: The Poetry of Matthew Arnold* (New Haven: Yale University Press, 1966), p. 176.

6. For the importance of this passage in Carlyle's thinking about Scott and Byron, see above, pp. 206–9.

7. See James Insley Osborne, *Arthur Hugh Clough* (Boston: Houghton Mifflin, 1920), p. 66.

8. These references are in *The Letters of Matthew Arnold to Arthur Hugh Clough*, ed. H. F. Lowry (Oxford: Clarendon Press, 1932), pp. 75, 111.

to rupture this tradition in order to replace its self-perpetuating morbidity with the resonant tragedy of the Greeks, who were counseled in such matters by "their exquisite sagacity of taste" (*CPW*, I, 7). And yet what Arnold wrote, both before and after composing the Preface, are works that, at least as scenarios, duplicate the tragedy of revolution as observed by Scott, Byron, and Carlyle.

The reason for this outcome is surely not difficult to define. The sense of oppression, the "continuous state of mental distress," which Arnold finds so contrary to the splendor of literature written by "the unapproached masters of the *grand style*" (*CPW*, I, 5), has a double significance in the essay. For, on the one hand, Arnold is protesting against an aesthetic founded on mere pathos, but, on the other hand, as the rest of his work clearly shows, he is thinking of a condition that inheres in the *Zeitgeist*. Arnold is calling for renewed sagacity of taste so that the poetic spirit will not be infected by the enervating paralysis of the age—the very theme upon which the poetic spirit must deliver its discourse. *Empedocles on Etna* rendered this theme. The 1853 Preface renders a warning against the insidious process by which theme has internalized itself as style and thus brought within the citadel of the aesthetic consciousness the frightful morbidity of the times, "its true *blankness* and *barrenness, and unpoetrylessness*."[9] The source of this morbidity, as we shall see, is the age's deadening polarizations.

Arnold's skirmishing with Scott, Byron, and Carlyle as exemplars of the Romantic tradition occurs, then, because he sees the self-indulgent melancholia of Romantic pathos as a miming of the age's paralysis. And he commends Greek tragedy as a cure. But this analysis does not take us away from the practice of Scott, Byron, and Carlyle. It returns us to their practice. Once again, tragedy is being set up against the blankness and barrenness of a world in deadlock. The tragic vision has become equipment for living through a

9. Ibid., p. 126.

spiritual and cultural void. To be sure, Arnold is dissociating himself from the manner and style of Romantic pathos, and advocating the manner and style of the Greeks. But he does this precisely so that tragedy may become a "fit mode" for dealing with a world—not just a literature—where suffering finds no vent in action. By placing so much stress on the capacity of Greek tragedy to "inspirit and rejoice" (*CPW*, I, 2), he is, in effect, valorizing tragedy for the grandeur it bestows upon the Empedoclean man who is engaged in unremitting struggle with his milieu. And so, while Arnold was explicitly trying to recapture the style of the Greeks in order to make modern poetry efficacious, he was implicitly trying to appropriate the world's most prestigious tragic tradition in order to generate "incident, hope, [and] resistance."

I do not mean that Greece is invoked only for the sake of voltage. Arnold did have a serious commitment to the classical tradition. The indispensable feature of that commitment, however, is its reverence. If Arnold was offering a learned alternative to the vague, uncanonical, and naively romanticized tragic sense of his predecessors, he was also claiming, as they had done, that the tragic attitude is in some sort a guardian of being in an age enamored of emptiness.

Perhaps it would have been an anomaly altogether had Scott, Byron, and Carlyle not left a trace of their influence even in the 1853 Preface. They had contributed substantially to the character of Matthew Arnold's imagination. The intriguing nature of Carlyle's influence has been studied in several essays that have reshaped our understanding of Victorian literary history.[10] Although Arnold's reactions to Carlyle are notoriously difficult to

10. See Kathleen Tillotson, "Matthew Arnold and Carlyle," *Proceedings of the British Academy*, 42 (1956), 133–53; David J. DeLaura, "Arnold and Carlyle," *PMLA*, 79 (1964), 104–29; and DeLaura's sequel to this essay, "Carlyle and Arnold: The Religious Issue" in *Carlyle Past and Present: A Collection of New Essays*, ed. K. J. Fielding and Rodger L. Tarr (London: Vision Press, 1976), pp. 127–54.

summarize, their basic tendency is reflected in his essay "Emerson" (1884). Speaking of his own formative years, he wrote: "There was the puissant voice of Carlyle, so sorely strained, overused and misused since, but then fresh, comparatively sound, and reaching our hearts with true pathetic eloquence. Who can forget the emotion of receiving in its first freshness such a sentence as that sentence of Carlyle upon Edward Irving, then just dead: 'Scotland sent him forth a herculean man; our mad Babylon wore and wasted him with all her engines'" (*CPW*, X, 166). That Arnold should praise Carlyle for his "pathetic eloquence," and then go on to quote, of all sentences, a perfect instance of the Carlylean true man's tragedy, will indicate how much he derived from Carlyle in modeling the struggles of his own culture heroes in a revolutionary era.

Further evidence of the same point is available in Arnold's poetry, such as the numerous parallels between *Sartor Resartus* and the discourse of Empedocles. Most dramatically, for the purposes of our discussion at least, there is the pervasive echoing of Carlyle's "Characteristics" in "Stanzas from the Grand Chartreuse." As Kathleen Tillotson observes, even the key image of "Wandering between two worlds" is evolved from "Characteristics": "The doom of the Old has long been pronounced, and irrevocable; the Old has passed away: but, alas, the New appears not in its stead; the Time is still in pangs of travail with the new."[11] While Arnold believed that "the Time" would have to be transformed with alembics unknown to Carlyle, his consciousness of history was nurtured by Carlyle's reading of the age's tragic "signs."

Byron counted heavily in the same process, although the nature and endurance of Byron's influence continue to be in some dispute.[12] Kenneth Allott points out that Arnold, while he listened

11. Tillotson, "Matthew Arnold and Carlyle," p. 149; *WTC*, XXVIII, 32.

12. The best discussion of Arnold and Byron is Leon Gottfried's in *Matthew Arnold and the Romantics* (Lincoln: University of Nebraska Press, 1963),

to Carlyle's command "Close thy *Byron*; open thy *Goethe*," was quite unable to suppress "a sneaking admiration for Byron's defiant energy or pretend that he had no sympathy for the discontented aspiration of Senancour's Obermann."[13] No more could Carlyle, as we have already seen. Byron's portrayal of the derelict, the man of discontented aspiration, struck too close to the heroes of both Carlyle and Arnold for either to close his Byron completely. And so, if *Empedocles on Etna* owes a debt to *Sartor Resartus*, it also owes a debt to *Manfred*.

The young Matthew Arnold, like so many of his generation, was captivated by Byron. His Rugby prize poem, "Alaric at Rome," is an imitation of *Childe Harold*, and earlier still he won a competition at Winchester for his recitation of the death speech from a work that has been of considerable interest for us, *Marino Faliero*.[14] These triumphs of Arnold's adolescence might reflect no more than a passing devotion, but Arnold himself suggests otherwise. In 1881 he wrote: "How then will Byron stand . . . ? That is the question on which I, who can even remember the latter years of Byron's vogue, and have myself felt the expiring wave of that mighty influence, but who certainly also regard him, and have long regarded him, without illusion, cannot but ask myself, cannot but seek to answer." The answer he gave is striking: "Wordsworth and Byron stand, it seems to me, first and preeminent in actual performance, a glorious pair, among the English poets of this century" (*CPW*, IX, 221, 236).

This final judgment came, it might be supposed, when Arnold realized that not even his lifelong censoriousness of both profligacy and bad grammar could drive Byron from him. The terms of

pp. 75–115. I offer some corrections in "Arnold, Byron, and Taine," *English Studies*, 55 (1974), 435–39.

13. "A Background for 'Empedocles on Etna,'" in *Essays and Studies, 1968*, ed. Simeon Potter (London: John Murray, 1968), p. 86.

14. See Thomas Arnold, *Passages in a Wandering Life* (London: Edward Arnold, 1900), p. 16.

his summing up are crucial. They make of Byron not a poet drowning in "Werterism" but a companion of those figures, struggling nobly against the barrenness of a world in deadlock, who represented what Arnold actually perceived as tragic experience:

> As the inevitable break-up of the old order comes, as the English middle class slowly awakens from its intellectual sleep of two centuries, as our actual present world, to which this sleep has condemned us, shows itself more clearly,—our world of an aristocracy materialised and null, a middle class purblind and hideous, a lower class crude and brutal,—we shall turn our eyes again, and to more purpose, upon this passionate and dauntless soldier of a forlorn hope, who, ignorant of the future and unconsoled by its promises, nevertheless waged against the conservation of the old impossible world so fiery battle; waged it till he fell,—waged it with such splendid and imperishable excellence of sincerity and strength.   [*CPW*, IX, 236]

Were it not that it is Byron about whom these words were written, we might have less difficulty in recognizing what they convey—a self-portrait of Matthew Arnold. That Arnold should see a Byron who mirrors himself indicates the depth of his identification with a writer who, for all his perversities and inadequacies, exemplified the essential condition of modern tragedy. The rhetoric and spirit of this passage are borrowed, as will be clear, from the conclusion of "Falkland."

One further anticipation of "Falkland" brings us to the third figure in the scene, Scott. The "Falkland" essay cites Edgar Ravenswood as an important example of the wanderer between two worlds. Arnold's allusion to Ravenswood is not casual. Though Arnold's comments on Scott are widely scattered and rather sketchy, they are surprisingly respectful. This is especially true if we remember the infrequency of Arnold's attention to novelists.

Writing to Clough in March 1853, Arnold reported the reception of Thackeray's recently published *Henry Esmond*. The general opinion, he says, is that the book is a failure: "—but I do not think so. [It] is one of the most readable books I ever met—and Thackeray is certainly a first rate journeyman though not a great artist;—It gives you an insight into the *heaven born* character of Waverley and Indiana and such like when you read the undeniably powerful but most un-heaven-born productions of the present people—Thackeray—the woman Stowe etc."[15] I take it that Arnold composed these remarks with reference, conscious or unconscious, to Fichte's distinction between the literary journeyman and the highest kind of genius.[16] If this is the case, then Arnold is reversing Carlyle's judgment on Scott, a judgment he is likely to have had clearly in mind since he was writing his letter within a few months of writing the 1853 Preface. Certainly, at this period in his life, for Arnold to pair any novelist with George Sand is tantamount to enshrinement in his personal pantheon of redeeming spirits. For Scott to be so enshrined—in 1853—is further evidence that Arnold's skirmishing with his Romantic predecessors did not cancel his sense of spiritual kinship with them.

Though he remained generally unaffected by Scott's poetry, Arnold continued to read the novels. His 1873 reading list is, remarkably, dominated by seven of Scott's novels, including the three we have discussed. But perhaps a letter he wrote the previous year gives us the best measure of the place Scott held in Arnold's imagination. He had been asked to support a petition requesting that F. D. Maurice be buried in Westminster Abbey. Arnold declined to sign: "I have a strong opinion against too free a concession of the honour of burial in the Abbey. There is hardly an Englishman in this century,—among those whose eminence is in letters,—whom I would have put there, except Scott and Wordsworth: to put Dickens there, for instance, seemed to me a monstrosity."[17] No doubt Arnold believed that Tories of the old

15. *Letters to Clough*, pp. 132–33.
16. See above, p. 205. Carlyle discussed Fichte's *Über das Wesen des Gelehrten* in his essay "State of German Literature."
17. *From a Victorian Post-Bag; Being Letters Addressed to the Rev. J. Lleweleyn*

school, to use Ruskin's phrase, had the most appropriate claim to
the Abbey. But this alone would not have qualified Scott if he had
represented no more to Arnold than emaciated "Götzism."

Carlyle's publication of *On Heroes and Hero-Worship* partly accounts for the fact that the subject set for the Newdigate competition in 1842–43 was Oliver Cromwell. Arnold's "Cromwell"
won the competition. One of the poem's verse paragraphs is
given to a panoramic survey of notable men in the English Revolution. Included among them is Lord Falkland:

> There Falkland eyed the strife that would not cease,
> Shook back his tangled locks, and murmured—"Peace!"
>
> [ll. 173–74]

Even this fleeting reference indicates that Arnold's hero was not
Carlyle's. Arnold would eventually dismiss Cromwell as England's "Philistine of genius in politics" (*CPW*, VIII, 206). But
Falkland remained with him as an extraordinary historical precedent for the moderate as tragic hero.

"Falkland" was first published in *The Nineteenth Century*
(March 1877), and two years later was reprinted in *Mixed Essays*.
As in three of the other selections in *Mixed Essays*, Arnold approaches his subject through the work of another writer, in this
case Clarendon. He takes Clarendon's admiration as typical. The
aim of his essay, Arnold says, is to explain why Falkland, whose
literary and political accomplishments were minimal, impressed
Clarendon and has continued to impress later generations. His
method is to show that Falkland has, in his character and situation, something that charms the imagination and something that
appeals to the intellect. The method is significant since the fusion
of imaginative and intellectual qualities is the grand synthesis in
whose interest Arnold shaped his critical principles. The essay

---

Davis by Thomas Carlyle and Others, ed. C. L. Davis (London: Peter Davies,
1926), p. 76.

also makes clear that in Falkland Arnold found much of himself. After giving an account of Falkland's early years, Arnold dwells on his retirement to a life of contemplation among a small group of friends at Great Tew, his Oxfordshire estate in the Scholar-Gipsy country. He was forced to abandon this life in 1639 by "Charles the First's expedition to suppress the disturbances in Scotland" (*CPW*, VIII, 193). Falkland, a born constitutionalist, could not remain indifferent in such circumstances. But he was also offended by the "violent proceedings of the court" during the Long Parliament. "He acted with the popular party. He made a powerful speech against ship-money. . . . He spoke vigorously for the bill to remove the bishops from the House of Lords" (*CPW*, VIII, 193). In a word, Falkland had no liking for the feudal authority to which the king and his court were so partial.

Having established this point, Arnold is ready to deal with Falkland's subsequent enlistment in the cause of the king. As the Long Parliament continued, the real motivations of the reformers made themselves known. The popular party "had professed at first that the removal of the bishops . . . was all they wanted; that they had no designs against episcopacy and the Church of England. The strife deepened, and new and revolutionary designs emerged. When, therefore, the bill against the bishops was reintroduced, Falkland voted against it" (*CPW*, VIII, 194). To Falkland the vote was a matter of conscience, not a matter of politics. Arnold is setting before us a portrait of the disinterested man, a historical embodiment of those human qualities that all his life he had urged upon his countrymen. The king's party eagerly began to press Falkland into service, but he resisted because "he was for great reforms" and he "disliked Charles's obstinacy and insincerity" (*CPW*, VIII, 194). Feeling a sense of duty, however, he overcame his reluctance and accepted a position as secretary of state. Several months later the Civil War broke out, and in September 1643 Falkland died a hero's death on the field at Newbury. During his tenure of office, he was extremely unhappy. As the war went on, this usually affable man, in Clarendon's description, " 'became on a sudden less communicable, and thence very sad, pale, and exceedingly affected with the spleen' " (*CPW*, VIII, 195).

With this review of Falkland's career completed, Arnold proceeds to develop his thesis: "In the first place, then, he had certainly, except personal beauty, everything to qualify him for a hero to the imagination of mankind in general. He had rank, accomplishment, sweet temper, exquisite courtesy, liberality, magnanimity, superb courage, melancholy, misfortune, early death" (*CPW*, VIII, 196–97). The ordering of this list is revealing: it begins in the seventeenth century but it ends in the nineteenth century. Having smuggled Falkland into his own era, Arnold, very significantly, goes on to compare him to "the Master of Ravenswood, that most interesting by far of all Scott's heroes." Like the Master of Ravenswood, "Falkland has for the imagination the indefinable, the irresistible charm of one who is and must be, in spite of the choicest gifts and graces, unfortunate,—of a man in the grasp of fatality. . . . He is surely and visibly touched by the finger of doom. And he knows it himself." For the imagination, then, "Falkland cannot but be a figure of ideal, pathetic beauty" (*CPW*, VIII, 198).

Arnold turns next to Falkland's ability to appeal to our "judgment." This involves him in a dispute with the Dissenters (he quotes from the *Nonconformist*), who see Falkland as weakly inconsistent in comparison to Hampden, whose death " 'was a martyr's seal to truths assured of ultimate triumph.' " Here Arnold has the real question of his essay established for him. "*Truths assured of ultimate triumph*! Let us pause upon those words. The Puritans were victors in the Civil War, and fashioned things to their own liking. How far was their system . . . an embodiment of 'truth?' " (*CPW*, VIII, 200). Arnold's point, of course, is that humanity won no victory with the triumph of Puritanism. The "right answer" to his question, he says, is to be found in the historical writings of Bolingbroke.

Cavaliers and Roundheads had divided the nation, like Yorkists and Lancastrians. To reconcile these disputes by treaty became impracticable, when neither side would trust the other. To terminate them by the sword was to fight, not for preserving the constitution, but for the manner of destroying it. The constitution might have been destroyed under pretence of prerogative. It was destroyed under pretence of liberty. We might have fallen under absolute monarchy. We fell into absolute anarchy. [*CPW*, VIII, 200]

In other words, the alternatives offered to England for its historical development were equally catastrophic. History had become a tale of ignorant armies clashing by night, leaving a Falkland to wander in some crepuscular no man's land. "To escape from . . . anarchy, the nation, as every one knows, swung back into the very hands from which Puritanism had wrested it, to the bad and false system . . . of the Stuarts" (*CPW*, VIII, 200).

Falkland's "judgment" is to be honored because he knew that the truth was not with the Puritans (for Arnold, of course, an indispensable discovery). He joined with the king because "he thought the triumph of the Parliament the greater leap into chaos" (*CPW*, VIII, 204). What Arnold wants to make clear, however, is that Falkland was not saved by having been wise enough to choose the lesser evil.

The final victory was neither for Stuarts nor Puritans. And it could not be for either of them, for the cause of neither was sound. Falkland had lucidity enough to see it. He gave himself to the cause which seemed to him least unsound, and to which "honesty," he thought, bound him; but he felt that the truth was not there, any more than with the Puritans,—neither the truth nor the future. *This is what makes his figure and situation so truly tragic.* [*CPW*, VIII, 204; italics added]

Falkland's figure and situation, as I have indicated, are mirrored in *Empedocles on Etna, Balder Dead, Merope,* and the unfinished drama "Lucretius." These poems differ according to Arnold's various intentions, but the experience of Falkland is central to the form of each. Their common concern is with the spiritual erosion that comes of protracted wandering between two worlds. Using "Falkland" as a guide, one may say that the tragic condition for Arnold consisted in the loss of options that led to such wandering. Tragedy is the doom visited upon those noble and attractive men who are left without fulfillment because they are caught in a revolutionary climate in which the engaged forces have become hardened and polarized into equally repugnant camps.

Behind Arnold's meditation on this condition lies a deeply felt personal experience. Indeed, he does not conclude his essay until he has pointed out the relevance of Falkland's "figure and situation" to the Victorian world.

> One might sometimes fancy that the whole English nation, as in Chillingworth's time it was divided into two great hosts of publicans and sinners on the one side, Scribes and Pharisees on the other, so in ours it was going to divide itself into two vast camps of Simpletons here, under the command, suppose, of Mr. Beresford Hope, and of Savages there, under the command of Mr. Henry Richard. . . . What we have to do is to raise and multiply in this country a third host, with the conviction that the ideals both of Simpletons and Savages are profoundly inadequate and profoundly unedifying, and with the resolve to win victory for a better ideal than that of either of them.   [*CPW*, VIII, 205]

To understand fully why Arnold would see a historical order dominated by the contention between Simpletons and Savages as a tragic condition, it is necessary to recall his career as a writer. Arnold had begun his career as a man bitterly alienated from his world, but at some point he realized that the burden of isolation was too great to bear. By the mid-1850s he was convinced that he needed to engage his world rather than repudiate it. As Madden says, "Unlike the early letters, in which he warned Clough that it was better to do and be nothing than engage in philistercy . . .

the later letters and the criticism were firmly set against 'quietism.' "[18] In carrying out this transformation, Arnold looked for an indication that his age was not implacably hostile to all his values. He saw, or thought he saw, such an indication in the *Zeitgeist* or "the modern spirit." More and more he stressed the idea that the historical process in the nineteenth century was building a mandate for cultural renewal. In "The Function of Criticism," for example, he clearly rested the case for his values on the argument that history was working in their favor.

Arnold's optimism, however, was never very vigorous. If some signs of the time promised that an era of rebirth was at hand, there were other, more urgent signs that the revolution actually being promoted by the historical process was dominated by the fruitless and enervating clash between Simpletons and Savages. This clash appeared to Arnold, therefore, as terrifying for more than its power to destroy noble souls. It was an action that seemed to demonstrate that appeals to history were futile. The forces working for a meaningful and elevating revolution were viable, but, in the vast and obscure operations of the historical process, their fruition was likely to be indefinitely deferred as the revolutionary energy of the nineteenth century dissipated itself in the kind of struggle described in "Falkland." This struggle issues in tragic consequences, then, not only because of its inherently catastrophic nature, but also because it makes faith in history—that last source of optimism for such a man as Arnold—almost impossible to maintain. This is what Arnold had learned as he meditated upon the historical process during the decade of the fifties, when all four of the works we shall discuss were written. Though he emerges in the sixties as a critic who made frequent appeals to history, his appeals are compromised by a persistent tone of despair. Arnold's desperate need to believe in history, as

18. *Matthew Arnold*, p. 135.

well as the agony of enduring ceaseless betrayals of his faith, are poignantly evoked in the last paragraph of "Falkland."

> Let us return to Falkland, to our martyr of sweetness and light, of lucidity of mind and largeness of temper. Let us bid him farewell, not with compassion for him, and not with excuses, but in confidence and pride. Slowly, very slowly, his ideal of lucidity of mind and largeness of temper conquers; but it conquers. In the end it will prevail; only we must have patience. The day will come when this nation shall be renewed by it. But, O lime-trees of Tew, and quiet Oxfordshire fieldbanks where the first violets are even now raising their heads!—how often, ere that day arrive for Englishmen, shall your renewal be seen! [*CPW*, VIII, 206-7]

ARNOLD AGONISTES

Empedocles on Etna deals mainly with its protagonist's immense struggle to preserve his perception, as Arnold put it, of "the truth of the truth" (*TL*, p. 291). Empedocles is Arnold's most impressive portrayal of the guiltless hero brought to calamity by some inadequacy inherent in his temperament. But while the poem's major interest is focused on the nature of Empedocles' failing, Arnold sees the crisis on Etna as precipitated by the revolutionary climate of Empedocles' age. He even has Empedocles suggest that in some earlier, ideal age the pursuit of truth was attended by no adversity.

> And yet what days were those, Parmenides!
> When we were young, when we could number friends
> In all the Italian cities like ourselves,
> When with elated hearts we join'd your train,
> Ye Sun-born Virgins! on the road to truth.
> [II, 235-39]

The historical background that Arnold provides for the drama is derived from the same sense of history that produced "Falkland."

The background is, one might say, an elaboration on what Arnold meant when he wrote, "I do not think any fruitful revolution can come in my time," a statement made in the midst of his work on *Empedocles.*[19]

Pausanius, who naively believes that Empedocles can allay "the swelling evil of the time," makes some pertinent remarks on the ethos of the age. "Broils tear us in twain," he says, "since [the] new swarm / Of sophists has got empire in our schools" (I, i, 121–22). Pausanius himself represents precisely the kind of thinking that the sophists have risen to attack. He is a Simpleton of the first order, and is rebuked by Empedocles for his dependence on *Aberglaube* (I, ii, 27). Arnold said that *Empedocles on Etna* displays an "impatience with the language and assumptions of the popular theology of the day" (*TL,* p. 288). Pausanius is the object of that impatience.

The sophists whom Pausanius fears populate the camp of the Savages. Arnold saw gathered in this camp highly heterogeneous groups allied, finally, in their common appeal to rationalism. When Arnold invoked "the modern spirit" he was himself appealing largely to the spirit of rationalism. He recalled Pascal's warning to the Jesuits that the world no longer believes what is not evident to it. "In the seventeenth century, when Pascal said this, it had already begun to be true; it is getting more widely true every day" (*CPW,* VII, 200–201). But Arnold profoundly distrusted the rational intellect. This distrust is made clear by his hopeful and arresting claim that "the main element of the modern spirit's life . . . is the imaginative reason" (*CPW,* III, 230).

The Savages were those reformers in religion, philosophy, and politics whose thought was guided by the *un*imaginative reason and whose sophistries would imprison the human spirit in a net-

19. *Unpublished Letters of Matthew Arnold,* ed. Arnold Whitridge (New Haven: Yale University Press, 1923), p. 14.

work of liberal cant. That Arnold saw the work of this group as
in fact savage is evident in his denunciation of such enterprises as
Bishop Colenso's biblical criticism. Colenso seemed an omen:
"all reticence is to be abandoned," a surge of liberal speculation
will proclaim every doubt and broadcast its conclusions "in the
crudest shape, amidst the undisciplined, ignorant, passionate,
captious multitude" (*CPW*, III, 54).

A third host could never gain way among a multitude so infa-
mously educated. Yet to Arnold the work of the Savages had an
even more disturbing feature, and that was its undeniable co-
gency. Empedocles is disabled by the influence of the sophists, as
he shows when the problem of "mind" and "thought" brings
him to a philosophical impasse:

> they will be our lords, as they are now;
> And keep us prisoners of our consciousness,
> And never let us clasp and feel the All
> But through their forms, and modes, and stifling veils.
> [II, 351–54]

The nullity of Pausanius on the one hand and the efficacy of the
sophists on the other move Empedocles toward his lugubrious
end. By evolving the historical framework of the poem out of the
"broils" between the Simpletons and Savages, Arnold suggests
how intimately connected this clash of ignorant armies was with
his understanding of tragic action. Empedocles quite explicitly
warns Pausanius to be "neither saint nor sophist-led" (I, ii, 136).
And in those climactic moments that depict Empedocles in his
last anguish, we hear him rail at both sophistry and superstition.

> The brave, impetuous heart yields everywhere
> To the subtle, contriving head;
> Great qualities are trodden down,
> And littleness united
> Is become invincible
> [II, 90–94]

And then:

> —Lie there, ye ensigns
> Of my unloved preëminence
> In an age like this!
> Among a people of children,
> Who throng'd me in their cities,
> Who worshipp'd me in their houses,
> And ask'd not wisdom,
> But drugs to charm with,
> But spells to mutter—
> All the fool's-armoury of magic!
> [II, 109–18]

Incapable of wandering any longer between the two worlds denounced in these passages, Empedocles has left no place to receive him but the isolated summit of Etna. There he has no alternative but to confront the root of suffering in himself.

In 1855 Arnold remarked to Wyndham Slade: "I am full of a tragedy of the time of the end of the Roman Republic—one of the most colossal times of the world, I think" (TL, p. 342). This work, with Lucretius as protagonist, was never completed, though Arnold showed interest in it for a period extending from at least 1849 to 1866. As Tinker and Lowry show, the connections of the poem with *Empedocles on Etna* are very close (TL, pp. 294–97). The two figures of Empedocles and Lucretius shared in Arnold's imagination very much the same character.

"On the Modern Element in Literature" (1857) presents a Lucretius hardly distinguishable from Empedocles:

> With stern effort, with gloomy despair, he seems to rivet his eyes on the elementary reality, the naked framework of the world, because the world in its fulness and movement is too exciting a spectacle for his discomposed brain. He seems to feel the spectacle of it at once terrifying and alluring; and to deliver himself from it he has to keep perpetually repeating his formula of disenchantment and annihilation. [*CPW,* I, 33]

268

Revolution as Tragedy

The sense of history that informs this passage belongs less to Empedocles or Lucretius than it does to Arnold. When Arnold attributed to Lucretius the need to discover an elemental reality immune to the historical process for the reason that the movement of history seemed by turns alluring and terrifying, and thus exasperating, he was synthesizing the major elements in his own attitude toward history. We note, too, what Arnold himself pointed out: Lucretius lived in a revolutionary time.

Although we do not know a great deal about Arnold's conception of "Lucretius," certain interesting information has survived in the form of manuscript notes for the play. A. Dwight Culler has examined these notes and has reported their content. The notes refer mainly to historical background and deal with "the public careers of the various characters—Pompey, Clodius, Milo, Cicero, Scaurus, Caesar, and others."

> From these materials it is possible to gain a fairly good idea of what the drama was about. It was to deal with "the events at the end of 53 [B.C.]"—i.e. with the contest for power between the two political gangsters who represented the parties of Pompey and Caesar—T. Annius Milo and Publius Clodius. . . . Two pages in Arnold's notebook which divide the characters into "Milonians" and "Clodians" suggest that this struggle was to be the main political backdrop to the play. [*Imaginative Reason*, p. 219]

By 53 B.C. Milo had for several years been the head persecutor and mob agitator for Rome's conservative party. His long and violent rivalry with Clodius, self-proclaimed deliverer of the democratic faction and chief ward organizer for Caesar, had erupted with renewed brutality while both were seeking political office in the year 53. The division of Rome's political forces into Milonians and Clodians indicates that Arnold was contemplating the same kind of hideous struggle between an effete conservatism and a preposterous radicalism that he described in "Falkland." And he could discover in the event that brought their fierce antagonism to a climax a literal instance of ignorant armies clashing by night.

At a little crossroads on the Appian Way, Milo and Clodius, each in the company of armed guards, met and fought. Clodius, after finding retreat in a nearby tavern, was murdered at Milo's command and mob rioting quickly ensued.

Just how Lucretius would have entered upon this dismal scene we do not know. But we do know the place he held in Arnold's imagination. In what may well have been an important source for Arnold's work on "Lucretius," Theodor Mommsen's *History of Rome,* the following estimate is made of *De Rerum Natura:*

> It was composed in that hopeless time when the rule of oligarchy had been overthrown and that of Caesar had not yet been established, in the sultry years during which the outbreak of the civil war was awaited with long and painful suspense. If we seem to perceive in its unequal and restless utterance that the poet daily expected to see the wild tumult of revolution break forth over himself and his work, we must not with reference to his view of men and things forget amidst what men, and in prospect of what things, that view had its origins.[20]

Whether Arnold was influenced by Mommsen or not, some similar view of Lucretius he undoubtedly had in mind. One of the surviving fragments from the drama, which refers to Lucretius, proposes very much the same image of the protagonist as Arnold had used in *Empedocles on Etna:*

> It is a sad sight when the world denies
> A gifted man the power to shew his gift;
> When he is tied and thwarted from his course;
> When his fine genius foams itself away
> Upon the reefs and sandbanks of the world,
> And he dies fruitless, having found no field.
> [TL, pp. 345–46][21]

20. *The History of Rome,* trans. W. P. Dickson (London: Everyman's Library, 1921), IV, 553.
21. Culler, *Imaginative Reason,* p. 220, shows that these lines refer to Lucretius.

While "Lucretius" lay dormant, Arnold was diligently at work on *Balder Dead*. The cosmic revolution augured by the death of Balder and known in Norse mythology as Ragnarok (the Doom or Twilight of the Gods) intimated in an ancient imagination a tragic knowledge of the conditions that beset Arnold's world. Arnold could hardly fail to respond to the *Prose Edda,* and he was pleased with what he had made of it: " 'Balder' perhaps no one cares much for except myself; but I have always thought . . . that it has not had justice done to it."[22] He had written it, for the most part, in 1854 and published it in the next year as the leading poem in his new volume. It was obviously, in his eyes, a major effort.

Balder Dead is throughout marked by allusions to the doom that has been prophesied for the Gods and Heroes in Valhalla's court. The anguished Hermod recalls the prophecy most poignantly:

> Yet here thou liest, Balder, underground,
> Rusting for ever; and the years roll on,
> The generations pass, the ages grow,
> And bring us nearer to the final day
> When from the south shall march the fiery band
> And cross the bridge of Heaven, with Lok for guide,
> And Fenris at his heel with broken chain;
> While from the east the giant Rymer steers
> His ship, and the great serpent makes to land;
> And all are marshall'd in one flaming square
> Against the Gods, upon the plains of Heaven.
>   [III, 471–81]

These lines envision the coming of the Giants from Jotunheim to overwhelm Asgard. The Giants are odious, of course, representing as they do the forces of evil. In Lok (Loki) Arnold had a uniquely interesting figure for the purpose of his theme. Al-

---

22. G. W. E. Russell, *Matthew Arnold* (London: Hoder & Stoughton, 1904), p. 42.

though Lok was a Giant, he was permitted to inhabit Asgard for a reason never explained in the myth. The Gods loathed him and attempted to keep him in check. But Lok was not cowed. As Hela, his grim daughter and mistress of the underworld, boasts: "Yet he shall one day rise, and burst his bonds, / And with himself set us his offspring free" (II, 222–23). There is more than a hint here of the movement of popular democracy against the old order. Whenever Arnold treats Lok and the Giants in *Balder Dead*, he concentrates on the viciousness of their temper, as in Lok's vile speech upon seeing Hermod return from his pathetic journey to the underworld to visit Balder ("Like as a farmer, who hath lost his dog / . . . So Hermod comes to-day unfollow'd home" [III, 8–19]). The impression that emerges from the poem is that the victory of Lok and his tribe will signify the victory of vulgarity and smallness of temper over a noble tradition.

But it must be pointed out, too, that the Gods are represented as a good deal less than perfect themselves. Thor, in lamenting at Balder's funeral, grieves most for the loss of Balder's pacifying presence:

> For haughty spirits and high wraths are rife
> Among the Gods and Heroes here in Heaven,
> As among those whose joy and work is war;
> And daily strifes arise, and angry words.
> [III, 79–82]

And Balder himself, speaking to Hermod in the underworld words that are wholly Arnold's addition to the story, says:

> For I am long since weary of your storm
> Of carnage, and find, Hermod, in your life
> Something too much of war and broils, which make
> Life one perpetual fight, a bath of blood.
>   . . .
> Inactive therefore let me lie, in gloom,
> Unarm'd, inglorious; I attend the course
> Of ages, and my late return to light,

In times less alien to a spirit mild,
In new-recover'd seats, the happier day.
[III, 503-13]

Balder's description of life in Asgard is reinforced by an earlier
reference to the pastime of the Gods and Heroes, which was to
hack each other to pieces during the day, knowing they would be
miraculously restored at night (II, 10-18).

Balder, then, may be found among that weary company of
wanderers between two worlds. The peculiar circumstances of
his death dramatize, with mythic power, the ominous configuration of the *Zeitgeist.* Balder is killed by a blind God whose arm is
directed by a savage Giant. They act simultaneously. Balder becomes the victim of this ironic cooperation because the Gods,
convinced that Balder could not be harmed, decide in their curious way to make a sport of throwing axes and spears at him. But
Balder *could* be harmed because Lok, the hidden curse in the
Gods' universe, had the malicious cunning to discover the only
object to which Balder was vulnerable. The myth spoke to Arnold of perils he knew too well. He had been stricken by the
blindness of one order to its fatal weaknesses, and stricken, too,
by the impending success of another order destined to rule but
formed and fostered in a spiritual wilderness.

The death of Balder is a mythic correlative of the theme of
"Falkland." The connection between the two works is evident in
the similarity of their conclusions. Speaking from the mists of
Hela's realm, Balder invokes some remote future and the promise
of "Another Heaven" that no one yet has reached. Anticipating a
favorite phrase in Arnold's late prose, Balder declares that
"Thither, when o'er this present earth and Heavens / The tempest of the latter days hath swept, / . . . Shall a small remnant of
the Gods repair."

There re-assembling we shall see emerge
From the bright Ocean at our feet an earth

More fresh, more verdant than the last, with fruits
Self-springing, and a seed of man preserved,
Who then shall live in peace, as now in war.
[III, 527–31]

These are the "saving remnant" or the "Children of the Second
Birth." They regenerate the world by preserving from the vicissi-
tudes of the *Zeitgeist* their integrity and their humanity. They are
the third host.

Arnold wrote a long "Historical Introduction" for *Merope*
(1858), which begins with a pointed statement: "The events on
which the action of the drama turns belong to the period of transition from the heroic and fabulous to the human and historic age
of Greece. The doings of the hero Hercules, the ancestor of the
Messenian Aepytus [Merope's son], belong to fable; but the inva-
sion of Peloponnesus by the Dorians under chiefs claiming to be
descended from Hercules, and their settlement in Argos, Lacedæ-
mon, and Messenia, belong to history."[23] The theme of *Merope* is
developed out of the tensions produced by the revolutionary
structure of the age. The heroine's plight is Falkland's: she is
forced to commit herself either to the barbarism of the old order
or to the ravages of the new.

Cresphontes, Merope's husband, claimed a right to one of the
kingdoms of Peloponnesus by virtue of his kinship to the "fabulous" Hercules. Of the available kingdoms, he secured the fertile
Messenia by deceit. It was after establishing himself in Messenia
that he married Merope, a native of Arcadia, and thus imbued
with a pastoral innocence that leaves her untainted by the barba-
rous past. The Dorian lords became dissatisfied in time with the
policy of Cresphontes. Headed by Polyphontes, "himself a de-
scendant of Hercules," they formed a cabal against him and assassi-
nated him. His two eldest sons were also killed, but the youngest,

23. *Poetical Works of Matthew Arnold*, p. 326.

Aepytus, was saved by Merope and escaped. After the assassination Polyphontes assumed the throne. Arnold's play begins in the twentieth year of Polyphontes' tyranny, with the king trying to subdue his still unsettled and divided country by marriage with Merope, and with Aepytus, unbeknown to either, returning to Messenia to take vengeance on his father's murderer.

Merope is forced to choose, for the sake of peace, between an alliance with her husband's killer and acquiescence in the policy of blood revenge upon which her vigorous but puerile son is implacably bent. These choices are seen in the play as a conflict between the two modes of political life which converged to form Arnold's "period of transition." The transitional period about which Arnold is thinking, however, is his own. The relevance of the play's headnote to Arnold's sense of history is suggested in one of his comments on the French Revolution:

> Whoever gives us a just and rational constitution of human society will also confer a great boon on us and effect a great work; but what has the French Revolution accomplished towards this? Nothing. It was an insurrection against the old routine, it furiously destroyed the medieval form of society; this it did, and this was well if anything had come of it; but into what that is new and fruitful has France proceeded to initiate us? A colourless, humdrum, and ill-poised life is a baneful thing, and men would fain change it; but our benefactor and initiator is the poet who brings us a new one, not the drunkard who gets rid of it by breaking the windows and bringing the house about his ears. [*CPW,* VII, 47]

In *Merope* the moral stupor of Aepytus brings down the house. It is true that by his insurrection and murder of Polyphontes the residual evils of the "fabulous" past are furiously destroyed. But it is quite clear in the play that the "human and historic age" of Greece, as the headnote calls it, would not have evolved from the transitional period of Merope's time had that period been dominated by such men as Aepytus. Merope is faced with the same constriction of alternatives that drove Empedocles to Etna, Lucretius to madness, and Balder to the underworld.

The insecurity of Messenia's civilized life is proclaimed in the play's major symbol, the "sacrifice axe" used in the community's religious rites. Polyphontes used the sacrifice axe to kill Cresphontes, and Aepytus uses it to kill Polyphontes. The usurper and the avenger are thus identified with each other, not only as murderers who believe they are redeemers but as murderers who defile the source of real redemption. Their identification through the symbol of the sacrifice axe resolves the central moral issue of the play: the question of revenge. Merope, though committed by her culture to the proposition that "blood requires blood" (l. 1987), has a moral intuition that revenge is unavailing to the human condition. In order to make clear the fact that Merope is right, Arnold places in her hand the much-abused sacrifice axe when, in a moment of confused passion, her moral vision fails her and she attempts to take vengeance on a young man who she believes killed her son. Her intended victim, of course, turns out to be Aepytus himself. Discovering her error and discovering, too, that Aepytus has come to murder Polyphontes, she cries, "Ah . . . revenge! / That word! it kills me" (ll. 1242–43). Unable to repudiate her son, Merope will eventually choose acquiescence in revenge. Yet as a wielder of the sacrifice axe herself, she is horribly aware that its use as a weapon makes it an instrument of moral disaster no less in Aepytus' hand than in Polyphontes'.

The character of Polyphontes is, as Arnold acknowledged, the most interesting in the play (TL, p. 280). Just as Arnold saw the tradition of European civilization, though damaged by its origins in an irrational past, as worthy of admiration for the real "culture conquests" in its long history, so he saw Polyphontes as a man whose barbarism had been ameliorated during his mature years and transformed into political wisdom. Only in a few passages (for example, ll. 1780–93) does Polyphontes betray himself as a feudal king. For the most part we find him struggling to arrest feudalism:

> The long repressive attitude of rule
> Leaves me austerer, sterner, than I would;
> Old age is more suspicious than the free
> And valiant heart of youth, or manhood's firm
> Unclouded reason; I would not decline
> Into a jealous tyrant, scourged with fears,
> Closing in blood and gloom his sullen reign.
>   [ll. 154–60]

Polyphontes is that miracle in which Arnold dared not believe: an aristocrat who had become accessible to ideas.

Aepytus achieves his dubious victory through little else than what seems his sheer inevitability. That he represents the revolutionary forces of the nineteenth century is a point unmistakably and dolefully made through the strategy he adopts, which is to win the support of the mob by killing Polyphontes. He expresses a sentiment with which Arnold would agree:

> A people, like a common man, is dull,
> Is lifeless, while its heart remains untouch'd;
> A food can drive it, and a fly may scare.
> When it admires and loves, its heart awakes:
> Then irresistibly it lives, it works.
>   [ll. 1342–46]

Aepytus is the fool who drives the people, not the leader who inspires. He calls this judgment upon himself when he announces that he will arouse the love of the people by "some signal, unassisted stroke, / Dealt at my own sole risk, before their eyes" (ll. 1353–54). His stroke is undoubtedly popular, but it is not edifying. Merope tells him: "I would now have Justice strike, not me" (l. 1472). Aepytus, however, declines to be deterred by appeals to such abstractions. He does his work, in damning contrast to Hamlet, while Polyphontes is making a sacrifice to Zeus in atonement for his "blood-guiltiness" (l. 1915). The Messenger's portrayal of the event puts in sharp detail the fear of visceral politics that *Culture and Anarchy* leaves in shadowy outline:

> from all sides a deluge, as it seem'd
> Burst o'er the altar and the Dorian lords,
> Of holiday-clad citizens transform'd
> To armed warriors; I heard the vengeful cries,
> I heard the clash of weapons; then I saw
> The Dorians lying dead, thy son hail'd king.
> [ll. 1937–42]

Merope's response to the calamity explains why Greece's development went well in spite of the minatory enthronement of Aepytus. The play had opened with Merope preparing to mourn at her husband's tomb in a ritual of grief she had maintained for twenty years. She was interrupted by Polyphontes, who came to her with his proposal of marriage. Now, at the end of the play, Merope completes her rites by praying over the body of Polyphontes (ll. 2010–13). Though she believes that Polyphontes had to die for his crimes of long ago, she sees no promise in the ethic of revenge. The spirit of Merope rather than the policy of Aepytus secured the future for Greece. For Merope herself, though, the journey to Periclean Athens has little reality. Hers is a stricken soul, and we see into it during those moments of confusion when she believes her son is dead. What we see is another Balder:

> Fain would I fade away, as I have lived,
> Without a cry, a struggle, or a blow,
> All vengeance unattempted, and descend
> To the invisible plains, to roam with thee,
> Fit denizen, the lampless under-world.
> [ll. 1027–31]

Although Arnold wrote poems, such as *Sohrab and Rustum*, in which the theme of "Falkland" does not appear, the theme occu-

pied a special place in his imagination. That he should come at last
to make explicit in the 1870s the theme of poems he wrote in the
1850s can be explained by the fact that he had by then entered
upon the period of his religious prose, whose main concern is the
clarification of an ethical ideal secure from the ineptitudes of orthodoxy, on the one hand, and on the other, from the subtleties
of rationalism.[24] If man's moral life could not find this security, a
time would come, Arnold feared, "when the mildness and sweet
reasonableness of Jesus Christ, as a power to work the annulment
of our ordinary self, will be clean disregarded and out of mind.
Then, perhaps, will come another reaction, and another, and another; and all sterile" (*CPW,* VI, 127).

A sterile future, indifferent alike to the example of Falkland
and the spirit of Jesus, is the tragic destiny toward which the historical process seemed to be moving with fearful alacrity. Arnold
was prompted to this vision not by maudlin sentimentality but by
the whole cast of his mind. It is illuminating to compare Arnold's
sense of tragedy with that of another writer, Hegel, whose theory of tragedy is also grounded in a view of history. Hegel believed that genuine tragedy arises from the collision of two ethical
forces each of which is in itself justified. Tragedy shows the resolution of this ethical contradiction through the reconciling agency
of Eternal Justice, which asserts itself against the "one-sided par-
ticularity" whence the contradictory ethical claims have issued.[25]
The theory, an application to tragedy of Hegel's philosophy of
history, has been criticized as providing, in effect, a rationale for
optimism. Out of the synthesis of the colliding forces comes a
fuller apprehension of the absolute; the future is nothing but
promising.

24. See William Robbins, *The Ethical Idealism of Matthew Arnold* (Toronto:
University of Toronto Press, 1959), pp. 30–31.
25. Hegel, *On Tragedy,* ed. Anne and Henry Paolucci (Garden City,
N.Y.: Anchor Books, 1962), pp. 46–51.

In Arnold's tragic vision the colliding forces, far from being justified, are menacing, and man is offered a future not because tragedy makes an alliance with history but because it offers a defense against fierce transition. Arnold sometimes seems to resemble Hegel in his frequent use of dialectical terms to describe reality. Hegel, however, is committed to the dialectic he postulates, and so he can make the tragic experience a mode of man's dialectical progress. But Arnold, despite his apparent relativism, invariably concludes his discussions of dialectical structures by locating reality in an absolute that is the synthesis of his operating terms. The synthesis, "Culture" or "the imaginative reason," for example, is urged upon us as an ideal; we see that the dialectic has been created only to be resolved.[26]

Arnold followed the impulses of his whole thought by defining tragedy as a condition in which access to the ideal is blocked by an antithesis that cannot be resolved. Tragedy can end in a sterile future because the essence of tragedy is historical stalemate. Like Schiller and Tocqueville, Arnold regarded this situation with profound dejection because he believed it would drain even the most advantaged creative power of its force and majesty. It would make of the heart, as it had made of the world, a foul rag-and-bone shop, and this could not be, for Arnold, an invitation to recruit his spirit. So he recruited his spirit within the exalted tradition of tragedy, placing his faith in the miracle of consolation he associated with the poet's office. Tragedy, Arnold might say, is "part of the *consolatio philosophiae*. It is . . . a ritualistic way of arming us to confront perplexities and risks."[27] Such, at any rate, is the value he assigned to tragedy as he saw himself and his age

26. A point frequently noted, as in Walter J. Hipple, "Matthew Arnold, Dialectician," *UTQ*, 32 (1962), 1–26.
27. The comments are from Kenneth Burke, *The Philosophy of Literary Form: Studies in Symbolic Action*, 3d ed. (Berkeley: University of California Press, 1973), p. 61.

perplexed by a suffering that found no vent in action. In doing so, he followed a path whose general direction had been marked by Scott, Byron, and Carlyle.

We may remain unimpressed by Arnold's attempts to make authentic tragedy out of these motives. Clearly, he failed to reinvigorate tragic drama in his age. But Arnold's tragic vision, in both his poetry and his prose, led him to his bracing and sensitive account of what has been called the ordeal of humanism in the nineteenth century. Arnold belongs to a humanistic tradition that founded itself on an attempt to relate the inspirations of the past to the aspirations of the modern temper. In any historical movement dominated by the nullities of the past and the aberrations of the modern temper, this illuminating relationship is exposed to destruction. Perhaps more than any other English writer, Arnold has given us the tone, the terms, and the imagery for identifying the cultural dislocations that emerge when humanistic thinking is "clean disregarded and out of mind," when all songs of what is past, passing, and to come are placed beyond human hearing by the din and frenzy of fierce transition.

Tragedy and Ideology

It has been said that Gladstone had as many cards up his sleeve as other politicians, but Gladstone was convinced his had been supplied by God. The same sort of thing might be said of the way our writers looked upon tragedy: by claiming the high cultural prestige of tragedy, they simply adopted an aesthetic mystification in their struggle against the political mystifications that divided their historical environment. Tragedy, so understood, is but another ideology, a formula for achieving control over the "belief system" of a social group. This is a crucial point, one that involves the most complex issues in Romantic and modern critical theory. I do not propose to treat these issues in any detail, but rather to suggest a schematic way of looking at the central problem as it emerges in the works of Scott, Byron, Carlyle, and Arnold. A few clarifications are first in order.

Throughout this study I have, of course, been indicating that tragedy did in fact become for our authors a way of achieving control. Their appropriation of tragedy's prestige for the sake of defending the position of the moderate has been a prominent theme. But this sort of control is formal; it is what Kenneth Burke would call a strategy for dealing with a situation. "Form, having to do with the creation and gratification of needs, is 'cor-

281

rect' in so far as it gratifies the needs which it creates."[1] Certainly our writers created form in this sense. The additional question is whether they also believed themselves to be magically free of ideology because they worked within an aesthetic rather than a political mode of discourse. To do so would be, of course, to claim that art is wholly autonomous, that it stands outside of other cultural systems, and that it has some primary access to value.

In practice, much rests on what one means by ideology. Two distinct usages of the term are relevant. Marx often spoke of ideology as meaning false consciousness or belief in a set of illusions widely shared by a particular class at a particular time. Marx exempted the proletariat of the future from subjection to ideology in this sense, though how the exemption is attained is problematical. The example illustrates the difficulty of distinguishing between ideology as false consciousness and transideological epiphany. Literary theory cannot resolve this issue, though much that was seminally important in Romantic aesthetics was offered in an attempt at resolving it. In the schematic analysis of the postures taken by Scott, Byron, Carlyle, and Arnold which I shall presently sketch, more will need to be said about this most radical form of the art–ideology antithesis.

But another, indispensable meaning of ideology is also pertinent. Our writers opposed tragedy to ideology to the extent that ideology bears the meaning that is now most commonly assigned to it: the organization of the social order around a highly integrated and rather narrow system of values coupled with an imperious demand for a high level of subscription to those values. Ideology so conceived sustains itself through the categorical elimination of experience.[2] It is against ideology in this sense that the moderate makes his protest by invoking the tragic spirit. Tragedy

1. Kenneth Burke, *Counter-Statement* (Berkeley: University of California Press, 1968), p. 138.
2. For a discussion in these terms, see William Earle, *Public Sorrows and Private Pleasures* (Bloomington: Indiana University Press, 1976), pp. 10–21.

acknowledges the repertory of possibilities that structure man's fate, including the possibility that social violence and injustice may be generated by ideologies founded on the noblest aspirations. The moderate, appealing to tragedy, insists on the value of his own experience and does so both in his own name and in the name of all those whose experience ideology would minimize or eliminate.

This opposition represents a lateral rather than a hierarchical separation of art from ideology. Implicitly, it makes the traditional claim that the artist is more deeply, more sensitively attentive to the spectacle of life than proponents of values that have been derived from empirical data or abstract systems. The separation is crucial for nineteenth-century writers who repeatedly defended the authenticity of art on the grounds of its special and strenuous way of remaining morally alert to the intricacies of experience.[3]

The lateral separation is itself, however, not in all minds above suspicion. Two forms of criticism have generally been made, one far more complex than the other. The simpler kind is well represented by Lewis S. Feuer in his essay "What Is Alienation?: The Career of a Concept."[4] Though Feuer does not address the art-ideology question directly, his comments are interestingly analogous to the sort of attacks often made in the nineteenth century on the so-called aesthetic "cult of inaction." Feuer writes:

> Like a true metaphysician, the intellectual projects his "alienation" upon every facet of discontent in the social universe. A universal indictment, however, provides no lever for social action; it expresses the mood of disaffiliation. . . . "Alienation" thus lends

---

3. This valuation, of course, remains central. It appears, not unexpectedly, in a recent controversial book that is apposite to our subject: Bernard-Henri Lévy, *Barbarism with a Human Face*, trans. George Holoch (New York: Harper & Row, 1979).

4. *Marx and the Intellectuals: A Set of Post-Ideological Essays* (Garden City, N.Y.: Anchor Books, 1969), p. 98.

> a distinctive emotive-dramatic metaphor to experiences of social
> frustration. It imposes on them the metaphor of prophets who
> failed. It conveys a mood of pervasive tragedy rather than the pos-
> sibility of effective action.   [p. 98]

Though Feuer has in mind not the artist but the intellectual in
politics, the terms of his discussion reveal how much the literary
theme of tragedy and revolution has bestowed upon our received
notions of the alienated man. And his discussion points to the frequently heard criticism of the artist: he separates himself from
ideology only by withdrawing into an aesthetically protected enclave where he can both indulge his narcissism and avoid delineat-
ing "the clear goals and foci for action that a political movement
requires." Feuer concludes by arguing that " 'alienation' remains
too much a concept of political theology that bewilders rather
than clarifies the direction for political action."[5]

We have only to replace "political theology" by "art" and to
remember Tennyson's "Lotos-Eaters" to find our way to the
most common form of the dissatisfaction with the art–ideology
antithesis in the nineteenth century. The charge is that even the
lateral separation of these forms of consciousness is a mystification
that impedes action. The preceding chapters have, I hope, suggested that Feuer's line of argument does not apply to the literature that articulates the tragedy of revolution. Tragedy is not a
retreat from action. It is an amplification of action. It insists that
action is not only pragmatic but symbolic as well. The tragedies
of our writers acted out in a symbolic form conditions of existence that were being suppressed by the hypertrophy of revolutionary politics.

The far more complex problem is the characteristic claim of literature in the Romantic tradition to transideological epiphany,
its claim to stand above ideology in hierarchical separation from
it. This claim or desire clearly emerges as a possibility in the liter-

5. Ibid.

ature we have been discussing, especially because our writers threw so much stress on the honorific nature of tragedy. It well may seem that the tragedy of revolution, while it begins by opposing ideology as intellectual conscription, ends, at least in some instances, by advocating art's autonomy from false consciousness in the most general sense.

I earlier suggested that such an enlargement of the tragic vision does not actually occur in our writers, in spite of some powerful strains in that direction, and I would like to indicate here, by way of summary, the kind of constraints that operated against their presumption to pure epiphany. In doing so, one finds it possible to schematize the positions of Scott, Byron, Carlyle, and Arnold in a way that identifies (perhaps overly identifies) the major responses of nineteenth-century writers to the radical form of the art–ideology antithesis.

Scott and Byron, on the one hand, Carlyle and Arnold, on the other, form contrasting pairs. Scott and Byron developed their aesthetics through what could be called creative reckoning with ideology. Carlyle and Arnold eschewed this model and instead developed their aesthetics through creative tension with ideology. This general contrast yields four points of reference rather than two because Scott and Byron achieve their reckoning in reversed ways, just as Carlyle and Arnold build up tension in reversed ways. The scheme can be seen as an inventory of the constraints that prevented these writers from regarding their art as an utterly transcendent category.

Scott had the least difficulty with the problem because he was least threatened by the continuity between art and ideology or by any implications that the authenticity of the artist was put in question by the origination of his art in irreducibly ideological structures. He wanted tragedy to illuminate models of community which he saw disfigured in the ordinary politics of his day, and only in *The Bride of Lammermoor* did he imagine a condition in which the artist alone might be left to supply what ordinary ideological initiatives had banished from the purview of reasonable men. On the whole, Scott placed as much trust in the fellowship of reasonable men as he did in the subjective powers of the imagination. His sense of fellowship is precisely the dominant sign of his authorial presence; it is the means by which he comes to power as an author. Moreover, implicit in all of Scott's novels is the conviction that this fellowship is symbolically formed in the communal act that binds reader and narrator. Hence Scott's repeated use of complicated prefaces that narrate the story of the way in which he, or a surrogate narrator, got the story that is about to be told. The reader takes his place as the latest figure in the fellowship.

Scott's art is, then, formed in a way that pictures the artist making models of community. Narratively and thematically, Scott, in effect, closes the gap between art and ideology by modeling his art on what is for him a recessed ideology that he admired and to which he would have been glad to trace his aesthetic inspiration. In a basic sense, the politics Scott wished to see in the public realm is constituted by the politics of his narration.

Byron quite distinctly reverses Scott's attitudes, but his reversal also functions as a creative reckoning with the art–ideology antithesis. It is one of the most significant qualities of Byron that he often attacked poetry as harshly as he attacked politics. "Poetry," he once said, in a typical comment, "should only occupy the idle. In more serious affairs it would be ridiculous."[6] What is reflected in this trait is Byron's whole concern with the problem of autonomy. Recognizing that every assumption of autonomy, aesthetic or political, entails a rationale for some sort of tyranny, Byron converted the post-Enlightenment search for spiritual authority, of which the art–ideology antithesis is a prodigious instance, into an account of the self-betrayals that can occur in that

6. Cited from Pietro Gamba, *A Narrative of Lord Byron's Last Journey to Greece* (London, 1825), in Andrew Rutherford, *Byron: A Critical Study* (Stanford: Stanford University Press, 1961), p. 6.

search. It was not to his purpose to publicize art's triumph over ideology or to lament the tainting of art by ideology.

However much Byron might have desired the victory of the poet—and *Sardanapalus* seems filled with that desire—he inevitably kept the desire in check or maintained it as a secondary impulse because he had to construct his art upon resistance to absolute hierarchies. Tragedy for Byron is specifically a criticism of man's dangerous passion for hierarchies. Byron reverses Scott by disengaging himself from the art–ideology antithesis in an act that images the existential consciousness underlying his creative effort. If Scott's art reaches out to mirror and embrace a recessed ideology, Byron's art resists all attempts, even the aesthetic attempt, to reach final stability.

As ideological strife increased in the nineteenth century, it became urgent for writers who were more threatened by the potential disintegration of art into propaganda than Scott, and less confident with risking its status than Byron, to deal head on with the question of art's relation to ideology. Carlyle and Arnold are clearly key figures here.[7] They certainly reflect in their uses of tragedy an overt tendency to represent the artist's accession to transideological epiphany that is not apparent in Byron and Scott. In his early essay "The State of German Literature," for example, Carlyle argued that literary men are "the dispensers and living types of God's everlasting wisdom." (*WTC*, XXVI, 58). Nevertheless, neither Carlyle nor Arnold settled in this position; each developed a rather haunted form of engagement with the problematics of ideology, and it was this very engagement that helped them forge their art. Though each at times seems willing to divorce art violently from ideology, each also knew that the palace of art is really a tomb, and that the literary imagination requires foundation in the living enterprise of social discourse.

7. See Lawrence J. Starzyk, "Arnold and Carlyle," *Criticism*, 4 (1970), 281–300.

We have seen in some detail how Carlyle moved quite self-consciously from an idealist vision of the artist to a proclamation of his role as a social prophet. The poet becomes akin to the revolutionary and shares the same fate: he works in chaos, amid wild ruin, and does his part in the downpulling and emergency house pargeting that becomes the lot of all true men in a revolutionary ethos. The very image of tragedy arises for Carlyle as an embodiment of this fate. Carlyle, with great effort, put his back to the transcendent, continued distantly to feel its radiance, but leveled his eye on the fallen world where, as he knew, false consciousness is in some sense always inescapable.

Arnold reverses this situation. He is always within the fallen world waiting for the spark from heaven to come. Though Arnold conceived of no actual heaven, his work as both poet and critic persistently generates the sense that transideological epiphany is only deferred, and that man is not exhaustively determined by the cultural systems that structure his environment. His longing is the longing of Empedocles, who wishes to know what in the universe can receive mind as the earth receives the body.

Though no transcendent realm ever appears for Arnold, he does see a horizon. Or rather, the poet sees it, for as William Madden has carefully shown, Arnold made the aesthetic consciousness an exceptionally privileged power of apprehension. This power, however, can never be entirely dissociated from ideological consciousness. One of the key terms in Arnold's vocabulary to describe supreme human endeavor is "study" (the "study of perfection," the "study of poetry"). The term, which Yeats would later brilliantly exploit, captures the image of man constrained by the school of the world which requires not only his attendance, but his allegiance. Yet man always seeks to discover in his study something magnificently other than the world's "*unpoetryless-ness.*" He follows the poet's eye and studies the horizon.

Arnold thus looks in the opposite direction from Carlyle. He locates himself within the cultural systems where all ideologies appear, but he discerns at a great distance a form of consciousness that is almost perfected, almost beyond ideology. When Arnold's imagination of this scene is burdened by the sense of study made dry and futile, tragedy emerges. Though working from the opposite perspective with respect to Carlyle, Arnold also created his art out of the tensions between the epiphanic and the ideological. They are tensions that he deliberately documented and exposed in his poetry, and nowhere did he do so with more ardor than in his poetic tragedies.

The deepest sources of the creative imagination cannot be schematized. My diagram is only intended as a way of looking at the possibilities for understanding how the tragedy of revolution, while an ideology in the broadest sense, is also an attempt to wrestle with false consciousness by keeping the imagination open to the play of experience. It is not too much to say that "tragedy" for writers in the tradition described here is essentially a brooding account of how ideology can contract into idolatry. By resisting this contraction, and by resisting as well the temptations of mystical aestheticism, they discovered the enabling instruments of their art.

In their art they faced the question of how to render the meanings of revolution and reaction. Both forces, though in certain ways as old as social history itself, were inscribing modern culture with its chief signs. Carlyle called these signs "characteristics," by which he meant features that pointed to meaning but did not constitute meaning. To realize meaning a code was needed, but in a state of fierce transition codes were not easy to come by. In their effort to make this crisis intelligible, writers turned to a code they called tragedy. The code did not allow them to understand all that fierce transition had made inscrutable. But it disclosed to them the points at which the inscriptions seemed densest and most forbidding. These were the points passed and repassed by the moderate in his alienated wanderings. Our writers identified these places in different ways: as the quagmire below Wolf's

Crag, as the base of Teufelsdröckh's tower, as the edge of Eden, as the summit of Etna. For this task of mapping and interpreting, ideology was of no use. An ideology is only a criticism of ideologies. What they needed was a criticism of life.

Index

Abrams, Meyer H., 42, 49, 192;
   Natural Supernaturalism, 49
Allott, Kenneth, 254–55
Anderson, Warren, 249n
Arendt, Hannah, 40, 44–46, 219–20
Arnold, Matthew, 19–20, 36, 39,
   49, 52, 63–68; aesthetic
   consciousness of, 248, 252, 288;
   and Byron, 63–68, 150, 250–56,
   280; and Carlyle, 63–68, 192–93,
   250–55, 280, 285–89; on French
   Revolution, 274; and Goethe,
   248; and Hegel, 278–79; and
   history, 262–64, 268, 278;
   humanism of, 280; and ideology,
   265, 281, 285, 287–89; letters
   of, 251–52, 256–57, 265, 267,
   270; on the moderate, 258; on
   novelists, 256–57; and
   polarization, 252, 262–63, 280;
   and Romanticism, 250–52; and
   Scott, 63–68, 116, 250–53,
   256–58, 260, 280; and third
   host, 250, 262, 266, 273; and
   tragedy, 247–49, 252–53, 256,
   262–63, 278–80, 289; and
   transition, 273–74, 280

Arnold, Matthew (*cont.*)
—works of: "Alaric at Rome,"
   255–56; *Balder Dead,* 249, 261,
   270–73; "Bishop and the
   Philosopher," 266; "Byron,"
   255; "Cromwell," 258; *Culture
   and Anarchy,* 277; "Dover
   Beach," 33; "Emerson," 254;
   Empedocles on Etna, 249, 253,
   261, 264–69; "Falkland," 249,
   256, 258–64, 272, 277; "French
   Critic on Goethe," 250;
   "Function of Criticism at the
   Present Time," 42, 263; *Merope,*
   247, 249, 261, 273–77; *Mixed
   Essays,* 256; "On the Modern
   Element in Literature," 267–68;
   Preface of 1853, 150, 247–53;
   "Renan's 'La Réforme
   intellectuelle,'" 274; *Sohrab and
   Rustum,* 277; "Stanzas from the
   Grand Chartreuse," 249, 254;
   unfinished drama on Lucretius,
   249, 261, 267–70
Arnold, Dr. Thomas, 62–63
Ashton, Thomas, 156n
Auerbach, Erich, 24

291

REVOLUTION
AS TRAGEDY

Designed by G. T. Whipple, Jr.
Composed by Metricomp
in 12 point Compugraphic Bembo, 2 points leaded,
with display lines in Bembo.
Printed offset by Thomson/Shore, Inc.
on Warren's Number 66 text, 50 pound basis.
Bound by John H. Dekker & Sons, Inc.
in Holliston book cloth
and stamped in All Purpose foil.

Library of Congress Cataloging in Publication Data

Farrell, John Philip, 1939–
   Revolution as tragedy.

   Includes index.
   1. English literature—19th century—History and
criticism. 2. Authors, English—19th century—Political
and social views. 3. Politics and literature.
4. Literature and revolutions. 5. Tragic, The.
I. Title.
PR469.P6F3   820'.9'007   79-26000
ISBN 0-8014-1278-1